SURPRISE, UNCERTAINTY, AND MENTAL STRUCTURES

SURPRISE, UNCERTAINTY, AND MENTAL STRUCTURES

Jerome Kagan

HARVARD UNIVERSITY PRESS
CAMBRIDGE, MASSACHUSETTS
LONDON, ENGLAND
2002

Library of Congress Cataloging-in-Publication Data
Kagan, Jerome.
Surprise, uncertainty, and mental structures / Jerome Kagan.
p. cm.
Includes bibliographical references and index.
ISBN 0-674-00735-2 (alk. paper)
1. Schemas (Psychology)   2. Cognition.   3. Perception.   I. Title.

BF313 .K34 2002
153.4—dc21   2001051484

Contents

Surprise, Uncertainty, and Mental Structures

INTRODUCTION

The most satisfying explanations of natural events consist of descriptions of clearly defined entities, the conditions that alter their states or properties, and the consequences of those changes. Current interpretations of sore throats, eclipses, and rainbows are convincing because they satisfy all three criteria. When these explanations appear to be simple, consistent, and easy to apply we regard them as beautiful. Sadly, too many explanations of psychological phenomena feel inadequate because the psychological structures contained in the explanations are fuzzy. One aim of this book is to address this theoretical frustration by describing some of the psychological forms that mediate thought, action, and feelings.

Minds perform many tasks quickly and often without error. They detect transient changes in the sensory surround, assimilate transformations on permanent knowledge, integrate the present with the past, suppress acts that violate personal standards, invent causes, and manipulate symbols in a richly generative semantic system. Although many aspects of these functions are well understood, and measurable to some degree, the nature of the relevant psychological structures is puzzling. Loyalty to the serviceable principle of parsimony, which prefers simple to complex solutions, motivates some, fortunately not all, psychologists to favor the view that minds do their work with one entity, often called an amodal cognitive structure, that combines the products of perceptual experience, feeling, and language in a seamless configuration.

Even the ancient Greeks recognized that they needed four different forms to explain the world's material substances. Advances in our understanding of matter and life over the last two millennia were made possible by procedures that detected the different structures that were the foundation of the phenomenal world. I shall argue that the extraordinary diversity of psychological functions also requires more than one psychological form.

There are at least two reasons for the current indifference to specifying the distinct configurations that make behavior, emotion, and cognition possible. Until recently, most psychologists studied only functions, like memories, perceptions, feelings, and actions. The small number of laws that have been generated—such as the Weber-Fechner function and the relation between frequency of responding and the schedule of reinforcement—are silent on the underlying forms.

Methodological immaturity is a second reason for the lack of concern with form. Psychologists do not command many techniques that permit them to quantify mental configurations with the specificity and accuracy that characterize the biologist's measurements of neurons, glia, and myelin. Although discovery of the brain structures that are the foundation of mental activity might provide some clues to the psychological forms, the former cannot be a substitute for the latter. The psychological structures that permit me to recognize a friend's face are not isomorphic with the pattern of neurons activated when I see this friend at an airport. That is, the two must be described with different vocabularies.

There is a competition in every discipline between the network of concepts that provide a coherent, minimally complex understanding of a family of phenomena and the number and seriousness of the facts that are inconsistent with that network. No theory is completely free of inconsistency. Controversy arises when the rebellious facts become so numerous that scholars admit to a need for theoretical reform.

A recognition of the importance of form, and discovering and measuring the major psychological forms, will lead to deeper understanding. The most fundamental distinction, I believe, is between schemata and semantic structures. The former retain some of the features of the events that created them, while the latter do not. Equally important is the fact that a schema is often linked to a motor action, called a sensorimotor structure. The schema for a pet beagle, for example, is likely to evoke an intention to stroke its fur. Also, the schema for the animal is not part of a hierarchy of symbolic categories. The semantic representation for the pet is a member of a network that includes the semantic forms dog, mammal, animal, and living thing. Although schemata and semantic forms are usually combined as the mind does its work, the former do not lose their features when they combine with semantic networks.

Because semantic structures are so closely linked to schemata (for example, my schema for the Statue of Liberty automatically triggers a semantic network referring to immigrants arriving in America), it is easy to be persuaded that the mind possesses only one type of structure. The belief in one mental form permits each guild of scholars to exploit their special talents and intuitions. Connectionist theorists can continue to simulate mental processes; psycholinguists can analyze linguistic rules; social psychologists can evaluate attitudes; and developmental scholars can probe the acquisition of the concepts of number and living things. Although this working premise has led to interesting discoveries, certain phenomena remain stubbornly inconsistent with that position.

The most troublesome fact is that infants do not have semantic structures. In addition, most adults are able to recognize over 90 percent of a large number of photographs of faces or scenes examined briefly an hour earlier, and brain-damaged patients who cannot understand language nonetheless can recognize pictures, sounds, and smells; for example, they can name a picture of a familiar object or animal.

Almost all attempts to understand puzzling phenomena begin with an idealized, usually parsimonious, assumption that is presumed to extend to a large number of related events, if not to the entire domain. The premise of determinism in classical mechanics and conservation of symmetry in the first version of quantum mechanics are two examples from physics. John Watson's assertion that conditioning was the only mechanism for acquiring habits and Freud's positing of libido as the primary source of psychic energy are two examples from the human sciences. However, empirical data revealed the flaws in all of these beliefs.

The suggestion that a single amodal structure is the basic unit in mental activity is also inconsistent with the evidence, but social scientists are less willing than physicists to accommodate to empirical facts because psychological results, usually less robust, permit continued loyalty to flawed, but favored, concepts.

A second aim of this book is to argue that events that are transformations of an agent's psychological forms are significant incentives for brain activity and its psychological consequences. Important implications flow from acknowledgment of the power of transformations of different mental forms to produce particular states. Events that are discrepant from schemata create a state one might call *surprise*. By contrast, verbal propositions that are inconsistent with semantic networks create a state one might call *uncertainty*. Surprise and uncertainty are distinct brain and phenomenological states. Surprise is brief, uncertainty is more often prolonged. Surprise has an immediate, almost reflexive, effect on autonomic and motor systems; the consequences of uncertainty are less predictable. The sudden sight of a child without arms evokes a distinct brain and mental state that is different from and more predictable than the state created by reading: "Children born to mothers who took thalidomide during pregnancy often have no arms."

The notion of transformations of an agent's knowledge penetrates this book because minds, and the brains which are their foundation, are provoked into activity by events that share some features with, but do not completely match, a person's schemata or semantic networks. There is some resistance among those who study behavior to acknowledging the significance of unfamiliar events because this idea implies that a given event will have different consequences for agents with different knowledge. This fact complicates the already difficult task of doing psychological research. Imagine what biology would be like if molecules of hemoglobin reacted to blood-borne oxygen in different ways depending upon what bodily events had occurred over the past twenty-four hours. It is not possible, however, to understand a culture or historical changes in its beliefs without acknowledging the motivating force of discrepancy and inconsistency. The changes in mood that accompany aging are as much a function of fewer surprises and states of uncertainty as they are the inevitable consequence of compromised organs and the wearing away of the ends of chromosomes.

Chapter 1 describes the concepts of schemata, sensorimotor structures, and semantic networks and explores the nature of schemata and the processes that follow encounters with events that are discrepant from this class of knowledge. I argue for a sharp distinction between a psychological form and its neural foundation and against a simple determinism between brain and mind. The psychological structures that emerge from brain activity have to be described with their own vocabulary, especially the quasi-logical properties that characterize semantic networks.

6

Chapter 2 probes the nature of semantic structures and affirms the distinction between schemata and semantic networks. The attraction to generality inherent in semantic structures often leads to classification of different phenomena into the same category. For example, the empirical bases for inferring a fear state in rats are sufficiently different from the evidence used to infer that state in humans that scientists should not assume a fundamental resemblance. And the concern with a person's identity, a concept Erikson introduced a half-century ago, owes its vitality to historical changes that created particular semantic inconsistencies in the categories for self.

Chapter 3 summarizes evidence from event-related potentials that affirms the distinction between schemata and semantic forms. Event-related potentials are patterns of waveforms produced by the synchronized activity of large numbers of neurons to a particular stimulus. The ability to measure these waveforms has altered our conception of the relation between schematic and semantic features and made it possible for scientists to ask questions about the different contributions of the left and right hemispheres to the sequence of brain events that accompany detection, recognition, evaluation, and decision. A similar revolution occurred in astrophysics when new techniques permitted scientists to measure the profiles of energy in the cosmos. To their surprise, they discovered that most of the energy in the universe, so-called dark matter, is invisible. This fact, impossible to know before physicists had the tools to measure this energy, has changed their theories of the cosmos. The data from event-related potentials and the new brain-scanning technologies have forced a reevaluation of the relation between language and perception.

The final two chapters concern the implications of the distinction between schemata and semantic forms for several issues, including psychological development, creativity, and personality measurement and theory. Chapter 4 examines the nature of the infant's knowledge of the world, the young child's moral sense, and the process of identification. My claim that the infant's schemata need not be an early form of the semantic concepts of the older child is especially relevant to the popular assumptions that infants possess a concept of number and understand some physical principles.

Chapter 5 applies the lessons of the first three chapters to the factors that lead audiences to judge a book or a scientific idea as creative. I suggest that concepts that transform the less essential features of the structures of an audience are most likely to be acclaimed. In the chapter's final sections I argue for a new approach to personality that supplements the current emphasis on semantic structures derived from questionnaires. I also pose a question that cannot yet be resolved. Is human restraint on asocial behavior mediated by the visceral schemata for guilt, shame, anxiety, and remorse, or by the semantic networks for self that demand consistency between one's actions and the judgment of personal virtue?

This book could have been a thousand rather than two hundred pages if I had summarized all of the pertinent literature on this broad set of themes. My purpose here, however, is to use an essay format to urge colleagues in the social and behavioral sciences to pay more attention to unfamiliarity and to the different consequences of engaging schemata or semantic structures.

DISCREPANCY AND
SCHEMATA

The popular conception of causality in the physical world assumes perfectly predictable relations between a specific event and an equally specific outcome. A boy kicks a pebble and it moves; heat is applied to water and it boils. But heating a pebble will not make it move; kicking water will not make it boil. The specificity of the relation between cause and effect affirms the intuition that each outcome requires a particular set of prior conditions. Some relations in the life sciences, however, fail to honor the principle of absolutely specifiable causes. The most obvious exceptions are those occasions in which a change in behavior or physiology is due to a detected change in the individual's sensory surround (such as the unexpected dimming of a light bulb) or a transformation of the individual's knowledge (such as reading that taking vitamin supplements has no beneficial effect on health). In both instances the condition for a change in thought and neuronal activity is a relation between an event and the mind of the agent.

The infant's distribution of attention provides clear evidence of the influence of unexpected change. Four-month-olds will look longer at a blue cube than at a green sphere if they have just seen the latter, but will look longer at the green sphere if first exposed to the blue cube. The physical characteristics of the object that recruit attention are irrelevant; the power to alter behavior rests with events that are transformations of the immediate past. The power of change to alert and to arouse is operative in the oldest mammals. An animal sated on a particular food will begin to eat again if presented with a different food. A male rat who has ceased copulating with a particular female will become sexually active if given a new partner. Adults are most likely to remember a word—whether read or heard—if an unexpected event occurred as they were processing the word. Our first memories are usually of events that were transformations of the familiar. Czeslaw Milosz's earliest recollection was of a chamber pot rocking in an odd, unstable fashion on a train in which he and his parents were traveling.[1]

The recollections of the writer Elias Canetti offer a persuasive example of the potency of events that are inconsistent with one's strong beliefs. On July 15, 1927, the twenty-six-year-old Canetti, who was studying chemistry at the University of Vienna, read in the newspaper that a court had acquitted a group of men who had killed some workers. A crowd, believing the verdict to be unjust, marched on the Palace of Justice and burned it down. The police, trying to stop the violence, killed ninety members of the crowd. Canetti, who witnessed the murders, was profoundly affected by this experience. "Fifty-three years have passed and the agitation of that day is still in my bones."[2]

Canetti's mind was especially vulnerable to these events because the crowd's behavior violated his deep conviction in the power of the human will to control wildness. I suspect that other witnesses that day, who were not surprised by the inability of individuals to resist a crowd's passion, were affected less deeply by the violence. One must know the mind of the agent in order to predict the psychological consequences of an infrequent event. It is the relation between an event and an agent's representations, not the event as recorded by a camera, that affects thought, feeling, or action. There is an analogous truth in immunology. If the body does not detect an antigen, there will be no immune response. The incentive power of change is as fundamental to psychology as the physical principle that an imposed force causes an object to move.

The Biology of Novelty

The brain of every animal is exquisitely sensitive to change. Tiny hairs on the posterior appendages of a cockroach are sensitive to subtle perturbations in airflow that might indicate the presence of a predator. Even the tiny nematode worm *C. elegans*, which has only 302 neurons, reacts to change in its sensory surround, for it displays a reflex withdrawal if the petri plate in which it rests is tapped. Although this reaction vanishes with repeated tapping, the reflex reappears if the nematode is relocated to a plate containing a different chemical environment. The simplest of unexpected events perturbs the biochemistry of genes within the activated neurons. A novel sound, for example, provokes production of a protein called *c-fos* in the rat's cochlear nucleus. Similar activity occurs in the inferior lobe neurons of sheep who are looking at photos of humans.[3]

The novelty of an event can, on some occasions, be as important as its hedonic quality. In the brains of rats, for example, the increase in corticotropin-releasing hormone within the central nucleus of the amygdala, which usually occurs following stress, is equally large when the rats are unexpectedly restrained, which they do not like, and when they are unexpectedly fed, which they do like.[4]

The human sensitivity to what is new is mediated by neuron ensembles in many parts of the brain, including frontal, parietal, and temporal areas, and especially the medial temporal area and entorhinal cortices, hippocampus, and amygdala. Neurons in these sites typically respond to events that, from the perspective of the agent, are unfamiliar, unexpected, or transformations of the products of past experiences.[5]

Although both places and objects can be unfamiliar, the hippocampus is usually more responsive when animals are in unfamiliar places; the amygdala is more reactive when they encounter unfamiliar objects. Strangers, as well as facial expressions that are not seen frequently, usually provoke the primate amygdala.[6] Because most adults do not regularly encounter people displaying the large eyes characteristic of a fearful expression, a presentation of this facial pattern that prevented subjects from consciously perceiving the fearful face elicited greater activity in the amygdala than a smiling face.[7] But when the state of uncertainty created by a discrepant event dissipates because the event has become familiar, amygdalar activity decreases, often rapidly.[8]

A failure to appreciate that unexpected events usually activate the amygdala can lead to a misinterpretation of evidence. Adults lying in a PET scanner were first shown a series of pictures that were neutral in content (for example, cups), then a series with pleasant connotations (food), and finally pictures with unpleasant content (a bloody person, a dirty toilet). The unpleasant pictures produced the largest increase in metabolic activity in the left amygdala.[9] There are two ways to interpret this result. The investigators concluded that the unpleasant pictures produced an aversive emotional state resembling fear and, as a consequence, activation of the amygdala. An equally reasonable explanation is that the subjects did not expect the unpleasant scenes after the long series of neutral and pleasant pictures. The resulting state should have activated the amygdala in the service of resolving the uncertainty. When subjects in another study viewed unpleasant and pleasant pictures alternately, rather than unpleasant scenes after pleasant ones, activity in the amygdala was greatest when extraverted women were viewing pleasant pictures.[10]

This result is not consistent with the assumption that amygdalar activity reflects a state of fear or anxiety.

The argument that a state of surprise is a more reliable incentive for amygdalar activation than a state of fear is bolstered by other studies that assessed metabolic activity in the amygdala. Adults who had been given electric shock while looking at a particular type of picture, and therefore should have acquired a conditioned fear reaction to that class of event, did not show increased PET activity in the amygdalar area when such pictures appeared. Further, adults undergoing eye-blink conditioning using an aversive air puff to the cornea showed decreasing amygdalar activity as the trials proceeded, because the test situation became predictable. Further, adults who saw a blank screen on some trials and nonaversive or aversive pictures on others showed more amygdalar activity to the pictures than to the blank screen, and equivalent activity to the aversive and nonaversive scenes.[11] The appearance of any picture was accompanied by increased excitability of the amygdala. For the same reason, increased skin conductance and a larger eye-blink startle—both reactions mediated by the amygdala—occurred when an unexpected but nonaversive light was presented within a series of identical tactile stimuli.[12] Because unexpected events can prime the amygdala, inferences regarding the presence of a fear state that are based only on physiological indexes of amygdalar activity should be treated with caution.

Variation in Reaction to Novelty

The specific reaction to a novel or unexpected event depends on the agent's gender and past experiences, the immediate context, and always the perceptual and response biases of the species. Blue jays are reluctant to approach objects with bold, black bands; as a result, moths who possess these bands are protected, to some degree, from predation by the jays. The size of an unfamiliar object is often a critical feature modulating an animal's reaction. Monkeys usually avoid large unfamiliar, inedible objects, but approach small ones. Ravens show a fear reaction to the carcass of a large unfamiliar animal, but not to a small piece of unfamiliar food. One-year-old infants cry or withdraw if an unfamiliar adult walks toward them slowly, but remain calm, and may even smile, if the stranger is a child, a midget, or a puppy. Rabbits produce four distinct patterns of neural activity in the dorsal hippocampus and frontal cortex to four novel but different events: (1) a new environment, (2) a new object, (3) an object (a stuffed hawk) that shares attributes with events encountered in the past, and (4) an unfamiliar but live animal (a cat).[13]

The most common behavioral reactions to unexpected or unfamiliar events that the agent cannot control are immobility, prolonged attention, approach, avoidance, escape, attack, and any one of a variety of species-specific responses (a smile or exclamation in humans, a grimace in monkeys). Aggression and sexual activity are restrained when animals are in an unfamiliar place because these contexts usually lead to a period of immobility. Stallions, for example, are less likely to approach a female in an unfamiliar environment. This restraint is weaker in primates, however, if a conspecific, preferably a familiar one, is present. Nonetheless, infant guinea pigs placed in an unfamiliar environment will secrete more cortisol if alone than if with an unfamiliar member of their species.[14]

Rats who repeatedly received a dose of amphetamine after first being taken to an unfamiliar cage showed increased motor activity following each administration of the drug. However, rats who received the same amount of the drug while in their familiar home environment showed minimal behavioral changes to the drug. Apparently, the brain state created by being in an unfamiliar place enhanced the behavioral reaction to the drug.[15]

15

The unexplained fact that males of most mammalian species are less avoidant of unfamiliar places than females may be due, in part, to the ability of androgen in the CA1 region of the hippocampus to mute reactivity to a novel event. Male rats deprived of androgen (as a result of castration) displayed larger increases in several messenger RNA products when exposed to an unfamiliar place than normal rats did.[16]

There can be intra- or interspecific variation in the reaction to unfamiliarity even when the event and the context are identical.[17] This variation has been observed in fish, octopuses, birds, mice, rats, dogs, foxes, cats, monkeys, and humans. For example, wild strains of fowl are more reactive to unfamiliar events than are domestic ones.[18] Every sample of children reveals variation in the propensity to attend, explore, withdraw, or cry to particular novel events. About 15 percent of one-year-old children— and, surprisingly, the same proportion of Bushbaby monkeys—became timid when confronted with an unfamiliar event.[19]

Titi and squirrel monkeys, who belong to the same family (Cebidae), do not respond similarly to unfamiliar situations. Titi monkeys, which form pair bonds, become emotional if they are alone in an unfamiliar place but remain calm if with another animal. Squirrel monkeys, who live in larger groups, behave more similarly whether alone or in the presence of a familiar animal.[20]

The pervasiveness of both intra- and interspecific variation in the reaction to unfamiliarity suggests that the profiles of brain chemistry that mediate the detection of and reaction to discrepancy are genetically labile traits mediated by alleles that are especially susceptible to mutation. Two examples are the alleles for the dopamine receptors (especially D2 and D4), which are associated with a rat's tendency to approach or to avoid novelty, and the genes responsible for brain serotonin and its receptors. Over forty years ago a Russian geneticist, Dimitry Belyaev, went to a silver fox farm in Siberia and selectively bred the small group of foxes who differed from the majority because they did not show a fearful, avoidant reaction to humans. Belyaev called these foxes tame. After fewer than forty generations of breeding tame animals with each other, 80 percent of the offspring were tame and one of their biological properties was a high level of brain serotonin.[21]

Although administration of cocaine or amphetamine produces an increase in motor activity if the rat is in an unfamiliar place, rats of the same strain vary in their susceptibility to becoming active following the administration of either drug. The drugs produce larger increases in locomotor activity, as well as greater dopamine concentrations in the nucleus accumbens, in those animals who usually explore an unfamiliar environment than in those who usually remain inactive in unfamiliar surroundings. This finding suggests that the animal's typical reaction to an unfamiliar place is modulated by alleles that also influence dopamine function.[22] This idea finds support in the fact that the C57BL/6 mouse strain has higher dopamine levels in the prefrontal cortex than the DBA/2 strain, after only one minute of exposure to an unfamiliar environment, despite no strain differences in basal dopamine level before the animals were placed in the unfamiliar location.[23] The corpus of evidence permits two robust generalizations: every animal is sensitive to unexpected changes in its surround, and there is considerable variation between and within species in the form and intensity of the response to such changes.

Functions Require Forms

The concepts "discrepant," "unfamiliar," "novel," and "unexpected" are defined by a relation between a brain/mind and an event and are not inherent in the event, as William James and Alfred North Whitehead understood. Therefore, one must know both the content of the agent's mind—the Greeks called it *lekton*—and whether the representations were created during the previous few seconds, the prior day, or years earlier, in order to predict the consequences of the experience. This truth requires an analysis of the different types of psychological structures that fill the mind of an agent.

Biologists with a philosophical bent appreciate that form is the fundamental riddle in nature, where form, or structure, is defined as a pattern of relations among a set of constituent features. Each time a new form is discerned, a puzzle of function is illuminated. Extraordinary advances in the understanding of heredity followed Crick and Watson's discovery of the structure of DNA. Equally stunning advances were made possible by Cajal's discovery of the neuron and his hypothesis of the synapse. These ideas were the foundation for later inquiry into the biochemistry of neural transmission.

Psychologists have been slow to recognize this truth because they typically study functions, such as actions, memories, feelings, categorizations, and perceptions, and are indifferent to the psychological forms—readers may prefer to call these patterns, structures, or configurations—that permit these functions to be actualized. The extensive explorations of the patterns of PET or fMRI activity to a specific task demand evaluate the brain areas that participate in particular psychological functions. These data do not tell us much about the psychological structures recruited by the task. Every mature science combines an understanding of forms with an understanding of their functions. Psychologists must discover the forms that mediate the functions they have been probing over the last 130 years.

Unfortunately, function does not reveal form. It is not possible to infer the anatomy of the retina, thalamus, or visual cortex from the perception of a soaring hawk or the Müller-Lyer illusion. The chemical structures of the male hormone testosterone and the female hormone estradiol, which have very different functions, have similar structures, for they differ in only two places. Almost a half-century ago Floyd Allport made this point forcefully in *Theories of Perception and the Concept of Structure*. Nature, he wrote, consists of functions and structures, and the former do not reveal the latter because "structures are lawful in a different way—in a way that quantitative functions are quite unable to state."[24]

Different Vocabularies for Brain and Mind

There is no consensus on the number or nature of the elementary psychological configurations that minds use to do their work.[25] Although discovery of the patterns of activated neuron ensembles that accompany psychological processes might illuminate the nature of the emergent psychological forms, the biological knowledge cannot be a substitute for the psychological configurations. The words used to describe the psychological structures that permit a child to recognize that the animal on the lawn is a dachshund, and not a cat, cannot be the same words that describe the temporal pattern of activated neuron ensembles that occurs when this perceptual decision is made. The relation between the pattern of brain activity in a woman who suddenly hears intermittent sounds coming from a windowpane and her conscious realization that it is raining remains a deep enigma. Although the former is the foundation of the latter, the two events have to be described with different vocabularies. This difference is reminiscent of the ancient distinction between matter and form. The atoms in the trunk of a cherry tree can assume many different forms, from cabinet to letter opener, none of which is knowable while one is looking at the tree.

The emergent nature of psychological events is analogous to the temperature and pressure of a closed container of gas. "Pressure" and "temperature" are terms that describe the emergent consequences of large numbers of molecular collisions and are inappropriate terms for a single molecule. Some neuroscientists assume, tacitly, that every lawful psychological phenomenon can be explained by or derived from the activity of particular ensembles of neurons, as the temperature and pressure of a vessel of gas are explained by Boltzmann's equations describing the collisions of large numbers of atoms. This analogy is flawed because the motion of each atom is assumed to be independent of the motion of every other atom. This assumption does not apply to neurons, for each is influenced by the activity of others; for example, a profile of activation of neurons in the occipital lobe is modulated by activity in the amygdala.

Anxiety is a property of a person and not of the neurons that participate in this emotion. Thus the scholar who acknowledges that thought, feeling, and action depend on and emerge from brain events, but who insists, nonetheless, that these events must be described in a language different from the one that describes the underlying brain processes, is not a metaphysical dualist. All of nature cannot be described with one vocabulary because brains have qualitatively different structures than schemata and semantic networks.

The need for different vocabularies for biological and psychological events has an analogue in Niels Bohr's insistence that physicists must use the concepts of classical physics, not those of quantum theory, to describe experimental results, even though the quantum concepts are the foundation of the measurements. When Edward Teller challenged this dualist position, Bohr replied that if the evidence were summarized in the language of quantum mechanics the two of them would not be sitting at a table drinking tea but imagining their conversation. Analogously, the molar psychological phenomena of emotion, action, and thought have to be described in psychological terms. The statement "The rat froze for six seconds when placed in the compartment where it had received one electric shock a day earlier" cannot be reduced to, or translated into, sentences containing words that refer only to events in brain and body.

This argument is not a rejection of attempts to understand the biological contributions to psychological processes. Even though complete translation of the latter events into the language of the former is probably impossible, research that tries to do so has two advantages. First, the products of this work deepen our understanding of the molar events. The discovery that connections between temporal and frontal structures mature during the last half of the first year of life implies that there should be a major improvement in retrieval memory at this time. This inference leads to a new conceptualization of the phenomenon Piaget called object permanence as well as of the universal display of fear of strangers and of separation from a caretaker.

A failure to find expected correspondences often provides fruitful seeds for new conceptualizations. The fact that lesions of the dorsolateral prefrontal cortex impair working memory but do not impair the retrieval of old motor habits invites a distinction among types of retrieval memory. The lack of a close correspondence between variation in behavioral signs of uncertainty or tension in ten-year-olds interacting with an unfamiliar adult and variation in theoretically relevant biological measures (EEG asymmetry, alpha and beta power, sympathetic arousal) implies that there can be a profound dissociation between the molar behavior of an individual and physiological reactions that are believed to be bases for the behavior. This independence invites the invention of concepts to describe the physiological states that do not have connotations for psychological terms like "anxiety" or "tension." Thus knowledge of the relation of brain activity to psychological events contributes to our theory even though a complete translation of mind events to brain events is probably not possible.

The argument against a strict causal determinism between brain and mental activity finds support in both empirical facts and logic. The empirical data gathered thus far reveal very loose connections between brain activity and most psychological events. Although proponents of a closer yoking of the two domains suggest that future technological advances will permit a tighter correspondence, there is an "in principle" argument against this view. A psychological phenomenon is the result of a cascade of many brain events that occurs over intervals usually ranging from a quarter-second to several seconds. The determinists believe that a complete description of the shared neural events displayed by a group of individuals to an incentive will make it possible to predict that most are about to speak, pick up a small object, or recall an obligation. Such a victory would be cause for jubilant celebration. However, each psychological intention has a target. Are these individuals about to speak a line of poetry, a greeting, or an obscenity? Are they trying to remember an appointment at a restaurant, a class to meet, or a gift to buy? It seems unlikely, at least at the present time, that the neuron ensembles activated when a person begins to reach for an object could specify that the target is a cup, rather than a glass, a pen, or a knife. Could any technology reveal in a student learning Russian that she is memorizing the Russian word for coffee rather than for tea? These uncertainties remind us of the reason for Wittgenstein's imperative for silence and why Niels Bohr realized that the complement of clarity of description was truth.

Further, a class of brain states, not a single state, is associated with a particular psychological phenomenon. Consider a specific brain state B and its derivative mental state M at a particular moment. If an investigator could remove one molecule of norepinephrine from a synapse or one spine from a dendrite that is a regular component of B, it is unlikely that these small changes would alter M in a measurable way. This thought experiment implies that different brain states can underlie the same mental state and that there is, necessarily, an indeterminate relation between B and M. The same principle holds for genes. An alteration in a gene does not always affect the organism's phenotype. The premise that any change in a constituent must alter the larger coherent phenomenon runs deep in Western thought. Fifteenth-century scholars assumed that any change in the words of a biblical sentence, no matter how subtle, implied a different meaning.

The relation between the minds of Americans and our society's functional institutions supplies an analogy. The beliefs, motives, and conflicts of contemporary adults between twenty and forty years of age are different from those held by the same age cohort fifty years ago. Nonetheless, the delivery of mail, the collection of trash, college registrations, commencement exercises, weddings, funerals, and a host of other societal activities have changed very little over the same interval. The minds of the agents participating in these activities have been altered, but the social functions carried out by those agents have changed far less.

An important reason why the description of a profile of neuronal activation is not a substitute for a psychological structure is that the context and the agent's past experience determine which particular neural pattern and therefore which psychological structures will be activated. The psychological representation of an event—or class of events—is a hypothetical network of many interrelated features that can include information from several sensory modalities, motor programs, and language. The particular subset of features activated in an individual at a particular time and in a particular place is not knowable until an incentive is specified. But different incentives activate different parts of the network. The features of the network for thunderstorms evoked in a person caught outside in a summer storm include visual and auditory schemata as well as motor programs. However, a different subset of features will be activated if the same person is in an office building or in an airplane while lightning is scarring the sky.

well-educated political activists; the second less well educated apolitical men. Although all the prisoners experienced similar acts of torture, more of the apolitical men developed anxiety, depression, or post-traumatic stress disorder.[29] The fact that fewer political activists developed stress disorder has to be due, in part, to their intellectual commitment to the ideological causes that led to their incarceration. The psychological state we call "intellectual commitment to a cause" cannot be translated into sentences whose words only describe brain processes.

These claims are neither bold nor counterintuitive. The structure of a protein is different from the structures of the DNA and m-RNA molecules that preceded it; the structure of a pyramidal neuron does not resemble the structures of the proteins that made it possible. The proteins of the major histocompatibility complex, which have one form, influence both the immune system and neural connections in the thalamus, each of which has a unique structure. Each entity in the complex series of cascades that eventuates in an agent acting in a context has a form that is described best with a vocabulary different from the one used to describe the structures that preceded it.

Forms of Knowledge

Because an agent's reaction to an event that transforms its existing knowledge depends on the form of that knowledge, one must know the nature of the agent's representations in order to predict the state and action disposition that follow an event. Humans create different kinds of representations, each with a distinct form that emerges from an equally distinct neurobiology. The most important forms are schemata (of two types: visceral and perceptual), sensorimotor structures, and semantic networks.

A person's network—or pattern—of possible representations for an event is analogous to the abstract physical notion of a phase space. A collection of gas molecules in a vessel can assume a very large number of states, only one of which can be measured at a given time. Similarly, a summer storm can activate a large number of representations. No member of this family is knowable until a scientist intervenes with a probe in order to measure it. No member is more essential than any other, and none is active while the person is sipping coffee on a sunny morning. Thus the neural pattern of activation in a person lying in a PET or fMRI scanner looking at pictures of bloodied soldiers and poisonous snakes is not to be regarded as the true, or only, neural configuration that these stimuli could provoke. These pictures would probably create a different brain state if the person were looking at them on a television screen at home. Just as there is no master clock for the universe, there is no God's-eye view of the brain's response to an incentive because each person has a particular frame of mind in each class of situation and that frame affects which neuronal ensembles and representations will be activated.

For example, a person reading alone in a quiet room at midnight is primed for one set of representations should he hear the sound of a crashing object, but quite another set if he hears exactly the same sound on a city street at high noon. If scientists could know the man's mind/brain and could measure every possible representation that could be evoked by the sound of a crashing object they would discover that the semantic representations for danger, animals, burglars, construction, bulldozers, and cranes were all potential candidates. The context of the room at midnight primes the first three; the street setting primes the others.

The influence of context may restrict the inferences scientists will be able to draw from measures of brain activity using an fMRI or

PET scanner. The representations that are primed while a person lying in a scanner is trying to remember a list of twenty-four emotional words presented minutes earlier may be different from those primed when the same person is sitting in his kitchen performing the same task. Should this speculation prove valid, generalizations about the brain circuits that are activated by cognitive tasks or emotional incentives will have to accommodate to the context of measurement. Genetically identical strains of mice administered identical procedures do not behave identically if tested in different laboratories.

A final reason why brain activity and psychological representations require different vocabularies is that no measured brain state, no matter how complete, can reveal all the relevant features of the agent's experiential history—and knowledge of that past history is necessary if we want to know whether the agent will treat an event as discrepant. The most sophisticated fMRI scan of my brain could not reveal the schemata for the most frightening event that occurred in my fifth year. The representation of that event guarantees that I will react to a picture of a rowboat on a lake in a special way. No sample of adults of the same age, sex, and health tested at the same time of day produces identical profiles of brain activity to a particular incentive. There is always variation, sometimes to an extraordinary degree, because each person brings a different history to the context of evaluation.

The patterns of neural activity in the prefrontal cortex of monkeys solving a series of difficult problems reflect both the current perception and the animal's prior successes and failures with the problem set.[26] A study of rats provides an example of the weak relation between neural events and behaviors as each changes over time. Electrodes placed in the striatum recorded neural activity as the animals learned to make a correct turn in a T-maze. A distinct tone signaled whether they should turn right or left in order to receive a

reward. After mastering the task, by the fifth day, they were given at least seven additional training sessions. Two results are relevant to this discussion. First, as the rats learned the correct turn fewer neurons became active when they were at the choice point and about to make a critical response. Surprisingly, over time more neurons became active when the animal was in the start box before a trial began. Second, the changes in neural activity over the sessions were not correlated with any single behavioral measurement, like speed of running or the probability of a correct turn. This extensive analysis of activity in a relevant brain structure did not permit prediction of behavior in a relatively simple, highly controlled situation.

Additional empirical support for this claim comes from a study adults exposed to twelve-second segments of two familiar melodies: one happy in content (from Saint-Saëns's *Carnival* *mals*) and one sad (Bruch's *Kol Nidrei*). The investigator r second-to-second changes in the 8–12 Hz band of the EE the subjects listened to the melodies. There was extraordin vidual variation among the EEG profiles to the two dif ments. It was not possible to determine, from this whether a person was listening to happy or sad music.[27]

The behaviors of two male lobsters, facing each ot been given identical injections of serotonin will diffe one animal has been defeated by the other.[28] Even t biological correlates of the prior defeat experience. ical data uniquely defines the experience of def this event must be described in psychological lan not possible to give a biologist a lobster and as with only biological measurements and no hi information, whether the animal has been def in the recent past.

Two groups of adults subjected to similar complex example of this important princip

SCHEMATA

The term "schema" (plural "schemata") refers to a representation of an event, often combined with features of the accompanying context, which retains, to varying degrees, the patterned features of the event—a relation called veridicality.[30] It is likely that schemata are the first psychological structures to emerge from the pattern of brain activity evoked by a sensory event.

The ability to recognize the face of a person encountered only once, without having imposed a verbal label on the stranger, is one reason to posit representations that retain some of the patterned features of the original event. Stephen Kosslyn's elegant studies on imagery provide another reason, as does the apparent retention of normal perceptual priming performance in an amnesic patient with severely impaired recognition memory.[31] Adults who describe a set of faces with words are less able to recognize those faces later than subjects who store them as schemata and do not describe them verbally.[32]

For the same reason, eleven-year-old Mayan Indian children living in a small, isolated village in northwest Guatemala performed as well as eleven-year-old Boston children when asked to recognize, following a two-day delay, color photographs of objects such as a telescope, a toaster, and a golf club—objects that the Boston children knew by name but that the Mayan children had never encountered before and, therefore, could not name. Both groups of children correctly recognized almost 90 percent of the pictures.[33] The excellent recognition-memory performance of the Guatemalan children was due to the creation of schemata for the pictures of the objects.

There are at least two different schematic forms. Visceral schemata, which originate in the activity of sensory receptors in body organs, skin, nose, tongue, muscles, and the inner ear, represent bodily states. Sensory receptors in these bodily sites relay information about physiological state, velocity of head and body, and muscular patterns to the medulla, limbic structures, and cortex. The information in these volleys, easy to recognize but often transient, produces representations that are difficult to re-create, and many are represented symbolically as pleasant or unpleasant after relevant semantic structures are acquired in the second or third year. Although we are usually unaware of these representations, they influence our decisions and actions.

It is well known that the memory of an event is preserved for a longer time if an emotionally arousing experience occurred at the same time. It appears that this phenomenon is influenced in part by activity in the nucleus tractus solitarius in the medulla, which receives visceral information and sends projections to the amygdala to enhance norepinephrine release from the amygdalar neurons and, as a consequence, to produce changes in heart rate, blood pressure, and other brain structures.

Patients with bilateral damage to the amygdala, for example, apparently fail to activate appropriate visceral schemata when they look at photos of faces that normal adults judge as untrustworthy, for they rate these faces as trustworthy. Neuronal ensembles in the orbitofrontal cortex, which receive information from the amygdala, contribute to the activation of visceral schemata that are part of an empathic reaction to the affect state of another. That is why patients with bilateral damage to this area cannot appreciate the class of comment we call *faux pas.* They would not recognize that Bill's comment to Mary in the following sentence is inappropriate: "When Mary, who gave Bill an expensive crystal vase, accidentally broke this valuable object Bill replied, 'I never liked the vase anyway.'"[34]

Every time we see a familiar friend, relative, or lover, a circuit that involves the hippocampus, amygdala, and orbitofrontal cortex is activated. Even though we do not consciously experience any distinct feeling, this neural activity contributes to our recognition of a person as someone we know. The rare patients for whom this circuit is compromised believe that a familiar friend is an impostor because they do not activate this circuit. Thus visceral schemata play an important role in the common human experience of seeing a friend.

Perceptual schemata are representations that originate in external events and are more easily retrieved from memory than visceral schemata. Most adults who can retrieve a rich visual representation of a Gothic cathedral visited years ago cannot re-create the pain of a past toothache or the taste of a chocolate mousse.

The fact that hippocampal lesions impair a rat's ability to acquire a conditioned fear response (such as freezing) if the conditioned stimulus is a state of hunger, represented by visceral schemata, but do not impair the acquisition of a conditioned freezing reaction to a light or a tone supports the need to award visceral representations of bodily states a distinct status.[35]

It is necessary, also, to distinguish between a schematic representation of the immediate sensory surround, which is constantly changing, and preserved schematic representations. Harry Helson noted many years ago that an animal is always at some momentary level of adaptation to its current sensory envelope.[36] A change in the components of the envelope that define the adaptation level usually leads to increased alertness, an automatic attempt to assimilate the change, and a distinct event-related potential.[37] Even newborn infants are alerted by a change in light, sound, or touch. Most of the time assimilation occurs and the individual establishes a new level of adaptation. When adaptation is not possible—for example, when a light is too intense—the individual does something to cope with the event.

Schematic representations of external events differ from the visceral schemata for hunger, rapid heartbeat, or cramps in two important ways. First, a person can choose to attend or not attend to most external events; that power is seriously compromised for bodily sensations. Second, visceral schemata have a weaker link to semantic structures than do those representing external events. Information from the body synapses primarily on the corticomedial and central areas of the amygdala, while visual and auditory stimuli synapse first on the lateral area. Reciprocal connections with cortical association areas are richer for the lateral than for the corticomedial and central areas. Hence associations between bodily sensations and language are less well elaborated. Languages have very few words to describe olfactory events. We usually describe a smell by saying "It smells like _____," where the blank refers to some other object, such as a rose. Adults presented either with fifteen familiar odorants or with the words for those odorants (coffee, cinnamon, rubbing alcohol), and asked to write down the memories evoked by the odors or the words as well as how often they had thought about each memory in the past, reported less frequent reflection or conversation about the memories evoked by the odorants than about those evoked by the words.[38] One reason why questionnaires and interviews are relatively insensitive indexes of human emotional states, and why scientists code changes in face, posture, and physiological reactions to aid inferences about a person's emotions, is that the English language has a limited number of words to describe the changes in bodily sensations that are the components of every emotion.

SENSORIMOTOR REPRESENTATIONS

Representations of coordinated motor sequences, a third structure, permit the skilled performances of violinists and athletes as well as implementation of everyday routines. Piaget called the goal-directed actions of infants sensorimotor schemes. However, one-year-old infants cry and thrash when the expected outcome of their reaching for an object does not occur, but show quiet interest when an expected perceptual event fails to occur.[39] The distinctively different reactions to these two forms of discrepancy affirm the suggestion that schemata and sensorimotor schemes are different structures.

Studies of six-and-a-half-month-old infants illustrate the ease with which distinctive sensorimotor representations are activated. The infants first saw either a small or a large hoop while simultaneously hearing a distinctive sound that accompanied the presentation of each object. After a number of familiarization trials, the room was darkened and the infant heard one of the two sounds but could not see whether the hoop was small or large. The infants adjusted their actions to fit the sound: they reached with both hands to the sound that had accompanied the large hoop but reached with one hand to the sound that had accompanied the small hoop.[40]

Alain Berthoz argues that, because neurons in many brain sites respond to more than one sensory input and facilitate sensorimotor structures, every object in the visual space activates, simultaneously, a motor response.[41] For example, some neurons in the superior colliculus are activated by both the sight and the sound of an object and contiguous cells send projections to motor centers. Some neurons in the parietal lobe respond to changes in the spatial location of an object as well as to somatosensory signals from the agent's limbs.

Each individual has acquired an envelope of actions to particular classes of events. The sight of a cup, for example, is linked to the representations for grasping, sipping, washing, and placing in a cupboard. Presumably each class of sensorimotor pattern involves a unique profile of brain activation. Two monkeys, with over three hundred electrodes in the prefrontal cortex, were taught three different cognitive tasks requiring the same simple motor action of moving the eyes to a particular location. One task required the animal to remember the location of a visual stimulus over a short delay and to move the eyes to that place. The second task required remembering the specific features of a visual stimulus over a delay and moving the eyes to that stimulus rather than another. The third task required learning to move the eyes to the right to one stimulus and to the left to another. Even though the motor action was identical for all three tasks, a unique profile of neuronal activation accompanied each task, suggesting that the animals had also learned a representation of the cognitive requirements of each task.[42]

Despite Berthoz's argument, perceptual judgments about the size and location of an object are very different from the scaling of skilled actions directed at the object. Perceptual judgment and visuomotor control are mediated by separate visual pathways in the primate brain—what we think we see is not always a guide to our actions.[43] The coordination between perceptual schemata and action schemes is likely for some events, but it is less obvious that this rule has no exceptions. Further research will be necessary to determine whether a motor program for reaching or touching is activated every time I see a flower on a table.

Psychologists have a choice in how they conceptualize schemata for events that have multiple sensory and motor contributions. They can follow Berthoz and conceive of a schema as a structure that combines all of its sensory and motor contributions. Alternatively, they can assume that the representations created by each modality retain their autonomy even though each is linked to others in the network. This suggestion means that the representations of the shape, sound, tactile quality, and motor programs linked to the sight of a silver dinner bell can retain their separateness even though they are coordinated. Nonetheless, Berthoz's insistence that perceptual and motor schemata are often coordinated implies that the most important distinction is between schemata and sensorimotor structures, on the one hand, and semantic structures, on the other.

THE INFANT'S SCHEMATA

The ability to establish perceptual and visceral schemata, present before birth, permits newborn infants to create schemata for some events in fewer than ten trials. Newborns can discriminate between recordings of their own cry and the cry of another infant; two-week-olds can discriminate the breast odor of a nursing woman from other odors.[44] Four-month-olds have acquired schemata permitting them to recognize many faces, voices, sounds, objects, and spatial patterns. Five-month-olds shown a pattern of three-dimensional geometric forms arranged in a row became attentive when the spatial pattern of the three forms was altered to form either a triangular or an oblique configuration.[45]

Infants are born with biases to attend to particular properties of objects. The behaviorists, who wrote in the early and middle twentieth century, were reluctant to award the brain any initial preferences. The infant, in this Lockean image, had to construct, from bits and pieces, schemata for a face, a cup, a door. But a new cohort of developmental scientists has rejected the tired metaphor of a blank slate for the young mind and has shown that the brain of each species is selectively attentive to particular events and, therefore, biologically prepared to favor the creation of particular schemata.

Young infants usually look longer at circular than at linear forms, at moving than at stationary objects, and at contoured than at homogeneous fields. It is not surprising, therefore, that infants create schemata for human faces, for faces are circular, are often in motion, and contain a great deal of contour. Infants also habituate faster to vertically symmetric designs than to asymmetric displays and by the end of the first year look longer at the former than at the latter. This bias may explain why newborns look longer at photographs of female faces judged as attractive than at those rated as less attractive, for attractive faces are more symmetrical. It may also explain why the eyes of the newborn will track a moving schematic face longer than most events, for this pattern has vertical symmetry around the pair of eyes.[46]

Young infants construct schemata for objects quickly because they are biologically prepared to perceive whole objects and do not have to connect lines with curves to create a representation of a cup or a hand. The mind/brain of young infants is biased to create a firmer schema for the shape of an object than for its color or surface pattern, even though they can discriminate among colors and patterns. Four-and-a-half-month-olds first saw a green ball on their left move to the right and disappear behind a broad screen. Several seconds later they saw a green box, not the ball, emerge from the right side of the screen. The green box then moved to the left and disappeared behind the screen, and a few seconds later a green ball emerged on the left side. Other infants saw the same objects move in the same way, but this time the screen was too narrow to permit both the ball and the box to fit behind the screen. The infants who witnessed this second sequence were more attentive to the objects than those who saw the same sequence with the broad screen, suggesting that they noticed that the object that emerged from the screen was not the same shape as the one that had disappeared several seconds earlier, for infants usually pay more attention to unfamiliar events. However, when the color or pattern of stripes on the ball or box was changed, the infants were far less attentive.[47] That is, the shape of the object had greater salience than its color or pattern. However, twelve-month-olds looked longer than younger infants when the ball had a changed color as it emerged from the screen, suggesting that, with age, infants are able to represent a larger number of features of an object.

But the distinctiveness of a feature, defined by its power to capture attention, is rarely absolute and is usually a function of the situation, the particular discrimination the agent is trying to make, and especially the total event of which the feature is a component. A shout is maximally distinctive in a forest but minimally distinctive on a city street. It should be possible therefore to arrange conditions so that infants look longer at a change in color or surface pattern than at a change in shape. When a human hand moved to touch a toy, six-month-olds were more attentive to a change in the shape of the toy than to a change in the path of motion of the hand. But when a rod moved to touch the toy, infants looked longer when the path of motion changed.[48] The context determined whether infants treated a change in object shape or a change in path of motion as the more distinctive feature of an event.

Every experience must be described as a figural event in a context. The distinctiveness of each feature is a function of the event of which it is a component; the distinctiveness of each event is a function of the context in which it appears, including the temporal delay since the last time it appeared.[49] The distinctiveness of the sound of moving water depends on whether the event is an open faucet or an open garden hose, and the distinctiveness of that event depends on whether a person is or is not monitoring the running water. Every description of an event must acknowledge, explicitly or implicitly, the context in which it occurs. The theoretical advantage of treating every event this way is analogous to the biologist's appreciation that every gene resides in the larger context of the genome, as well as the advantages in relativity theory of treating space and time as a unity. This truth motivated the philosopher Charles Travis to argue in *Unshadowed Thought* that the context of an utterance affects its meaning: "It is, irreducibly, the circumstances in which we speak that make *what* we say just what it is."[50]

The two hemispheres of the brain appear to assume different responsibilities during the processing of sensory information that contains substantial variation in the frequency of its components.

The right hemisphere more often elaborates the lower-frequency components of an event, while the left hemisphere elaborates the higher-frequency information in the array,[51] although these biases are modulated by the salience of the features.[52] This view assumes, for example, that the right hemisphere more completely processes the changing prosody of a speaker's communication, while the left hemisphere is biased initially to process the rapidly moving stream of phonemes in the vocal signal. Because the fetus, surrounded by fluid and tissue, hears predominantly low-frequency sounds, more auditory stimulation should be processed by the right than by the left hemisphere. This speculation could be one basis for the earlier development of the former structure in humans.

SCHEMATIC CONCEPTS

Infants create prototypic schemata that are psychological "averages" of a number of similar events—a phenomenon that is especially clear for the schemata that represent the phonemes of the local language.[53] Infants only eight months old have acquired prototypic schemata for the acoustic envelopes of the vowels and consonant-vowel combinations of their language and have lost the ability to distinguish phonemes that are not heard regularly but resemble sounds of the language they do hear. For example, if the adult speech does not make a distinction between *ra* and *la*, as is true in Japanese, older infants will cease to attend to a change from one to the other, even though they would have been alerted by the same change when they were two months old. These schematic prototypes, like the average schematic representation of two dozen successive sunsets over a bay, might be called schematic concepts.

One study of six-month-old infants provides an elegant example of a schematic concept. Each infant first repeatedly saw eight different female faces of equal attractiveness. If the infants created a schematic concept of the eight faces (that is, a mental average of the eight), they should look longer at an unfamiliar ninth face than at a constructed average of the eight which they had never seen, because infants usually look longer at unfamiliar than at familiar faces. That is exactly what the infants did, indicating that they must have created a schematic concept of the eight faces.[54]

Infants can also create schematic concepts for temporal patterns of unfamiliar vocal sounds. Seven-month-olds first heard a two-minute speech sample containing three representations of each of sixteen three-syllable utterances of the form a-b-a, but the syllables in each utterance were different. For example, on the first trial the infant might hear "ga-ti-ga," and on the next trial "li-no-li," and on the third trial "bo-gu-bo." The single feature shared by all the utterances was that the first and third syllables were identical. After the infants became familiar with this pattern they heard either an utterance with the same form—a-b-a—or a new set of three syllables having a new form, for example a-b-b, as in "wo-fe-fe." The infants were alerted by and displayed greater attention to the unfamiliar a-b-b pattern,[55] indicating that they had created schematic concepts for the temporal pattern of the vocal sounds.

Thus it should not be surprising that infants can create schemata for brief musical melodies, which are sound patterns of different frequencies in a particular rhythm. The schemata for an entire melodic pattern appear to be firmer than the schemata for the pitch of each note, for infants do not become alerted when the frequency of all the notes in a melody is altered, as long as the melody is preserved. Infants are alerted, however, if the frequency of one note in the melody is altered.[56]

These findings imply that the young human brain is biologically prepared to detect and to create representations for the spatial or temporal relations among discrete events and to award priority to these patterns. As we shall see in Chapter 2, the representations of the order of semantic structures define the syntax of a language.

The distinction between a schema and a schematic concept is captured by the comparison of a person's conscious categorization of physically similar but not identical spoken syllables with the brain's reaction to a deviant sound. There is a continuum of acoustic energy from the labial syllable *ba* to the dental *da* to the retroflex Hindi syllable *ḍa*. Adults often perceive physically different acoustic forms of *ba* (or *ḍa*) as perceptually equivalent and do not report hearing two different syllables. However, a clear brain response in the EEG occurs when a variant of *ba* is presented as a deviant stimulus following a string of identical presentations of a different variant of *ba*. Cats, too, show an event-related potential to a deviant tone even though they may not orient to it.[57] The brain detects subtle differences that consciousness ignores because the mind treats a set of different *ba* sounds as a schematic concept. The schemata for a friend's face and voice provide a plainer example. A person may not notice the difference in vocal timbre of a friend who says "hello" with a slightly hoarse voice, even though his brain may react with a distinct waveform to the friend's discrepant voice quality. These examples remind us of the gap between brain and psychological states.

The representations of features shared by events from two different modalities, called cross-modal processing, are also schematic concepts. Older children create such representations easily; for example, two-year-olds will detect a similarity between a loud sound and a large object. Three-year-olds will preferentially point to a sad face rather than a happy face after listening to a twenty-second excerpt from a Mozart symphony in a minor key, but will point to a happy face after listening to a segment in a major key.[58]

There is debate, however, over the infant's cross-modal capacity before eight or nine months because the integration of visual and auditory stimuli in the superior colliculus is immature at birth.[59] One-month-olds do not recognize an attribute presented visually, such as nubbiness (or smoothness), as the same attribute presented earlier in the tactile modality. Infants who sucked a pacifier that was nubby (or smooth) for ninety seconds did not show a special attentional preference to the visual presentation of a nubby (or smooth) pacifier.[60]

It is likely that a cross-modal competence matures in a major way after six months because the prefrontal cortex plays an important role in linking information from different modalities, and anatomical links among sensory association areas, the basolateral nucleus of the amygdala (which contains sensory information from many modalities), and the prefrontal cortex are immature during the first six months. As a result, cross-modal schemata may be possible, but fragile, during the first half-year.

We do not know whether a talent for creating schematic concepts is characteristic of all animals, only vertebrates, only mammals, or whether this competence was enhanced, in a major way, when primates evolved because of the dense sets of reciprocal connections among large numbers of neurons in the primate brain. Scientists do know that the primate brain is especially talented at detecting relations among events that occur over short periods of time or are spatially contiguous. The bias for detecting pattern permits the mind to move toward simplicity, even though there is always the risk of grouping events that should remain separate. For example, two-year-olds may create a schema for the spoken utterance "thankyou" that represents it as one word rather than two.

The events that occur within a short temporal interval, typically less than one second, are likely to be grouped into a pattern; as a result, the phonemes of a word and trios of notes in a melody will be grouped. Parts of objects that move together, such as the arms and legs of a tennis player, and spatially contiguous events, such as a cup on a saucer, are also grouped. But neither the critical temporal intervals nor spatial distances that bias each species to group particular features are well understood.

This discussion of schematic concepts does not mean that "concept" has one definition; rather, this term refers to a family of structures. Most philosophers are friendly to the a priori bias that the mind possesses only one kind of concept and have tried to invent a definition that covers all instances. This strategy has failed because the word "concept," like "truth" and "time," has multiple meanings.

Six-month-olds who have studied twelve different exemplars of a particular category (such as toy animals) will look longer at an exemplar of a new category (such as fruit) than at a new animal. This finding requires a term for the schematic concept the infants created for the animals. But this schematic concept will not explain why adults group together words that belong to the same semantic category when they recall a list of twenty-four words heard earlier that contained eight exemplars from each of three semantic categories (say fruits, animals, and vehicles). And the semantic concept that explains the adult memory performance will not explain why children treat large objects and loud sounds as if they belonged to the same category.[61] The empirical evidence demands the positing of more than one kind of concept, as other data demand the positing of more than one kind of fear state.[62]

Biologists, who are more pragmatic than philosophers or psychologists, adopt a less rational stance toward the assignment of natural phenomena to their conceptual homes. Until recently, most biologists agreed that a necessary feature of all infectious agents that caused human illness was a capacity for reproduction, which is a primary feature of living things. The recent discovery that proteins with anomalous shapes, called prions, may cause some diseases motivated some biologists to alter their traditional definition and acknowledge that some infectious agents need not have a seminal attribute of living things. The scientist who discovered prions was awarded a Nobel Prize, albeit with some controversy.

It would be aesthetic, in part because it is parsimonious, if the term "concept" had one set of defining features and a single meaning. Although formal arguments require a unitary meaning for each theoretical term, the behavioral sciences are years away from formal descriptions of most cognitive, emotional, and behavioral events. A majority of currently popular psychological constructs have multiple meanings.

ESSENTIALNESS OF THE FEATURES OF A SCHEMA

Recognition is rapid when the features of an event match those of the schema; recognition is slow when they do not. The features of a representation that permit rapid recognition of a class of event in a specific context might be called essential, although it is probably wise to treat essentialness as a continuum. A pair of eyes is a more essential feature of the schema for a human face than the ears. A pair of small closed geometric forms placed horizontally in the upper part of a circular frame is an essential feature of the seven-month-old infant's representation of a human face. Infants who had seen a schematic face consisting of two horizontally placed circles within the upper part of a larger circle attended to a vertical arrangement of the two small circles in the large frame, but did not attend to the same schematic face composed of two horizontally placed squares, rather than circles, in the larger frame; the pair of squares was easily assimilated to the schema for a face and, therefore, was not discrepant. Adults' schemata for human faces are so firm that adults display similar event-related potentials to a face with open eyes and one with closed eyes, but a different pattern of potentials to a scrambled face or to a hand.[63] Faces and eyes, but not lips, noses, and scrambled forms, elicit a distinct event-related potential with a latency between 150 and 200 msec.[64]

Events that alter the less essential features of a schema, which might be called discrepant, usually provoke more sustained attention than events that alter essential features, which might be called novel. Four-month-old infants were exposed to a mobile composed of objects of different form and color in order to assess their initial interest. Each infant was then assigned to one of seven groups. Six groups saw mobiles that differed from the one seen in the laboratory while they were lying in their cribs for thirty minutes a day for twenty-one days so that they could form a firm schema for that form of the mobile. The seventh control group did not see any mobile at home.

All infants returned to the laboratory after twenty-one days and were shown the same mobile they had seen three weeks earlier. Those who had been exposed to a spatial reorganization of the three objects, a change in less essential features, were most attentive to the original mobile. By contrast, the infants who had been exposed either to a subtle change in the arrangement of elements or to a major change that altered essential features were less attentive.[65]

Young children have difficulty recognizing events that do not contain the essential features of their schemata. Two-and-a-half-year-olds who watched an adult hide an object in a distinctive location in a miniaturized room did not recognize the correct hiding place when taken to an identical room of normal size. However, they were able to recognize the hiding place in the normal room if they had seen a photograph of the adult hiding the object in that room. It appears that the miniaturized room was so different from their everyday experience—that is, the essential features had been altered—that they created a unique schema when they saw the adult hide the object there.[66] Because so much of young children's experience is novel, they often fail to detect similarity between two events that share some features.

Over 90 percent of two-year-old children who enter a room they have never seen initially scan the location for ten or twenty seconds and then explore the area with no obvious signs of fear, suggesting that the size, shape, and color of the walls are not essential features of a new location.[67] But if the transformation had involved the essential features of a room, for example, if they entered a room with slanting walls and an unevenly ridged floor, they would probably cry because straight walls and a level floor are essential features of their schemata for rooms.

Most older children name snakes as the animal they fear most because this animal lacks the essential feature of two or four legs characteristic of the animals they usually encounter. The monsters that medieval citizens imagined to be real changed the essential features of the human form, for example replacing the arms with wings or the head with that of a dog. The sixteenth-century monster of Ravenna had a horn growing out of the head, bat wings for arms, a leg with reptilian scales, a foot of a bird, and the genitals of both sexes.[68] However, the emotions generated by these anomalies depended on the presumed reason for the pattern. The typical feeling was wonder if the object was believed to be the result of natural causes, but ranged from fear to horror if it was interpreted as a sign of God's anger over human sinfulness.

The essentialness of a feature for a class of schemata depends on how often it was experienced, its significance for the object's function, its perceptual salience, and always the context and the problem being solved.[69] But, as with the concept of distinctiveness, which refers to the power of a feature to recruit attention, no feature remains essential for all of the events of which it is a component. The metal nib is an essential feature of my schema of a fountain pen (the colors of the cap and barrel are less essential) because the nib is always a part of the object, is necessary for its function, and is perceptually different from objects with similar shape and function like the roller of a ballpoint pen. But the material composition of the pen, not the metal nib, is a more essential feature when I am differentiating inexpensive from expensive fountain pens. The shape and arrangement of eyes, nose, and mouth in a photograph are essential features if one is discriminating the faces of humans from those of dogs, but not essential if one is distinguishing men from women.

SEMANTIC REPRESENTATIONS

The fourth mental structure, and the only one that may be distinctly human, consists of semantic representations that combine the representations of words (lexical structures) with schemata and motor structures to form networks that are logically constrained, often hierarchical, and used to communicate information and to facilitate thought.[70] The distinction between schemata and semantic structures is of critical importance.

The relations among the features of my schema for a terrier in my neighborhood who barks early in the morning (the color, size, gait, sound of bark, and spatial relations among head, ears, eyes, limbs, and tail) are different from the relations among my semantic representations of this animal, which include close links among the semantic concepts "dog," "pet," "mammal," "domesticated," and "annoying." Support for this claim, as we shall see in Chapters 2 and 3, includes the performances of brain-damaged patients and differences in latencies, magnitudes, and sites of event-related potentials.

Schemata and semantic structures have different psychological functions. The former are used primarily for recognition of events, places, and objects experienced in the past. A person who has never seen a fire extinguisher will have a difficult time finding this object if told, "Please bring me the fire extinguisher," even if he understands the reason for the verbal request. Semantic structures are used primarily for classification, reason, inference, and communication, which are necessary for understanding causal sequences and maintaining social harmony. Schemata are woefully inadequate at these functions.

Although events discrepant from schemata and propositions inconsistent with semantic networks alert individuals and recruit attention, transformations of semantic structures containing minimal schematic components produce a psychological state different from the one created by transformations of semantic structures with a rich schematic contribution. The term "uncertainty" seems appropriate for the former; "surprise" an apt name for the latter. Uncertainty occurs if a person reads, "Justice for the majority cannot be achieved in any society." Surprise is more likely if a person reads, "Eating tomatoes is the sole cause of acne."

The Distinctiveness of Schemata and Semantic Forms

Some psychologists, recognizing the difficulty of measuring the separate contributions of different mental forms to a performance, choose to model cognitive processes with an a priori set of entities that have the same configuration. Connectionist theorists, who rely on amodal cognitive structures, would be frustrated if they had to acknowledge two different mental forms. Because it is not possible, given current methods, to know if an individual activates a schema or a semantic network to a particular event, most psychologists are loyal to the rule that cautions: "Do not reject a theoretical view, even if it is likely to be wrong, until you have an equally useful replacement." Because that replacement has not been invented there is some resistance to admitting that a person can have a schematic representation of the relations among parts of a scene without an accompanying semantic structure or any conscious awareness of that schematic knowledge.[71]

Some theorists assume that all mental activity consists of the manipulation of symbols; others argue that the mental forms are acquired associations. Neither group differentiates types within their preferred, but hypothetical, structure. Further, neither position solves the critical problem of predicting (or explaining) the degree of similarity among representations, in part because the similarity between two structures depends not only on the number of shared components but also on the specific context, as David Magnusson has argued.[72] For most Americans, semantic representations of cows and goats are more similar than those of cows and chickens if the context is the production of milk for human consumption; cows and chickens are more similar if the context is inclusion on restaurant menus. Most individuals regard turtles and crocodiles as dissimilar because of their different shape, size, habitat, and potential for harm. But biologists who study phylogeny regard them as similar because of their close genetic relationship.

Although certainty regarding the major classes of contexts eludes us, it is likely that some of the most important contrasting settings for humans include familiar versus unfamiliar, social versus solitary, safe versus dangerous, coerced versus freely chosen, engaged with a person of higher versus lower status, and engaged with someone belonging to the agent's defining social category versus someone from another category. That is why many social scientists insist that some of the behaviors displayed to a stranger in small laboratory rooms will not generalize to familiar real-world settings; hence the plea for ecological validity in the design of experiments.

A defense of the separate ontological status of schemata and semantic forms should not be required given the history of Western philosophical essays on knowledge. Bacon, Descartes, Hume, and Locke were convinced that the mind's representations of sensory information were the foundation of all knowledge. These patterns were Locke's simple ideas and, like our definition of schemata, were assumed to be veridical with experience. Complex ideas, in contrast, were derivatives of simple ones, and were suspect because they might not refer to real events. These are the semantic networks that have little or no schematic content.

Then Kant began to brood on this issue. The advances in mathematics in sixteenth- and seventeenth-century Europe, highlighted by the insights of Newton and Leibniz, made it impossible to defend Locke's experientially dependent conception of mental structures. Newton's inverse square law originated in a mind, not in sense impressions. Kant reversed the arrow of causation by making the semantically rich ideas of negation, reciprocity, possibility, existence, and necessity and the intuitions of space and time fundamental mental categories. Kant's a priori categories are implicit in the amodal representations that are basic constructs in a great deal of contemporary cognitive theory.

The distinctions among schemata, sensorimotor structures, and semantic networks have implications for current debates on the notion of consciousness, especially for the question of whether minds experience a number of qualitatively different conscious states or one unified state with different features.[73] As I have written elsewhere, humans are conscious of very different contents—or targets—including external and internal sensations, thoughts, intentions to act or to inhibit an action, and symbolic categories for self.[74] Awareness of a pink cloud at dusk can be mediated by schemata with a minimal contribution of semantic or motor structures. Awareness of one's posture while throwing a ball, which relies on schemata and sensorimotor structures, can be free of semantic networks. Put plainly, awareness of the taste of chocolate, the feeling of ice on the skin, and the pain of a cut finger, which chimpanzees also experience, differ in both profile of brain activity and subjective state from the awareness that accompanies remembering one's childhood home, deciding whether to have a second glass of wine, brooding about one's ethnic category, or trying to solve a spatial problem.[75] The combination of (1) conscious awareness of one's feelings, thoughts, intentions, and self-attributes, (2) inferences about the thoughts and feelings of others, (3) finger-thumb opposition, (4) an extensive episodic memory, (5) the ability to anticipate events in the distant future, (6) logical reasoning, (7) mathematics, and (8) a generative symbolic language distinguishes humans from every other species. Perhaps the most critical competence is the ability to imagine desired goals in the distant future and to work for years to achieve them. The awareness of a future desired state is as powerful an incentive for humans as encountering a desired event directly is for animals.

Because hominids split from their primate ancestor only about six million years ago, and *Homo sapiens* appeared about a hundred thousand years ago—a relatively short time in evolution—either most of these talents emerged at the same time or some represented a foundation for others. It is not clear, for example, whether language was the foundation of consciousness, episodic memory, and anticipation of the future, or whether the new brain organization of *Homo sapiens* permitted all eight abilities to emerge at the same time. Should the latter script be correct, it is not obvious which competences were most adaptive in the African savanna a hundred thousand years ago.

Both animals and humans rely on visceral and perceptual schemata to recognize a present situation and exploit sensorimotor representations to act in the world. By the second year of life, however, humans begin to exploit semantic structures in ways that radically change their interpretations of experience.

INCONSISTENCY AND
SEMANTIC NETWORKS

Semantic structures, which are so critical to human psychological function, begin their growth when infants begin to relate what they see to the words they hear, or, if deaf, to the manual signs that they see. By the final months of the first year most children display initial signs of understanding the meanings of some words, and during the first six months of the second year they speak their first words. Monkeys and children share the ability to detect patterns in the auditory stream that represents speech. Both monkeys and human infants would be able to detect and to create a schema for the sequence "bi-da-ku" if it occurred many, many times in a continuous three-syllable sequence of consonant-vowel combinations: "bidakupadotigolabubidaku . . ."[1] But only human children assume that a repeated pattern of speech sounds probably means that the speaker is referring to some event in the world.

Lexical and Semantic Structures

The representations of the auditory or visual patterns of words are called lexical structures. The fact that patients with particular lesions can recognize and read words but do not understand their meaning affirms the autonomy of lexical representations.[2] Infants who hear the phrase "What a good baby" hundreds of times in their early months create lexical representations for this sequence, even though these structures may have no strong link to schemata for events. Semantic structures are created when these lexical patterns gain meaning through associations with schemata. With the exception of onomatopoeia and sign language, the lexical components of semantic representations are not veridical with the events they represent. Fortunately, children form semantic structures easily, and the number of such structures expands dramatically from the first to the fourth birthday.

The following two sentences illustrate the difference between lexical and semantic representations:

1. Bill and Mary saw the mountains when they were flying to California.
2. Bill and Mary saw the mountains when they were covered with snow.[3]

In order to know immediately that the lexical form "they" in sentence (1) refers to Bill and Mary, but in sentence (2) refers to the mountains, it is necessary to activate the semantic knowledge that people fly and mountains are snow covered. Richard Shweder resurrects Benjamin Whorf's distinction between meaningful and meaningless words.[4] Americans associate the vocal sound "queep," which has no meaning in English, with the semantic forms fast (rather than slow), sharp (rather than dull), light (rather than dark), and narrow (rather than wide). But the meaningful word "deep," which has a similar sound, elicits the opposite set of associations because of the schematic and semantic forms linked to the sound.

The activation of semantic representations to words and events is automatic, even when the task requires an adult to attend only to the shape of a picture and not to its meaning.[5] The Stroop interference effect reflects this principle: children and adults are slower to say the word "red" when shown five letters printed in red ink that spell the word "green" than when the stimuli are simply five red Xs. Children are also slower to name the color of the outline of a series of aversive pictures if the semantic name for the picture is a single familiar easily retrieved word, such as "gun," "knife," or "snake," than if the picture does not automatically elicit a single-word description (for example, two boys fighting or a boy falling off a roof). Associating an unfamiliar lexical representation with a schema for an object is fragile before the first birthday[6] because the prefrontal cortex participates in this process and connections between temporal and sensory association areas and the prefrontal cortex are immature until eight or nine months. But these associations become easy after the first birthday.[7]

Acquiring Semantic Structures

The young child's first semantic representations are preferentially linked to schemata for objects, especially moving ones. English-speaking children have a more difficult time learning names for actions—for example, associating an unfamiliar word with a dynamic event, as when a toy car is pushing compared with pulling another object. Two-year-olds assume that if an adult speaks an unfamiliar word, say the word "spider," while pointing to an unfamiliar object on top of a sand pile, the word must be the name of the whole spider, and not the name for the location, the insect's legs or behavior, or the sand pile.[8] W. V. O. Quine did not acknowledge this inherent bias to attach words to whole objects when he wondered what a visitor in a foreign land would infer about the meaning of a novel word when a native, upon seeing a rabbit scurry for cover, exclaimed "Gavagai."

The attention of the one-year-old is recruited primarily by salient features of events, such as size, motion, and unfamiliarity. When a parent names an object with these features—for example a spinning top—while the one-year-old is either looking at or manipulating it, the child is likely to learn the new word and on a later occasion attend to the object for a longer time. But during the second year the direction of the adult's gaze becomes a salient feature. Two-year-olds infer that a word spoken while an adult is looking at an object is likely to be its correct name, even if the object itself has no salient features. But if the adult is not looking at the object the child is less likely to link the word with the object.[9] That is why many children do not improve their vocabularies very much by watching television alone.

It is not clear why two-year-olds automatically search the face of a parent to infer the adult's target of interest. Some might argue that they have learned that parental actions have emotional consequences; hence this habit could be a conditioned reaction acquired over the first year of life. Or parents could be salient objects because two-year-olds have created a schematic category that includes self and other humans. A third possibility is that maturation of brain circuits involving the temporal and frontal lobes renders children capable of inferring the thoughts of adults. Although these three explanations are not mutually exclusive, the last finds empirical support in the case of an infant who was observed at four, fourteen, twenty-one, and forty-eight months. This girl developed before her second birthday a profile of the autistic spectrum. Her behavioral profile at four and fourteen months was not atypical, but at twenty-one months she did not look at the examiner and her moods were labile. The dramatic behavioral change between fourteen and twenty-one months implies that a compromised brain prevented her from engaging the gaze of the examiner as normal children do.

The problem facing a young child trying to understand adult speech can be described easily. A two-year-old listening to her mother chat with a friend hears the mother say "Have one more scone" as she removes the baked object from a basket and places it on the neighbor's plate. The fact that the word "scone" is unfamiliar and is articulated with vocal emphasis leads the child to infer that the object is the referent for the word. If children had no initial cognitive biases favoring objects and words spoken with emphasis, the word "scone" could refer to the basket or the act of placing something on a plate. Young children not only assume that an unfamiliar word spoken in the presence of an unfamiliar object must name that object; they also assume a new meaning must be intended if a new word is applied to a familiar event. The power of change to attract a child's attention is the main reason why the language of two-year-olds is rife with words that refer to transformations, especially the sudden appearance or disappearance of objects ("more," "gone"), the movements of objects ("go," "off"), and changes in an object's state ("break," "fix").[10]

In addition, inferring the meaning of a new word is aided if the child knows the meaning of other words in an utterance. If the two-year-old knew the meaning of "eat" and the mother said "Eat one more scone," the child would find it easier to assume that "scone" referred to an edible object and not to the basket or the plate.[11] Further, the child who knew the word "bread" and initially thought it was the name of the object would accommodate to the perceptual difference between the spoken words "bread" and "scone" and learn, at that moment, the correct name for this new food.

Human languages differ in the degree of distinctiveness awarded to nouns, verbs, adjectives, and adverbs. English contains many words for objects that usually occur in either the initial or the final position of an utterance and are given vocal emphasis ("See the big *tree*"; "The *tree* is big"). Also, many English verbs fail to specify the details of an event ("give," "take," "hold," and "get" could apply to many different objects and movements). Hence it is not a coincidence that children learning English speak many more nouns naming objects than verbs naming actions. By contrast, Mayan dialects have more words that specify a particular action with a particular object (for example, the Mayan language has a verb that refers specifically to eating tortillas), and Mayan verbs occupy a salient position in adult utterances. As a result, Mayan children's vocabularies show equally large increases in nouns and verbs during the second and third years of life.

Nonetheless, many students of language believe that words for objects (nouns) and words for actions (verbs) are psychologically different structures. Some stroke patients with localized brain damage lose the ability to comprehend one of these syntactic forms more profoundly than the ability to comprehend the other. One patient's comprehension of nouns might be seriously compromised, while another might show a more serious impairment for verbs. Because the semantic representations of nouns are usually richer in schemata than those for verbs, the pattern of impairment in stroke patients might mean that semantic forms that are rich in schemata and forms that are lean in schemata are represented in different brain circuits.

Schemata become more firmly integrated with semantic structures as the child grows. Fourteen-month-old infants, who have just begun to acquire language, often use the physical features of objects (for example, presence or absence of legs) to guide their sequential touching of a set of toy animals. Two-year-olds, by contrast, more often use semantic structures, such as the names "dog" and "bug," to guide their touching, and are less likely to touch a dog and a bug sequentially because the two objects have different names.[12] And from childhood to senility semantic structures increasingly dominate schemata when individuals classify experience into meaningful categories. That is one reason why the number of verbal descriptions of childhood memories increases dramatically after six years and why adults, asked to recall an autobiographical incident evoked by a particular olfactory stimulus or the verbal name for that stimulus, retrieved more memories to the actual odor if the remembered event occurred before age ten but recalled more memories to the words if the event occurred after age ten.[13]

Syntax

This chapter is concerned primarily with semantic structures; hence I do not consider in detail the controversies surrounding the nature of the representations of the syntactic rules of the child's language. I noted in Chapter 1 that humans create representations of temporal patterns of sounds, sights, and motor acts. A violinist who has practiced a Bach partita has a representation of the proper order of hand and finger movements for the entire composition. An experienced air traffic controller has acquired representations of the temporal order of events on a monitor when a plane is approaching an airport.

The syntax of a language consists of the representations of the permissible orders of linguistic forms in well-formed sentences. These rules are Platonic ideals. Imagine the parents of a six-year-old watching their child kiss a pet puppy. The syntactic ideal for a query the mother might ask of the father is "Why did Kim kiss the puppy?" However, if the mother says "Kim kissed the puppy, why?" the father will understand that question to have the same meaning.

Readers will recall that infants younger than one year can create a schema for the auditory pattern a-b-a in trios of syllables. This talent could be related to the ability to learn that in the English language nouns usually occur before words referring to actions. But we should not assume that the schematic concept for any temporal

house and home, sick and ill, drunk and smashed. For example, the schemata linked to the word "fair" are likely to refer to a conflict in a noninstitutional setting, while "just" is more often associated with schemata for a judge in a courtroom. The word "house" is likely to be associated with the schema for a residence as viewed from the outside, while "home" is more often linked to schemata of a residence as viewed from the inside. Should this intuition be affirmed by evidence it would support the importance of the particular schemata that penetrate a semantic structure. It is likely that this intuition led Quine to write in *Two Dogmas of Empiricism* that propositions that described empirical events were not qualitatively different from analytic definitions because matters of fact influence all meanings. Although the pope is an unmarried male adult, few would classify him as a bachelor because his other properties render odd the sentence "The pope is a bachelor" but not "The mayor is a bachelor."

This hypothesis implies that the members of a culture that provides opportunities for varied experiences with a particular event, or a variety of actions with a particular object, possess a family of schemata for the same event category and, presumably, more synonyms. A half-century ago the term "death" had one consensual meaning for Americans and their physicians. Then a technological advance allowed patients in a coma who were about to die of natural causes to continue breathing with a machine that supplied oxygen to the body. In an attempt to cope with the possibility of large numbers of comatose patients remaining in the hospital in a vegetative state, a new term, "brain-death," was invented. Among physicians this semantic form is penetrated with schemata for an EEG recording without brain waves. This feature was not part of the semantic network for death before 1960. Thus when the referent for a word changes, as it has for words like "rap" and "fuzz," schemata change, too, and meaning is altered.

Elizabeth Warrington and Rosaleen McCarthy used evidence from lesioned patients to distinguish concepts heavily weighted with schemata from those with a weak schematic contribution, and speculated "that the relative importance of weighting of values of different channels of sensory motor evidence could possibly form the basis of category specificity in the brain."[16]

A picture that engages a schema (for example, a color photo of a tomato) has more efficient access to the semantic network than a printed word with the same referent. Thus adults are faster at naming the category to which an object belongs if the latter is presented as a picture rather than a word.[17] Evaluation of the truth or falsity of a statement is also faster if the statement engages a schematic representation; for example, adults are faster to answer "false" to "The color of carrots is blue" than to "The function of vitamins is social justice."[18] Adults even hold different understandings of the word "above" when the context is a picture than when it is a sentence.[19]

The different qualities of semantic and schematic representations are due, in part, to differences in activity in the right and left hemispheres. The right hemisphere processes words with a rich schematic contribution more efficiently than it does abstract words.[20] Subjects were asked to decide if pictures presented either to the left or to the right hemisphere portrayed objects that were either (a) living or nonliving, which is a semantic judgment, or (b) bigger or smaller than a cat, which is primarily a schematic judgment. Decision times were faster for the first task if the pictures were presented to the right visual field and, therefore, to the left hemisphere, but faster for the second task if the pictures were presented to the left visual field and, therefore, to the right hemisphere.[21]

Brain activity is greater in the right medial temporal lobe when individuals are activating a schema to name objects, especially unfamiliar ones, but greater in the left medial temporal lobe when they are reading words.[22] Even when the cognitive requirements of a task do not change, the pattern of PET activity is different when the information is presented verbally from when it is presented pictorially.[23]

Because the visceral schemata linked to an emotion are more fully represented in the right than in the left hemisphere, it is likely that events that engage schemata more often provoke activity in targets of the autonomic nervous system. Adults were asked to imagine that the police suspected them of having participated in a murder. Some subjects were then shown photographs of the murder victim and of faces that varied in the number of features shared with the victim. Faces that were similar to that of the victim provoked larger skin conductance reactions than faces that shared no features with that of the victim. However, when instead of looking at photographs subjects were given a verbal description of the victim and presented with verbal descriptions that varied in the number of features shared with the victim, the skin conductance responses did not vary as a function of the features described.[24] It appears that peripheral sympathetic activity is activated more easily by schemata and semantic representations penetrated with schemata than by semantic representations lacking a rich set of schemata.

The individual's momentary internal state, as well as the immediate context, can influence the semantic representations activated by an event. Adults heard single words that had homophones differing in their affective connotation (for example, "bored" versus "board"; "dear" versus "deer"; "bridal" versus "bridle") and were asked to spell the word on a piece of paper. If subjects had previously heard music that usually induces a sad mood, they spelled the word whose meaning was less joyful ("bored" rather than "board"). But if they had heard happy music, they more often spelled the word with a joyful meaning ("bridal" rather than "bridle").[25]

Events that share no obvious perceptible features—such as a cake and a sunset—are often placed in the same category if they induce the same feeling state in an agent.[26] Wittgenstein ignored this possibility when he argued that "game" was not a concept because its exemplars shared no observable features. In fact a playful psychological state, which is private and not easily measured, is shared by all the events we call "games."

Meaning

Perceptual and visceral schemata, sensorimotor structures, and semantic representations combine to form networks whose meaning is defined by the pattern of interrelations among the components. This definition of meaning places it within the person rather than in the community. Of more importance is the fact that sentences do not always capture, and occasionally distort, the meaning of the thoughts they are intended to express because schemata often contribute to the semantic representations that are the foundation of, but not isomorphic with, a thought. There is no guarantee that an agent possesses, or has immediate access to, the words needed to describe the schematic contribution accurately. This lacuna is especially characteristic of young children and adults with limited vocabularies.

Although the essential attributes of semantic and schematic representations are often dissimilar, some psychologists and philosophers are reluctant to distinguish among semantic representations that vary in their schematic contribution.[27] For example, the essential features of the semantic network for "woman" include the biological capacity to conceive and to give birth to an infant. These qualities are not the most essential features of the schematic representation "woman," which include body build, costume, and amount and arrangement of hair. A woman with a crew-cut wearing cowboy boots is discrepant from the schematic representation for woman but not from the semantic one. The newspaper reports that

Susan Smith drowned her children in a lake are discrepant from the semantic representation of woman but not from the schematic one.

The behavior of a woman who had lost her right amygdala and had a seriously compromised left amygdala affirms the difference among perceptual, semantic, and motor structures. Although the woman could correctly name the emotion that matched a written sentence and could simulate the correct facial expression for six different emotions, she could not judge the level of fear in a photograph of a face with a fearful expression. Surprisingly, however, she could assess the intensity of emotion in photographs of faces displaying surprise and anger.[28] Apparently a face with a fearful expression did not engage her schemata for this concept, even though the printed word "fear" did engage the proper semantic network.

The schematic contribution to a semantic representation can change as new knowledge is acquired. Sometimes the schematic contribution is enhanced; sometimes it is diminished. The semantic network for the concept of a gene is an example of the former. The meaning of "gene" was bereft of well-articulated schemata before electron microscopes and X-ray crystallography. Many contemporary adolescents have a rich schema for the double helix. The concept of a structural gene is rich in schemata. The concept of a functional gene is far leaner. The concept of an atom in the minds of early twentieth-century physicists was penetrated with a schema for Niels Bohr's model of a sphere surrounded by orbiting electrons. Contemporary physicists hold a mathematically abstract conception that is difficult to visualize and, for some, may be relatively free of schemata.

This distinction between semantic structures that are rich in schemata and those which are lean in schemata is affirmed by an experiment that found that subjects who hear a list of words belonging to a common category (such as foods that taste sweet) are vulnerable to a recognition-memory error when, during a later test phase, they have to say whether a word was or was not in the original list. While listening to the initial list of words, they create the semantic category "sweet-tasting foods." Then when they hear a word for a sweet food (such as "honey") during the test phase they are likely to report that they heard it earlier even if they did not— because it fits their semantic category. However, subjects who, in the first phase of the experiment, see a picture of the object as they hear the word (for example, a picture of a cake appears as they hear the word "cake") are far less likely to make this type of error.[29]

The tendency to overextend semantic concepts affects the accuracy of a person's memory for the distant past. Because a verbal request to remember an early experience is semantic in form, subjects are biased to activate semantic structures. As a result, any event that might be a member of the semantic category, whether or not it actually is, may be recalled. Imagine a thirty-year-old man who has stored a childhood memory of being stung by an insect. If a psychologist asks "Were you ever stung by a wasp?" the man is likely to say yes, even if the actual culprit was a bee.

Five-year-olds have no difficulty appreciating that the semantic categories "sick" and "healthy" can change over time. But if shown two pictures of the same individual, one appearing to be healthy and the other ill, children deny that the two pictures could be of the same person because the schemata provoked by the pictures dominate the semantic meanings.[30] Furthermore, the meaning of the word "big" depends on the schemata activated. If the child activates the schema for trains, big means long. If the child activates the schema for pumpkins, big means a large area. And if the schema for a building is activated, big means tall.[31] These results, as well as the anxiety adults experience when they recognize the face of an old acquaintance through the activation of schemata but cannot retrieve the person's name, support the distinction between schemata and semantic networks.

The lack of correlation between the essential features of schematic and semantic representations of the same family of events, more common than psychologists acknowledge, has implications for one popular description of human memory. One of the most widely cited models, attributed to Jeroen Raaijmakers and Richard Shiffrin and called "search of associative memory" or SAM, assumes that events are encoded in terms of their features and aspects of the context.[32] This position, like most connectionist models of cognition and empirical studies of categories motivated by a preference for simplicity, fails to make a sharp distinction between the schematic and semantic features of the encoded representation. This claim finds support in the finding that adults spent more time viewing part of a scene that, on a prior exposure, was subtly different (for example, an object in the scene was deleted or added) than they spent viewing scenes that were unchanged, even though they were unaware that any scene had been changed. Their schematic representation of the scene caused their eyes to focus on the location that had been changed, although they had no semantic representation of that knowledge.[33]

Walter Kintsch, too, ignores the contribution of schemata when he asserts that verbal propositions are the primary structures individuals use in understanding text.[34] A proposition, according to Kintsch, is a predicate with an argument. Kintsch admits that his reason for indifference to the schematic contribution to semantic structures is that it makes it easier to write a description of text comprehension. He is also indifferent to the context in which a proposition appears. Consider the sentence "Grizzly bears can approach tents quietly at night." A reader who is camping in the Canadian Rockies is likely to brood about the aggressive potential of bears and have an emotional reaction. A reader sipping wine in a Chicago apartment is likely to focus on the remarkable ability of bears to move without making noise.

Elinor Ochs and Bambi Schieffelin provide a persuasive example of the different features of semantic and schematic forms.[35] The Samoan word "sau" is similar in meaning to the English imperative "come." Although young Samoan children hear this phonologically simple word frequently, it is absent from their speech because "sau" is usually spoken by a person of high status to one of lower status. Children, who belong to the latter group, recognize that it is inappropriate for them to use the word "sau." The child's schemata for adults with high status—two-year-olds cannot have a semantic structure for this concept—influence the expression of this semantic form.

The distinction between schemata and semantic forms is also relevant to the debate over whether categorization is based on features or rules. Feature-based categorizations more often rely on schemata or semantic structures penetrated with schemata, while rule-based categorizations more often rely on semantic networks with weak links to schemata.

Individuals will use physical features, functions, names, origins, feelings, and algorithms, along with other attributes, in categorizing events. This talent is fundamental to our species. The Wechsler Intelligence Scale includes a series of questions requiring the subject to name the similarity between two objects, for example a fly and a tree. Humans are so adept at detecting a basis for similarity that it is difficult to think of a pair of events or objects that would frustrate someone determined to find at least one shared attribute. Objects as different as a cup and a lung share the function "capable of being filled with liquid." Many of the magic rituals of ancient Greece and Egypt were based on a single shared feature. For example, a woman who wanted to attract the ardor of a man would melt a figurine of wax on the premise that wax and the human heart shared the "capability of being softened."[36]

Some of the semantic features that render two representations similar are unavailable to consciousness. Seven-year-old children, for example, evidently possess a tacit semantic network in which the concept "female" shares features with the concept "natural."[37] A group of children were seen on two different occasions. On the first, the examiner enhanced the salience of the concept "natural" by requiring the child to learn two different nonsense syllables to two series of pictures, one series illustrating natural objects and the other artifacts. All the children learned the distinction easily. One week later the children were given a similar task, using different nonsense syllables, in which they had to apply one word to male and another to female objects. When they had mastered this task, new pictures of natural scenes and artifacts were introduced. Most children of both sexes applied the "female" syllable to the pictures of natural objects and the "male" syllable to the artifacts. For example, over 80 percent treated a plant, a seashell, and clouds as "female" but street signs and a television set as "male."

The Logic of Semantic Structures

An important distinction between schemata and many semantic structures is that only the latter imply both the essential features of the referential event and the features the event does not possess. That is, most "is" statements are also "is not" statements. This logic does not apply to schemata. The sentence "The leaf is on the ground" implies that there was a time in the past when it was not on the ground. The schema of a leaf on a lawn does not contain that extra knowledge. A person who reads or hears for the first time "Banana is a tasty fruit" knows two facts simultaneously: the object is edible, and it is not a vegetable or an animal. However, the schemata of bananas have none of this extra information. If a semantic category is salient for a linguistic community, the phenomena that are not members of the category, no matter how varied, can belong to a complementary category for which there may be no comparable schematic concept. The semantic forms "insufficient," "unending," and "nonrefundable" are examples.

A second distinction is that most of the time schemata can be transformed without an accompanying cognitive tension. Dreams and reveries provide classic examples. The image of a smiling face can turn into a pumpkin without any of the dissonance that would occur if a person read "A smiling face is a pumpkin." Einstein's image of riding a light wave is said to have been one of the origins of his theory of special relativity. But the printed sentence "Humans can move at the speed of light" would evoke in most readers an immediate sense of impossibility.

THE BIAS FOR SEMANTIC CONSISTENCY

Historians writing about an era long before their birth, as well as biographers writing about individuals they never met, are limited to textual statements that, like magnetized iron filings on a sheet, are pulled into patterns that must honor semantic consistency. Thus a biographer's interpretation of a life based only on written documents is vulnerable to the distortions that the logic of language requires. For example, the author of a recent biography of Lenin notes that Lenin had excellent grades in school. The biographer uses this fact to infer that Lenin was "an extraordinarily ambitious and determined young man." This attribution is semantically consistent with the good school report, but the academic achievement could have been used to infer conformity to parental values or exceptional intellectual talent compared with other pupils in the school. I suspect the author preferred the words "ambitious and determined" because he knew these were salient qualities in Lenin's adult personality and wished to imply preservation of these traits.[38]

Freud's arguments were appealing because of the consistency of the schematically rich semantic networks evoked in his readers and not because they had robust empirical support. Piaget's appeal to developmental scientists was based on the opposite profile. The semantic networks for Piagetian terms like "ensemble," "assimilate," and "accommodate" are minimally schematic and difficult to comprehend. But because Piaget's empirical evidence was so reliable and visualizable, readers attributed to the abstract semantic structures some of the validity characteristic of the schemata created by the descriptions of children solving a conservation-of-mass problem.

The appeal of theoretical arguments in the social sciences and humanities too often rests on consistency among semantic networks that have ethical connotations that are not rich in empirical support. By contrast, the appeal of propositions in the natural sciences is more often based on semantic networks penetrated with the schemata created from the descriptions of empirical observations. Semantically coherent texts and natural events are different, but equally legitimate, bases for claims of truth. The preference for one or the other differentiates the two cultures C. P. Snow described many years ago.

It is not obvious why inconsistency among semantic networks evokes a state of cognitive uncertainty. The members of each language community learn the transitional probabilities between the words in a narrative, along with the frequencies of the large number of associations among words. A violation of either of these probabilities elicits uncertainty and, as we shall see, distinct brain responses. That may be one reason why magicians in ancient Greece used unfamiliar combinations of words in their incantations.

Some might argue that this uncertainty is an inherent property of the brain, analogous to the fact that dissonant musical chords produce a distinct profile of evoked potentials in the cochlear nucleus, different from the one produced by consonant chords, and motivate four-month-old infants to turn away from the former.[39]

A third view is that the cognitive uncertainty is built on early experiences of seeing that an object cannot be simultaneously big and small, up and down, light and dark, or inside and outside of a container. Six of the ancient Sumerian gods represented three pairs of opposites: earth/sky, sun/moon, and salt water/fresh water. However, this account does not explain the occasions of uncertainty created by statements that do not contain antonyms (for example, "Dogs are vegetables"). No current explanation of this phenomenon is satisfying.

The agent's cognitive frame always influences the semantic structures activated in a particular situation. This influence is less obvious for schemata. Each listener must make at least three assumptions when interpreting a communication. The first is the speaker's intention. A person at a dinner table who hears someone say "The salt" assumes the speaker wishes to have the salt shaker passed rather than to announce that some salt was spilled on the tablecloth.

Each person must also make an assumption about the meanings of the words immediately prior to a particular word. The meaning of "right" in the statement "He thought he was right" is different from the meaning in "He thought he turned right." Finally, the listener must make an assumption about the topic under discussion. The word "shot" in the utterance "He took too many shots" has one meaning if spoken in a bar, a different meaning on a golf course. The statement that a moving object approaching a screen with two small openings in it cannot pass through both openings is true in a Newtonian world, but not in quantum theory. As noted earlier, Quine recognized that all definitions assume some facts and none is true simply because of the relations among the semantic forms

RELATIONS AMONG REPRESENTATIONS

Perhaps the most important difference between schemata and semantic structures has to do with their relations to other structures.

The relations of *similarity*, *part-whole*, and *contingency* apply to both schematic and semantic representations, even though the specific attributes that define these relations can be different for the two structures. For example, judgment of the degree of similarity between men and women can refer either to schemata for body shape or to semantic representations of dominant motives. The contingent relation between force and acceleration can refer to schematic representations of a sailboat on a windy day or to semantic representations of Newton's equation linking force, mass, and acceleration.

Some relations, however, apply only to semantic structures.[40] Only semantic representations possess the quasilogical relations that take the form of hierarchically nested categories for objects and events (hyponyms) and opposites for qualities (antonyms). These relations assume prominence after the age of five or six years. When asked to say the first word evoked by a noun, children under six usually respond with a verb (dog—bite; sun—shine). After age six or seven they usually respond with another noun that belongs to the same category or is an antonym (dog—cat; sun—moon).

Most adults treat the semantic representation "dogs" as a logically necessary member of the semantic category "animals." These hyponymic relations are richest in English for words referring to living things, especially animals; a bit shallower for words naming plants and manufactured artifacts; and least frequent for verbs of action. The fact that the verbs most often linked to nouns for living things do not form hyponymic hierarchies implies that the mind/brain treats representations of actions as different from representations of objects, even though individuals possess schemata for dogs and for the act of barking.

A puppy named Max belongs to at least five hierarchically organized categories—puppy, dog, mammal, animal, and living thing. Even if the technical term "mammal" is ignored, a hyponymic hierarchy of four categories remains. It is difficult to find comparably rich hierarchies for most verbs or manufactured objects, suggesting that living things, and especially animals, represent a special class of object.

The reports of patients with lesions in different brain areas are in partial accord with this distinction. One patient had greater difficulty retrieving the names of animals, fruits, and vegetables than the names of many nonliving objects;[11] another patient more often matched the correct word to pictures of animals and fruits than to pictures of objects.[42] A third patient could not generate the names of animals, whether the features were described in speech or in print, or describe verbally the attributes of animals (for example, she could not name the color of an elephant). However, she could distinguish among the physical attributes of different animals when each was presented in pictorial form.[43] For example, she could tell the difference between an animal that was colored correctly and one that was colored incorrectly (a gray elephant versus a pink one). The mind honors the distinction between animate and inanimate things, and this talent emerges during the second year.[44]

Artifacts, unlike living things, are classified primarily by their function rather than by their appearance. Although hammers and cups have distinctive shapes, their functions are their salient features. Snakes, dogs, and elephants are as dissimilar in shape as hammers and cups but share animacy as a salient feature. One reason why animacy is a distinctive feature of living things is that self-initiated movement is the most obvious quality humans share with animals. A second reason for animacy's distinctiveness is that it creates uncertainty as to what an animal or a person will do. Finally, the brain is especially prepared to award salience to motion. A moving object alerts infants more consistently than almost any other visual event. Animacy awards the semantic network for living things a special structure that children honor early in development.[45]

The most important point, however, is that schemata do not nest into a consensual set of hierarchical categories. My schema of the place in which I work is a gestalt of a tall white concrete building close to a busy street. It is not a member of, or subsumed by, a more abstract schema. Although the semantic representations for "sweet" and "sour" are antonyms, no comparable relation of oppositeness exists for the visceral schemata produced by these two tastes. Individuals do not experience cognitive dissonance if the two taste sensations occur simultaneously. Similarly, the semantic forms for "good" and "bad" are antonyms in every language, but the schema of an adult striking a child is not linked to a uniform set of semantic networks among individuals of different ages or cultural backgrounds.

All philosophical arguments must honor the logical constraints that are inherent in semantic networks but absent from schemata. That is one reason why philosophers of language try to defend a particular definition of meaning and are often forced to take an extreme position that is consistent but vulnerable to critique. The perennial philosophical debates on realism, consciousness, justice, and morality remain enigmas because each involves a complex semantic network. However, a person who has just cut his finger on a knife and watches the blood ooze over his palm has no uncertainty about the existence of objects that can cause blood to flow and is certain that he feels different than he did moments earlier. Chimpanzees adapt well to their niche without semantic structures to confuse them over what they should worry about when the sun begins to rise over their forest home.

All explanations require semantic networks. The reasons for the American Revolution cannot be conveyed with pictures alone because schemata are not efficient at expressing causal sequences. Monkeys experience events but do not have representations for the causal relations among them; humans comprehend the contingent relations among events through construction of a semantic glue that holds the schemata of experience in patterns of causality that are occasionally true.

An investigator's initial representation of an unexpected empirical result that is not yet understood is penetrated with schemata. Darwin's representations of the external features of the tortoises and finches he saw on the different islands of the Galápagos chain were rich in schemata. A contemporary college student who reads that reproductive isolation of members of a species often leads to mutations that produce anatomical novelties stores this idea in a semantic network that can be lean in schematic features.

When further inquiry following an initial discovery leads to broad generalizations, the semantic networks describing these new principles can lose their originally tight link to the earlier schemata. Interpretations of patterns of cerebral blood flow using fMRI, for example, rest on evaluations of colored pictures illustrating gradients of activation in different brain sites. The scientists scanning these computer-generated pictures store their observations in semantic structures rich with schemata. This knowledge will be freer of schematic contributions after a deeper understanding of these data is attained.

Experienced psychotherapists who are not involved in research possess representations of patient profiles that are rich with schemata for the patient's posture, tempo of speech, vocal timbre, facial expressions, and mode of dress. These structures are seminal components of each therapist's representations for concepts like "depression," "anxiety," "schizophrenia," and "obsessive-compulsive disorder."

By contrast, the representations of these concepts among academic investigators who study these categories with standard questionnaire schedules, often administered by graduate students over the telephone, but rarely see patients, lack the rich schemata of the clinician. As a result, the two groups do not always agree on who is depressed or anxious. The clinician distinguishes between reports of depression by an obese adolescent living in poverty who is failing in school and a thirty-five-year-old successful, attractive, happily married lawyer who is also experiencing a prolonged bout of deep sadness. The epidemiologist is likely to conclude that both are suffering from the same major depressive disorder.[46]

The Meaning of "Know"

This caricature of the difference between clinicians and investigators engages the more general issue of what it means to "know" a domain of nature. Most scholars eager to learn about an unfamiliar domain begin by reading appropriate books and papers. The resulting semantic networks do not contain the schemata of the experienced observer who has witnessed the phenomena of interest directly. Sándor Ferenczi, a prominent psychoanalyst and one of Freud's colleagues, read about Tourette's patients but had never seen one of them. Ferenczi suggested that the patients' tics were due to a repressed urge to masturbate—a guess that evokes a smile in modern readers. My generation of graduate students who had not seen an autistic child believed in 1950 that autistic symptoms could be produced by a rejecting mother.

I began to read about event-related potentials ten years ago. My representations of these phenomena became much richer with schemata, and different from the ones I had created from reading the technical papers, when my laboratory began to gather event-related potentials on children and adults.

My colleagues and I have been studying the category of "high reactive infants" for over twenty years, and I have watched videotapes of more than six hundred four-month-old infants react to a battery of visual, auditory, and olfactory stimuli. Students who read journal articles stating that high reactive infants show vigorous motor activity and distress to unfamiliar stimuli construct a semantic representation that is much leaner in schemata than the one I hold. I suspect that one reason we attribute wisdom to the elderly is that their understandings of love, sadness, loss, vanity, envy, and desire are richly plaited with schemata that add texture to the more limited understanding words alone provide.

Each mind faced with a proposition can retrieve semantic structures bleached of or penetrated with schemata. Readers encountering the sentence "A fear state is a characteristic of all mammals" have a choice in the meaning they extract. Most natural scientists will retrieve semantic structures penetrated with schemata for the behavioral and biological phenomena (for example, rats freezing to a light that had been paired with shock, monkeys grimacing to an aggressor, children running from a large dog).

Philosophers, writers, poets, and historians are more likely to retrieve semantic structures that are synonyms for fear (words like "anxious," "terrified," "uncertain"), have a hyponymic relation to the word "fear" ("emotion"), or are antonyms ("serenity," "pleasure," "joy"). The retrieval of these networks will lead these readers to abstract concepts, such as "anxiety," that are popular in the social sciences and psychiatry.

The problem is that semantic summaries of evidence in support of a construct strain toward a generality that the phenomena may not possess. Like band-pass filters, they distort our perceptions and conceptions and, in T. H. Huxley's view, are "noise and smoke until the referent is specified."[47] "Intelligence," "neuroticism," "arousal," "regulation," "anxiety," and "attention" are popular examples of overextended semantic terms. The psychological concept of positive affect provides an obvious example of this unfortunate habit. Pride, laughter, ice cream, a log fire, sleep, sexual release, an embrace, wine, a raise in salary, and learning that a rival has had an accident are all potential members of this semantic category. However, these experiences are linked to very different physiologies, thoughts, and schemata. The concept of positive affect, which is not theoretically fruitful, appears frequently in psychological journals because of a semantic network that links the terms "pleasure," "desire," and "approach" in a coherent, consistent structure. The same critique applies to the concept of negative affect.

The extensive research on fear provides a better example. If a rat hears a tone and then receives a shock that it cannot control, it quickly acquires conditioned reactions of freezing and accelerated heart rate to the sound of the tone. Investigators assume that the tone, which warns of an imminent shock, elicits a state of fear in the animal. However, if the amygdala is removed before this training these reactions are not learned. Because an intact amygdala is necessary for the acquisition of conditioned freezing or increased heart rate, many neuroscientists believe that an intact amygdala must also be necessary for a fear state.

However, rats display other reactions to conditioned stimuli paired with shock: they also defecate, urinate, and show a rise in core body temperature when the conditioned stimulus appears. (The last two responses also occur when a rat is placed in an unfamiliar place.) Surprisingly, rats without an amygdala who are shocked in a distinctive chamber defecate and urinate when placed in that chamber at a later time.[48]

These facts require the positing of at least two different fear states. One represents the state of an animal with an amygdala; the other represents the state of an animal without an amygdala. It is tortuous to argue that a rat that defecates in a distinctive chamber where it was shocked is not in a state of fear but a rat who freezes is in such a state.

Further, the assumption that activation of the amygdala in these conditioning paradigms generates a fear state is vulnerable to a critique. Juvenile female rats without an amygdala will approach and lick rat pups while intact females avoid them.[49] Few scientists would conclude from this fact that the amygdala mediates a state one might call "suppressed maternal nurturance." The more likely interpretation is that the amygdala mediates suppression of approach to unfamiliar objects, such as rat pups. But the brain state that accompanies suppression of approach to unfamiliar objects is not to be equated with anticipation of imminent shock.

Because the amygdala is activated by unexpected or unfamiliar events, an explanation of the acquisition of a conditioned freezing response may not require the concept of fear. A sudden tone and the tingling sensation of electric shock on the paws are both unexpected, uncontrollable events that provoke the amygdala and its projections to the motor and autonomic sites that mediate freezing, a rise in heart rate, and other reactions. Hence, when the tone occurs a second time, the learned association between it and the shock leads the rat to freeze and show a rise in heart rate. It is not obvious that the brain or psychological state of the rat a few hundred milliseconds after hearing the tone is fundamentally similar to the state of a person who sees a tornado on the horizon or the state of a driver who sees a trailer truck bearing down on him at eighty miles an hour. Adults who voluntarily agreed to experience painful but predictable increases in heat applied to their skin showed enhanced brain activity in many structures as the pain became intense, but not in the amygdala. Another group of adults agreed to have an aversive air puff applied to their cornea as an unconditioned stimulus for an eye-blink reflex. Activity in the amygdala decreased over the 198 trials as the situation became predictable, even though the air puff remained aversive.[50] The amygdala reacts to the unpredictability of an event, not always to its aversive quality.

Most humans understand the word "fear," or its synonyms in other languages, to mean the conscious state of a person facing an imminent threat to his welfare—a grizzly bear on a trail and a tornado on the horizon are two classic threats. None of these events is a conditioned stimulus, for the fear state will occur the first time any one of these events occurs. Further, the probability of a fear state requires semantic knowledge about the danger inherent in these events and depends on the estimate of control the individual believes he has over the potential danger. Hostages vary in their degree of stress depending, in part, on their interpretation of their level of control. The semantically based estimates of danger and control of the situation seem irrelevant to the paradigm used with rats.

Neuroscientists have a choice when they reflect on what word to use to name the brain state of a rat that freezes to a tone that had been followed by shock. Although they have chosen the term "fear," this may not be the theoretically most fruitful way to conceptualize the animal's state. Pavlov did not claim that the dogs he trained to salivate to a metronome were in a state of hunger when they heard the sound that had been associated with delivery of food. Conditioned engorgement of the genitals of women watching an erotic film, which is also a classically conditioned reaction, is not to be equated with a state of sexual arousal. Most women who showed a pulse of engorgement did not report any increase in felt sexual desire.[51]

A human fear state, like the perception of pain, combines activity in brain, peripheral body structures, and thought—it is not just a brain state. It is a documented fact that varied strains of mice and rats show different patterns of avoidance to varied incentives presumed to generate "fear" (elevated maze, open area, electrified probe). A strain that failed to explore an unfamiliar area might not avoid an electrified probe. The presumed fear state that mediates avoidance is specific to a target.

Further, male and female mice of the C57BL/6 strain showed significantly different amounts of bodily freezing when put in a chamber where twenty-four hours earlier they had received an electric shock. The duration of freezing depended on when that shock was administered. If it occurred either five seconds or twelve minutes after they were placed in the chamber, male and female mice froze for equivalent durations. But if the shock occurred one minute after they entered the chamber, males froze more than females. It is difficult to argue that males are more fearful than females if they have been shocked after one minute rather than after twelve minutes.[52] The more reasonable conclusion is that there are sex differences in the forming of associations between the stimuli of the chamber and the shock.

The same principle applies to human children and adults. Children who are afraid of having an electrode put on their chest may not show fear of a robot or clown. I recently saw in our laboratory a three-year-old boy who had suffered serious burns on his face and arms and therefore had experienced frequent distress in the medical setting where he was treated. As a result, he was very fearful in our laboratory, even though his mother was present, when we tried to put heart-rate electrodes on his body. He said tearfully, "I want to go home." However, minutes later he showed no fear to a realistic toy snake and a person dressed in a clown costume, two incentives that often elicit fearful responses in three-year-olds. Fear, like anxiety, is not a free-floating state that can attach to any target. It is a family of states, each defined by a class of incentive. The idea of a single fear state characterized by a particular pattern of brain activity involving the amygdala reminds me of a saying attributed to Confucius: "The hardest thing of all is to find a black cat in a dark room, especially if there is no cat."

The critique of a single state of fear applies also to the concept of a reactive sympathetic nervous system. The evidence indicates low correlations among magnitudes of reactivity in varied target systems of the autonomic nervous system. A high heart rate is not correlated with a large pupil size, high blood pressure, or frequent galvanic skin reflexes on the palms of the hands. Each autonomic target is part of a loose confederacy, for it responds to local factors. And yet prose summaries describe the "reactivity of the sympathetic nervous system" as if the response of any one sympathetic target were an accurate index of the responsivity of the entire system. This is the error of the seven blind men exploring an elephant.

The habit of ascribing to animals human qualities that involve intentionality as part of the definition is easier when the animal is a primate. Three scientists concluded from a longitudinal study of macaque monkeys: "Early maternal rejection . . . can promote independence and the development of a less anxious personality."[53] The observations that lay behind this claim were that three of the nineteen adult monkeys who rarely retreated or bared their teeth when approached by an animal were more likely than the other sixteen monkeys to have had a mother who, during the first twelve weeks of the infant's life, made it difficult for the infant to attain bodily contact, either by moving away or by pushing the infant from her. The adjective "rejecting" when applied to a human parent assumes an attitude of dislike for the infant. The term "independence" when applied to humans assumes a desire to make autonomous decisions, and "anxiety" assumes worry about the future. Neither "rejecting," "independence," nor "anxiety" is an appropriate term for monkeys.

A final example of the seductive power of overextended semantic representations involves the interpretation of the potentiated startle reflex while a person is watching an aversive stimulus. An enhanced eye-blink reflex to a brief burst of white noise delivered while watching pictures symbolic of danger or harm (for example, a gun, a knife, or a snake) has been regarded as indicating an aversive or defensive emotional state. But there is no independent evidence to indicate that individuals who show large blink reflexes while watching unpleasant pictures are actually in an aversive feeling state.

Further, children who possess a temperament characterized by timidity and shyness over the first ten years do not show larger blink reflexes to aversive pictures than children who have been spontaneous and relaxed. An alternative interpretation of the variation in the magnitude of the blink to a burst of loud sound exploits the common experience of startling to an unexpected loud sound when one is deeply engrossed in thought. Some children showed their largest blinks to nonaversive pictures, such as two rabbits or an umbrella, while others showed their largest blinks to aversive pictures, such as a revolver or a snarling dog. Boys, who more often play aggressive games, showed larger startles to the nonaversive pictures, while girls showed larger startles to the aversive pictures. One interpretation is that the boys were surprised by the nonaversive pictures while the girls were surprised by the aversive ones. This interpretation is supported by the fact that adults showed enhanced startles when they were unexpectedly presented with a light following a large number of discrete tactile stimuli (vibration of the finger). The light was surprising, but was not an aversive event.[54]

Semantic summaries of relations between phenomena are often misleading because they imply linear relations even though many functional relations in the life sciences are nonlinear. Scientists often write about a positive, or negative, relation between two variables when actually the relation holds for only the top 10–25 percent of the sample. For example, the positive relation between age and the volume of the corpus callosum in children between six and thirteen years old is due primarily to subjects whose values were in the top and bottom 15 percent of the distribution of the two variables. There is no relation between age and size of the corpus callosum for children in percentiles 16–84. Similarly, the negative correlation between the sexual attractiveness of male guppies and their survival is due to the animals whose values fall in the top and bottom 10 percent of the distributions.[55] It is usually the case in studies of humans that if the correlation between two variables is less than 0.5, which is common in the social sciences, a minority of the sample is responsible for the significant correlation.

This principle also applies to timid, fearful behavior in children. There was no predictive relation between degree of inhibited behavior in the second year and a similar disposition at age four. However, the children in the top and the bottom 20 percent of the distribution of inhibition in the second year clearly differed at age four in their level of timidity, shyness, and sympathetic activation of the cardiovascular system. Thus the statement that an inhibited or uninhibited style of behavior is preserved from the second to the fourth year must be understood as restricted to children with extreme scores.

The probability that a verbal description will capture accurately a nonlinear relation between variables is as low as the likelihood that a person wearing large leather mittens will be able to pick up a half-dozen fragile glass sculptures without breaking any of them.

Identity

The state of uncertainty, or dissonance, created by inconsistency among the semantic networks for self has a special relevance for the popular term "identity." Edward Said, an academic who has championed the Palestinian cause, has written of the confusion he felt when he realized that his first name was linked to a semantic network implying a Western European family, while his last name belonged to a network implying an Arab pedigree. Said entitled his memoir "Out of Place" to convey the dissonance he experienced on realizing that the meanings of the two networks were inconsistent.[56] Similar cognitive tensions arise in adopted children when the adoptive parents belong to an ethnic group different from that of the child's biological parents, and in people who grow up in poverty and later, through effort and talent, achieve positions of high status, fame, or wealth. The conviction that a particular object, or person, cannot have two different names at the same hierarchical level is present in most children before they are five years old.

One of the major intellectual changes at adolescence is the detection of semantic inconsistencies in the corpus of beliefs about self. A state of uncertainty accompanies that discovery. Erik Erikson's suggestion in *Childhood and Society* that each adolescent is trying to find his or her identity elicited a feeling of truth because historical events had forced many young Americans to recognize that they belonged simultaneously to semantic categories that were not completely consistent.[57] Youth born in America to European immigrants during the first three decades of the twentieth century were forced to decide if they were primarily American, on the one hand, or Irish, Scottish, German, Jewish, Italian, Polish, Greek, or Russian, on the other.

Large numbers of working-class men returning from military service after World War II decided to train for professional careers rather than return to the blue-collar jobs held by their parents and other relatives. Women who worked in factories or served in the armed forces during the war added a masculine feature to the traditional semantic network for female. Accordingly, many young women had to decide whether they would retain the traditional female traits or adopt the qualities of professionalism, ambition, competitiveness, and sexual freedom as features of the concept "woman."

Further, many young people entered college rather than the work force after graduating from high school. As a result, many twenty-year-olds, who fifty years earlier would have assumed adult vocational and marital roles, were now in an ambiguous developmental category that was neither child nor adult. This was the first generation in America characterized by a large proportion of twenty-year-olds experiencing this ambiguous status. Erikson articulated, in graceful metaphors, his tension over the special inconsistencies in his semantic categories for self in ways that were deeply meaningful to young adults who were trying to resolve different inconsistencies in their own networks.

It may not be a coincidence that J. D. Salinger's popular book *The Catcher in the Rye*, published only a year after *Childhood and Society*, dealt with a similar theme. A recent biography by his daughter implies that Salinger, like Erikson, was trying to resolve inconsistencies in his self categories, for his father was Jewish and his mother was Irish Catholic.[58] The clash between these two semantic nodes was intensified by the virulent anti-Semitism in America during the 1930s when Salinger was an adolescent.

Attainment of the developmental stage Piaget called formal operations renders all adolescents vulnerable to detecting inconsistency in the semantic networks that represent their beliefs about certain moral issues. They recognize logical inconsistencies in their assumptions about sexuality, parental virtue, the price of honesty, and the existence of God. Twentieth-century history added dissonance over the proper semantic categories for one's social class, nationality, and developmental stage. A state of uncertainty over one's sexual identity has been added to this list over the past few decades. One lesbian, who had unexpectedly fallen in love with a male friend, told an interviewer that she did not know her current sexual identity. She described herself as "a lesbian involved with a man."[59]

A number of college-educated women who wish to enjoy professional careers experience more dissonance than their grandmothers did over the role of mother. The uncertainty created by the semantic inconsistency between the professional position and the maternal role leads parents who are also writers to describe the ordinary acts of caring for an infant as if they were the exotic practices of a newly discovered culture far from civilization.

The uncertainty over personal identity that Erikson addressed a half-century ago has been replaced by different uncertainties. Most contemporary American youth accept the necessity of a college education and therefore experience less conflict over their economically dependent role. Further, the recent celebration of the legitimacy of the values of all ethnic groups has reduced the ambivalence some minority youth of earlier generations felt over their family's ethnic category. There is, however, one critical change. A person's social-class category is now seen as reflecting historical forces outside the individual rather than implying the possession of inherent traits that are characteristic of a particular class position. Time has softened, somewhat, the rigid boundaries of religion, ethnicity, class, and gender, which earlier generations had treated as signs of fixed traits. Contemporary youth see these categories more accurately as no-fault accidents that can be repaired. The contemporary crisis among most young adults in industrialized societies is not "Who am I?" but rather "What will I become?" or, more cynically, "How much will I be able to get?"

A serious transformation wrought by historical events is the increasing anonymity among those who live in densely populated areas and the frequent geographical mobility from one city or neighborhood to another. These conditions, which were far less common before World War I and rare before the car and the train, pose a threat to a universal need to know that there are people outside the family who are aware of one's existence. This knowledge is as important as the evidence Descartes used to affirm the reality of his existence. When a person is unsure that representations of his personhood are present in the minds of others he feels an urge to do something to proclaim his presence and force others to acknowledge his existence. Some acts of asocial behavior can be motivated by this powerful need.

I interpret the modest commercial success of the film *Being John Malkovich*, despite its critical acclaim, to mean that American audiences under age forty were not emotionally moved by the film's harsh satirical analysis of those who are trying to adopt the properties of a different self. I suspect that the current young adult generation would not have nodded as approvingly as my own on reading Erikson's description of the conflict surrounding a search for one's "true" identity.

Metaphors

The speculation that transformations of the essential features of a representation and transformations of less essential ones have different consequences has implications for metaphors.[60] The essential features of the vehicle in aesthetically pleasing metaphors are less essential features of the topic. For example, in the metaphor "Humans are gorillas" the capacity to frighten is an essential feature of the vehicle "gorillas" but a less essential feature of the topic "humans." Note, however, that the pleasing quality of the metaphor assumes a particular context. If all gorillas lived in zoos and were drugged daily by managers the metaphor would not work. A metaphor is far less satisfying, if it is satisfying at all, when the features of the vehicle and the topic are either both essential or both less essential, as in "Tigers are scorpions" or "Redwoods are skyscrapers." This fact, together with a society's consensus about which metaphors are pleasing, means that the notions of essential and less essential features of a pair of events are useful. Even three-year-olds are sensitive to the difference between good and bad metaphors, for they process the former more effectively. For example, they remember "The chimney is a house hat" better than "The rain ate with three voices."[61]

Children's metaphors reveal that a semantic representation can function as a feature. One four-year-old girl, on noting her dresses packed tightly together in a closet, said, "Look, my dresses are friends." It is likely that the word "close" underlies this thought. But this representation has two different meanings: spatial contiguity and emotional intimacy. Apparently the sight of the dresses evoked the semantic network for the term "close," which, in turn, elicited the semantic representations that refer to the affective relationship between friends. The fact that a word with different sense meanings can be a shared feature tempts humans to categorize together objects and experiences that are very different in physical properties and functions. The diverse collection of events that humans label as good—friendship, chocolate cake, a promotion, honesty—is a classic example of Francis Bacon's "Idols of the Marketplace."

History continually changes the power of metaphors. If a particular concept becomes more richly schematic over time—the computer is a good example—metaphors in which it is a vehicle should become more satisfying. Conversely, a metaphor can lose its aesthetic power if the salient features of one of the concepts change. Metaphors involving the moon as a vehicle for romance are probably less pleasing today than they were a hundred years ago because today's generation of young adults, exposed to pictures of the pockmarked lifeless surface of the moon and the debris left by human visitors, has been deprived of the untouched mystery of this object. Metaphors involving a woman's foot, an erotic symbol during the Ming dynasty when young girls' feet were bound, have far less aesthetic power in contemporary Shanghai. The invention of trains and the need for accurate schedules of arrivals and departures made "time" a topic of concern and, following Einstein's rejection of absolute time, altered its metaphorical connotations.

The thirty-year popularity of animal magnetism or mesmerism in Victorian England, from 1830 to 1860, was helped by the invention of the telegraph, which made the idea of invisible transfer of ideas over space a possibility. It was easy to accept a metaphor in which a human magnetic force was the topic and the telegraph was the vehicle, for the success of the telegraph implied that humans could also transfer ideas from one person to another through the action of a mysterious force.

Because pleasing metaphors have a rich schematic component, and because the right hemisphere plays a more important role than the left in the processing of schemata, the following result should not be surprising. Subjects were shown pairs of words with brief delays between the first and the second word. Some pairs were related literally ("stinging-mosquito"), while others were related metaphorically ("stinging-insult"). Each pair was shown either to the right or to the left visual field and therefore to the left or the right hemisphere. When the two words were related metaphorically, the subjects tended to name the second word more quickly if the delay between the two words was relatively long (700–800 msec) and the words were processed by the right hemisphere. Presumably when the word "stinging" was processed by the right hemisphere, schemata for "feeling hurt" were evoked. By contrast, when the words were related literally, subjects named the second word faster if it was processed by the left hemisphere.[62]

The intuition that a particular declaration is correct has at least four distinct sources. A logically or mathematically derived conclusion from a set of formal statements is one criterion for truth. Correspondence between statements and observations is a second criterion. The ethics of the community provide a third foundation for the intuition that a declaration is true. Each cultural group regards a particular set of ideas as morally right, and any claim congruent with one or more of those ideas is felt to be correct. Copernicus's belief that the planetary orbits were circular matched the pleasing assumption that God used perfect forms to create the world. The possibility that humans were related to animals was not ethically pleasing to eighteenth-century citizens, and we had to wait until the late nineteenth century before many Europeans were prepared to consider Darwin's claim that humans were a close relation of apes. The fourth basis for an intuition of truth resides in the semantic relations among statements. When these relations contain metaphors that match the semantic structures of readers, the readers experience an immediate sense that the statements are valid. Freud's claim that the repression of sexual motives can lead to symptoms because it absorbs the psychic energy needed for adaptation seemed correct to many twentieth-century readers because the metaphorical relation between freed libidinal energy and health was popular. Although that metaphor is less pleasing today, the residual appeal of dynamic psychotherapy rests on the presumed similarity between citizens' inherent right to freedom from external coercion and their freedom to have any thought, simply because the word "freedom" occurs in both statements.

The popularity of Erikson's declaration that "infancy is the stage of trust" rested, in part, on the metaphorical relation between the primary feature of the state of "trusting another"—the conviction that a person who is necessary for one's well-being can always be relied on for help—and the infant's receipt of care from the biological mother. The latter is a secondary feature of infants because adults other than the mother can care adequately for the dependent infant. The primary features that distinguish infants from adults are the inability to locomote, to understand language, to feel guilt, and to anticipate the distant future rather than dependence on the biological mother for survival.

Formal arguments, correspondence with observations, accord with ethical premises, and pleasing semantic metaphors appeal to different audiences. Scientists are persuaded by the first two but resist the latter pair. Most citizens hold the complementary set of prejudices.

Style in Selecting Semantic Concepts

Adults vary in the degree to which they rely on semantic structures rich in schemata when they interpret experience and communicate with others. Some adults filter a great deal of their experience through abstract semantic networks for good and bad, rich and poor, high- and low-status, smart and dumb, honest and dishonest, pleasant and unpleasant. Others exploit semantic networks tied more closely to schematic structures. Aphasic adults who have suffered damage to the left hemisphere are less likely to rely on semantic categories and more likely to use schemata when trying to determine if a person is lying or telling the truth.[63] It appears that the second strategy is more accurate. Women may process scenes symbolic of fear and disgust primarily with semantic structures, while men may rely more on schemata, for the difference in recall of these scenes, compared with neutral ones, has been found to be correlated with greater metabolic activity in the left amygdala of women but in the right amygdala of men.[64]

Idealistic philosophical positions, such as John Rawls's in *A Theory of Justice*, persuade on the basis of semantic arguments concerning ethical ideas of fairness and justice that are lean in schemata. The first important paragraph in *A Theory of Justice* reads: "Justice is the first virtue of social institutions, as truth is of systems of thought . . . Each person possesses an inviolability founded on justice that even the welfare of society as a whole cannot override."[65]

Compare Rawls with John Dewey's more richly schematic opening to *Human Nature and Conduct:* "Habits may be profitably compared to physiological functions like breathing, digesting . . . Breathing is an affair of the air as truly as of the lungs . . . Natural operations like breathing and digesting and acquired ones like speech and honesty, are functions of the surroundings as truly as of a person."[66]

Kant's definition of beauty contains semantic concepts with a minimal link to schematic structures: "Beauty is the form of the purposiveness of an object, so far as this is perceived in it without any representation of a purpose . . . The beautiful is that which without any concept is cognized as the object of a necessary satisfaction."[67] This style motivated the members of the Vienna Circle to try to create formal rules for scientific prose.

Poets, too, can be placed on this continuum. The poems of Dylan Thomas are much richer in schemata than those of T. S. Eliot. Thomas often used words like "blood," "sour," "buds," "flow," and "cut." Eliot preferred words like "time," "eternal," "possibility," and "purpose."

On a recent visit to a museum I saw, in the same gallery, Rodin's sculpture of Balzac and Degas's *Dancer*. The aesthetic feeling generated by the former required evocation of rich semantic associations to the famous nineteenth-century French writer. The aesthetic satisfaction evoked by the *Dancer* seemed to rest more completely on schemata.

Categories for Observations

This discussion has obvious implications for the categories scientists select to classify observations. This process of conceptual invention is not well understood because of the long-standing tension between rationalists, who assume, a priori, the privileged status of certain categories, and pragmatic empiricists, who, being less committed ideologically, remain ready to change a category assignment in the light of new evidence.

The problem with the empiricists' approach, of course, is that facts do not speak. No corpus of evidence announces the semantic categories to which it should be assigned. For example, should the processes of human memory be carved into two categories of declarative and nondeclarative, three categories of declarative, implicit, and procedural, or four categories of declarative, implicit, procedural, and episodic? Homicide victims are more likely than most adults to be brain damaged or abusing drugs. Should we award these features significance when we classify those who have been killed by another? Such decisions have consequences for subsequent investigations of these issues.

The need to reflect on the best label for an observation is especially relevant for behavioral biologists and neuroscientists who borrow words like "aggressive" and "anxious," invented originally to name human intentions, emotions, and actions, and apply them to what seem to be similar phenomena in animals. When we describe a person as aggressive, we mean not only that the person acted in ways that harmed another but also that he did so intentionally. A two-year-old who bites a parent accidentally in play is not called aggressive. The attribution "anxious" was intended originally to name a private state of worry or uncertainty over a possible future calamity.

Although mice possess neither intentions to hurt nor a capacity to worry about the future, many biologists label a mouse who bites an intruder as aggressive and one who is reluctant to leave a familiar area to enter an unfamiliar one as anxious. Because the mice who bite intruders are also the ones likely to enter unfamiliar areas, biologists conclude that aggressive mice are minimally anxious.[68] However, most students of human behavior believe that the adults who are most aggressive toward others are those who are highly anxious about their security, status, virtue, or acceptability to others. The apparent inconsistency between mice and humans in the relation between aggression and anxiety disappears when we acknowledge that the words "aggressive" and "anxious" are inappropriate descriptors for mice. Biologists should invent other names to classify these interesting animal behaviors.

This claim is supported by a recent study of a behavior of eight strains of mice on the elevated maze. The animal is placed on the central platform of the maze, which contains closed arms that are dark and open arms that are full of light. An animal who spends a lot of time in the open arm is assumed to be low in anxiety. However, the three strains that spent the most time exploring the open arms possess a mutation that causes degeneration of the rods of the retina. Thus these animals spend more time in the open arms because they do not perceive light very well, not because they are "low in anxiety."[69]

One useful criterion to consider when deciding whether two events belong to the same (or different) categories is to ask whether the metrics for the phenomena are the same (or different). Most brain events are measured in microvolts, latencies, and changing sites of maximal neural activity. By contrast, actions, which are derived from sensorimotor structures, are measured in terms of speed, force, and the goal to which they are directed; schemata are measured in terms of accuracy and speed of recognition; semantic structures are measured in terms of information. The languages of measurement for the three classes of psychological structures do not map easily onto the metrics for brain processes.

The brain of a person who sees a semantically incorrect word at the end of a sentence (for example, "Carrots are easy to sleep") produces a negative waveform in the electroencephalogram at about 400 msec (called N4) after hearing the word "sleep." The person is unaware of this cortical reaction and will neither report a special feeling nor display an obvious change in posture or facial expression at the time the N4 occurred. In contrast, if a friend told the same person, "Guess what, you won the college prize of $1,000 for good citizenship," the person would be surprised at the news but probably would not produce an N4 waveform. Analogously, most infants shown a series of pictures of familiar and unfamiliar faces look longer at the latter, but show a larger negative waveform at 600 msec over frontal areas to the familiar faces.[70] Thus looking time, measured in seconds of behavioral orientation, belongs to a category different from the one used to classify brain events measured in milliseconds and microvolts. In the next chapter, which summarizes what scientists have learned about event-related potentials, I address this issue in more detail.

Event-related

Potentials

The detection of new structures in nature following the introduction of a novel technology is common in all of the sciences. The microscope revealed bacteria; the electron microscope revealed the structure of molecules; the radio telescope revealed the presence of the invisible matter that fills the cosmos. The amplifiers that permit measurement of synchronized neural activity to a stimulus have revealed facts that illuminate how the brain reacts to discrepant events.

The varied waveforms of the event-related potentials (ERP) in the electroencephalogram reflect the brain's response to sensory change, violation of short-term expectancies, and transformations of preserved schematic and semantic representations. The peaks in the waveforms are produced primarily by the synchronized activity of cortical pyramidal neurons. Amplification of the dipoles created by the synchronized activity permits recording of the neural excitation in the form of event-related potentials. The polarity of each waveform, negative or positive, is indicated by the capital letter "N" or "P," followed by a number that indicates the usual latency of the peak magnitude following stimulus onset. A dipole, which is a separation of charge in a volume conductor, occurs when an excitatory or inhibitory input from a neighboring neuron alters the charge of a post-synaptic cell. If the input is excitatory, positively charged ions flow into the cell, creating a negative charge in the contiguous extracellular space called the sink. The positive ions flow through a segment of the neuron and exit back into the extracellular space to create a positively charged area called the source. If the synapse is inhibitory, however, the sink has a positive charge. The disparity in charge between the sink and the source establishes a dipole.[1]

Over three decades of study of the ERP have revealed robust facts that support the distinction between schemata and semantic networks and the importance of distinguishing between semantic networks of high and low schematic content.

Response to Sensory Properties

It is not seriously incorrect to regard the cascade of waveforms that occur in adults over the first 1800 msec after the onset of a stimulus as reflecting four psychological stages (these latencies are slower in children). The two waveforms that occur during the first 70–80 msec index activity in sensory areas and represent the brain's reaction to the physical qualities of a stimulus (especially spatial frequency, amount of contour, motion, orientation in the visual modality) but not its meaning. That is, there is no evocation of schematic or semantic structures. These two waveforms are called P1 and N1. The waveforms of the second stage, typically between 100 and 250 msec and generated by neurons in the temporal cortex, reflect the brain's detection of the general category of an event—for example, whether it is a human face, an animal, or a house—but not a particular object. The third stage, between 300 and 600 msec and often involving the frontal cortex, appears to reflect the brain's reaction to particular events, such as the face of a particular person or

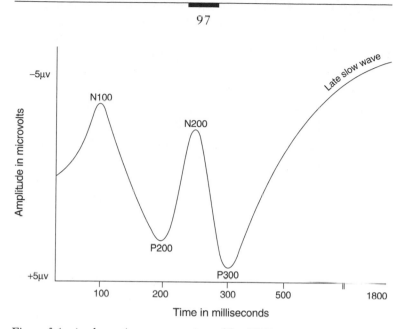

Figure 3.1. A schematic representation of five ERP components to a discrepant visual scene.

animal, as well as recognition of the relation of these events to stored knowledge. The waveforms of the last stage, between 600 and 1800 msec, reflect the brain's activity to evaluations of the prior stage when meaning was detected (see Figure 3.1).[2]

Recognition of a Meaningful Category

The brain's initial detection of the categorical meaning of a stimulus, accompanied by evocation of schemata or semantic structures for classes of events experienced in the past, usually occurs between 100 and 170 msec.[3] Activation begins in the occipital area for visual events and moves forward to temporal and prefrontal areas. The two waveforms that accompany this first appreciation of meaning are called P2 and N2. Magneto-encephalographic recordings reveal that the brain distinguishes between any face and another category of objects at about 140 msec. A distinct negative waveform occurs to human faces at about 170 msec, and adults who are experts at identifying birds show the same waveform to pictures of birds.[4] Thus rich experience with a particular set of events creates such a firm set of schemata that later appearance of a member of that set automatically elicits the negative waveform. The brain seems to detect some features of familiar faces before it recognizes the complete face: the component that appears at about 112 msec is larger to photos of famous people than to those of unfamiliar people.[5]

The distinction between semantic structures with rich and lean schematic contributions is supported by the finding that single words with a strong schematic contribution produce a larger N2 over the right than over the left hemisphere, while words with a weak link to schemata have a larger N2 over the left hemisphere.[6]

Figure 3.2. Subjects were instructed to attend either to the global "H" pattern or to the smaller "S" pattern.

The N2 is also larger over the right hemisphere when subjects are told to pay attention to a global design (such as the H shape shown in Figure 3.2), but larger over the left hemisphere when they are instructed to attend to the small component features (the letter S in Figure 3.2) making up the global design.[7] Readers will remember from Chapter 1 that global patterns are of lower frequency than the components. The N2 is also larger if the event is discrepant from the subject's corpus of acquired knowledge.[8]

Mismatch Negativity (MMN)

A change in a repeated stream of identical auditory stimuli, usually a change in the frequency or the duration of a tone, potentiates the N2 waveform to produce a component that usually peaks at 100–250 msec following presentation of the deviant stimulus. The enhanced amplitude of the N2, due to detection of the deviant event, is called mismatch negativity (MMN or N2a) and is believed to originate in the temporal cortex.[9] The MMN also occurs if there is a change in loudness, if a stream of auditory stimuli suddenly stops (indicating that the brain treats the pause as a discrepant event), or if the subject expects to hear a change in sound.[10] But the brain's detection of a discrepant stimulus need not be accompanied by an overt response or conscious recognition of a change in the surround. Adult English speakers show a distinct MMN to two physically different examples of the sound ba, even when they do not consciously detect a difference between the two ba sounds.[11]

The MMN is relatively, but not completely, independent of level of attentiveness, for it occurs in anesthetized rats, premature and newborn infants, and adults who are sleeping.[12] But the MMN is smaller if the person is distracted by a task (for example, required to attend to a visual stimulus) or exposed to pictures symbolic of a joyful or happy state.[13] Further, some individuals who showed a clear

MMN to a change in frequency or duration the first time they were tested failed to do so when retested two weeks later. This finding suggests that their psychological state, which was presumably different on the second visit, affected the magnitude of the MMN.[14]

There are constraints on how long the auditory cortex can hold the representation of a stream of auditory stimuli in sensory memory; the limit is estimated at about 3–4 seconds in adults, shorter in children. Although an intact temporal and dorsolateral prefrontal cortex is required for the MMN, surprisingly, an intact hippocampus does not seem to be necessary, for patients with hippocampal lesions do not show an attenuated MMN.[15]

The site of the largest MMN depends on the nature of the discrepancy. If the subject hears a tone of one frequency 97 percent of the time and a tone of a different frequency only 3 percent of the time, the MMN is largest over the temporal region. But the MMN is largest over a more central location when the rare event is a change in auditory pattern rather than frequency (for example, when a pattern like a-b-a-b heard 90 percent of the time is interrupted by a pattern like a-a or b-b 3 percent of the time). Further, infants show different waveforms to a change in phonemes (*ba* to *ga*) than they do to a change from a male to a female voice.[16]

The robust quality of the MMN has motivated scientists to exploit this phenomenon to diagnose children with academic difficulties. For example, children who have reading or spelling problems show an attenuated MMN when a stream of frequent words is interrupted by a novel word, and adult dyslexics show an attenuated MMN when the difference in frequency between the rare and frequent tones is very small (around 15 Hz) but larger if the difference is between 1000 and 2000 Hz, as in most studies.[17]

Evaluation of Meaning

The next two waveforms are called P3 and N4: the first occurs between approximately 250 and 800 msec; the second appears at 350–600 msec. It is believed that these waveforms reflect the evaluation of an event whose particular meaning has been initially recognized, including the fact that it may be a transformation of an existing representation. Direct recordings from neurons in the rhinal cortex revealed increased neuronal activation at 300 msec when individuals were reading meaningful words.[18]

Sometimes the P3 is larger when the event is discrepant from the person's long-term memory store than when it is discrepant from experiences in the laboratory over the last few minutes. However, the opposite result can occur: the P3 can be larger if the stimulus is discrepant from an immediately past experience.

My use of the terms "evaluation" and "recognition" as descriptors of brain events does not mean that these processes are conscious. Brain processes mediating the event-related potential can occur without awareness or focused attention to the stimulus.[19] Although discrepant events are often followed by a long period of behavioral orientation to the deviant stimulus, this meaning of "attentive" is different from the meaning of "attentive" based on event-related potentials. Four-month-old infants, who show differential attention to stimuli that vary in their frequency of presentation, showed similar waveforms to the frequent and less frequent events.[20]

In another study ten-year-old children saw, in random order, nine pictures of aversive scenes (snake, gun, bloody soldier), nine pleasant scenes, and nine neutral scenes, while ERP and heart rate were gathered. Because a heart rate deceleration of two to four beats per minute is a typical reaction to a discrepant or interesting event, psychologists usually assume a state of attentive surprise when a heart rate deceleration occurs. Thus one might expect a correlation between magnitude of the P3 waveform, which is also regarded as. indicative of a state of attentiveness that accompanies surprise, and magnitude of heart rate deceleration. However, that expectation was not affirmed. The children showed their largest heart decelerations to the aversive pictures, but the magnitude of the P3 was similar to all three classes of pictures. Further, the P3 magnitude was not correlated with the magnitude of heart rate deceleration. These findings imply that the "state of attention" that produces a P3, which usually occurs within 300 msec of stimulus onset, is not the same as the state that produces a heart rate deceleration, which occurs over a period of several seconds.

The P3 or N4 occurs to discrepant events in any modality, and the more surprising the event, the larger the magnitude of these components. A large P3 occurs, for example, when a person unexpectedly hears her name, is presented with nonidentifiable or novel sounds, or first identifies an object that was presented earlier as part of a series of six fragmented pictures that only gradually became clear.[21] However, the individual's expectations are as critical as the features of the event. The N4 can be larger to familiar than to unfamiliar faces if the person does not expect to see any familiar faces in a series of photos that are mostly of unfamiliar faces and houses.[22]

Because there should be individual variation in the specific events that are perceived as surprises, individuals should differ in the specific events that evoke large P3 waveforms. Recall the ten-year-olds who were shown three classes of pictures. Some of these children had been classified as high reactive infants at four months, fearful in the second year, and subdued in the laboratory at ten years. Children in this group, called inhibited, are biased to expect aversive or dangerous events, and therefore might be surprised by the appearance of neutral pictures. The inhibited children did have larger P3 waveforms to the neutral than to the unpleasant or pleasant pictures, while most of the children had their largest P3 waveforms to the unpleasant or pleasant pictures.

If the brain treats an acoustic profile of a meaningful word as discrepant from the agent's lexical representation (for example, the word "wagon" pronounced "w~gon"), a P3 will occur. An MMN occurs if the brain treats the sound only as a change in the sensory surround without a lexical or semantic referent. But if a sound is a change in the surround that also has meaning, both an MMN and a P3 waveform occur. Thus the psychological expectation of the agent, not just the physical qualities of the stimulus, influences the brain's reaction. That is why the appearance of a letter on a screen produces one profile of fMRI activity if it is a rare target but a different profile if the same letter is presented frequently.[23]

If the individual is psychologically passive without any instruction to detect and to respond to a target, the P3 to a discrepant event has its largest amplitude over frontal areas.[24] This waveform, called P3a, decreases in magnitude if the discrepant event is repeated many times. Marcel Mesulam has suggested that the hippocampus and parahippocampal gyrus, structures in the medial temporal cortex, participate in the evaluation of meaning of a discrepant event.[25] When information is discrepant from the agent's knowledge, these structures send cholinergic projections through the basal nucleus of Meynert to the prefrontal cortex. For this reason the P3a to discrepant events is usually largest in frontal areas.[26] Patients with lesions in the prefrontal cortex show reduced P3a waveforms to discrepant events.[27] The magnitude of the P3a is reduced by drugs that block the cholinergic projections from limbic sites to the prefrontal cortex but is enhanced to a discrepant sound if individuals believe they might experience an electric shock.[28]

However, if the person is instructed to detect and to respond to an infrequent visual target, usually by pressing a button, the P3 to discrepant events is slightly later than the P3a and is larger in posterior areas of the brain; this waveform is called P3b.[29] The popular interpretation of the P3b is that it reflects recognition of a target, often called updating. It is of interest that the P3b is a bit larger among persons living in the northern hemisphere during the summer months when the hours of sunlight are extended.[30] However, there is another way to interpret the P3b. If the P3a reflects the initial detection of an unexpected or unfamiliar event, the P3b may index the brain's preparation to cope with the implications of that detection. Put simply, the P3a is the neuronal component of an orienting reaction to an event that may have consequences. The P3b marks the beginning of an interpretation and/or the initial recruitment of a possible response.

The N4 is most often studied in the context of semantic inconsistencies. If a sentence, heard or read, ends with a semantically inconsistent word (for example, "Apples are cats") or contains a semantically anomalous word in the middle of the sentence ("The cat will not bake the food that Mary left there"), an N4 appears following the inconsistent word. But an N4 waveform will occur to other discrepancies, including incorrect answers to arithmetic problems, a picture that is semantically inconsistent with a previous non-semantic event (for example, a picture of a smiling face following the smelling of an unpleasant odor), and seeing a photo of a sad face while hearing a voice with an angry tone.[31] But the N4 does not occur to all violations of syntax.[32]

Pictures discrepant from a schema elicit an N4 slightly earlier than semantic inconsistencies. Thus if a series of words that might form a coherent thought ends with a picture that is incongruent with the meaning of the words, an N4 appears about 80 msec earlier than if the sentence fragment ends with an anomalous word.[33] Similarly, when a coherent narrative is composed of pictures and the final picture is inconsistent with that narrative, a negative waveform appears at about 300 msec over frontal and central sites. But when the coherent narrative consists of sentences and the final word is inconsistent, the negative waveform occurs later, at about 400 msec, and is larger over central and parietal sites. Finally, if the narrative consists of words and the final event is an incongruous picture, a negative waveform appears at 500 msec and is widespread across the entire head.

These results suggest that meaning is apprehended more quickly for events that engage semantic structures rich with schemata. One author concluded: "The different patterns of ERP . . . suggest that distinct representational systems are being accessed by the different types of materials . . . These findings support the modularity of semantic representations and semantic processing mechanisms in the human brain."[34]

The N4 is also larger when subjects reading sentences one word at a time encounter a concrete rather than an abstract anomalous word at the end of the sentence. For example, the N4 is larger to "Armed robbery implies that the thief used a rose" than to "Armed robbery implies that the thief used the fun."[35] Similarly, subjects reading a list of single words belonging to a particular category (for example, food) produced a larger N4 to a word from another category if the latter was rich in schemata (for example, "bird") than if it was lean in schemata ("court").[36]

Even when individuals are simply reading words one at a time (with no special task to perform), a large N4 occurs to a word that is discrepant from a prior one if the new word is rich in schemata. A smaller N4 or none at all occurs if the discrepant word is abstract.[37] This result, too, argues that semantic representations rich in schemata are a special mental form.

Later Cognitive Work

It is important to distinguish between recognizing a word's meaning and deciding on its proper semantic category. The additional cognitive work involved in deciding on a category is often accompanied by a later positive wave that occurs between 600 and 800 msec.[38] When individuals had to decide whether each of eighty words belonged to the category "pleasant" or "unpleasant," the positive waveform occurred even later, at about 1250 msec.[39] This late waveform reflects a third form of attention, in this case attention focused on the person's cognitive functions. Thus initial orienting, prolonged attention to an external event, and the cognitive work of categorization are three different phenomena often awarded the same attribution, "attentiveness."

The left hemisphere performs a finer semantic analysis of words than the right. Subjects read, one word at a time, the following two sentences: "The day before the wedding the kitchen was covered with frosting. Annette's sister was responsible for making the . . ." The subjects then saw in either the left or the right visual field, that is, in the right or the left hemisphere, (a) the word "cake" (which is expected), (b) the word "cookies" (a mild semantic violation), or (c) the word "toast" (a serious semantic violation). The N4 was larger over the left hemisphere to "toast" than to "cookies," but was of equal magnitude over the right hemisphere to both "cookies" and "toast,"[40] suggesting that the left hemisphere performed a more detailed analysis of the semantic distance between the words.

T. S. Eliot took advantage of the N4 sensitivity to semantic inconsistency in the opening lines of *The Waste Land*.[41] Each of the first five lines of this poem contains a second member of a word pair that probably would have elicited an N4:

April—cruel
lilacs—dead
memory—desire
dull—spring
winter—warm.

Dylan Thomas's poem "And Death Shall Have No Dominion" provides another example:

death—dominion
man—moon
stars—foot
sink—rise.

The final verse of Thomas's "If I Were Tickled by the Rub of Love" has three perfect examples:

fear—apple
bad—spring
thistle—kiss.

The meaning, and not the sound, of the word produces the N4. First-grade girls who were good readers displayed an N4 to visual presentations of both familiar and unfamiliar words; girls who were poor readers showed a much smaller waveform.[42] In a more persuasive study, adults first saw a category word (for example, "food") and 200 msec later saw either a word that could be a member of the category ("meat"), a homophone of such a word ("meet"), an orthographic control word ("melr"), or an unrelated word ("bank") and had to decide if the second word was a correctly spelled member of the category. Words that did not belong to the food category produced a larger N4 than words that were proper members, like "meat." But the homophone ("meet"), which was not a category member, also elicited a large N4. This finding suggests that the meaning of the word was determined by its perception and was not modulated by phonological recoding. If the homophone "meet" had been recoded phonologically, it would have been classified as a member of the category "food" and would have elicited a smaller N4.[43]

However, when the subjects in this study were asked to decide if the homophone belonged to the category (that is, they were asked to decide whether *meet* was a food), they took longer to make that decision than to decide about words that were not homophones, and 11 percent made errors. Thus the behavioral evidence (the judgment that a word was or was not a member of the category) and the brain evidence (the large N4) were not completely congruent. The behavioral data indicated that some subjects confused the homophone "meet" with a correct member of the category "food," while the N4 data indicated less confusion. Frege would have been delighted to learn that the results of this new technology, discovered over seventy years after his writings on meaning, support his controversial view that individuals grasp the semantic meaning of a sentence before they can evaluate whether it is true or false.

The N4 is also a sensitive measure of the degree to which two words belonging to different semantic categories share schematic and semantic features. Subjects first saw a category word like "fish" and then had to decide whether the next word was a proper member of the category. If a second word was from a different category but shared some schematic features with the first (for example, "whale"), the N4 was smaller, even though subjects knew that whales were not members of the category "fish." As expected, the N4 was larger when the second word did not share any schematic features with the first (for example, "car").[44]

Dissociation between Perception and Brain Response

These data motivate a closer analysis of the constructs psychologists use to describe neurophysiological and psychological events. A large N4 occurs when a subject reads a word that is semantically distant from a prior word (or series of words). This phenomenon, an automatic reaction of the human brain, is dependent on the individual's language history and not on earlier words in the test series. This conclusion must be tempered, however, when the data are behavioral rather than neurophysiological. If an individual must decide if a second word is an exemplar of the category named by the first word (for example, whether "table" is a member of the category "fish"), the time it takes to make that decision is affected by prior items in the test series. Decision times were longer if subjects had been viewing pairs that shared objective features, like "fish" and "whale," than if the series contained no semantically related items. That is, decision times were sensitive to the larger context in which a particular item appeared, but the magnitude of the N4 was less affected.

There was also a dissociation between the ERP and behavioral evidence when adults, viewing lists of words one at a time, occasionally saw three different kinds of discrepant events. Sometimes a word was printed in a larger type; sometimes it was framed with a red border; sometimes it was framed with a red border but there was a space between the border and the word. The accuracy of recall of words with any one of these discrepant features was equivalent and was superior to the recall of the nondiscrepant words. But the P3 was clearly larger to the words printed in large type than to the words framed with a red border.[45] Once again behavioral evidence, in this case accuracy of recall memory, led to a conclusion different from the one drawn from the ERP information.

This dissociation was also found in six-month-old infants who saw familiar and unfamiliar faces and toys presented in a random order. The largest negative waveforms occurred to the familiar events, even though other data imply that most infants would have looked longer at the unfamiliar stimuli. A second investigation also produced relevant evidence. Six-month-olds saw frequent and infrequent female faces on a monitor presented in an oddball paradigm. The ratio of frequent to infrequent faces was either 9:1, 8:2, 7:3, or 6:4. In addition, some infants saw equal numbers of the two faces. Fixation time was longer to the infrequent face, as one would expect. However, the two largest negative waveforms at frontal sites, which peaked at 600 msec, occurred to the frequent face that occurred just prior to an infrequent one, as well as to the infrequent face that occurred on the very next trial. The waveforms to the other stimuli were smaller.[46] The behavioral and ERP data from these two studies invite different conclusions regarding the psychological and brain states of the infant.

Because a word can activate different semantic networks in different individuals, the resulting waveforms might be used to measure the subjective meaning a particular individual imposed on a word. One ingenious pair of investigators used the P3 for that purpose by comparing groups of students who had decided on a career with students of the same age and gender who had not yet come to a final decision. Each student saw a pair of words on a screen (for example, "freedom" and "status" or "helping" and "money"). The students were asked which word they would use in choosing a career. Presumably, those students who had based their career decisions on a desire to help society realized that in that choice they were sacrificing the possibility of very large salaries. Hence for them the words "helping" and "money" would be inconsistent semantically, and they should show a P3 when they saw that word pair. However, the same pair of words should be less inconsistent semantically for those who were undecided, and therefore their P3 should be smaller. The evidence affirmed that prediction. Among those who had made a career decision, the larger the semantic distance between the two words in the pair, the larger was the P3, but there was no similar relation in the undecided group.[47]

Developmental Considerations

One intriguing developmental phenomenon warrants special attention. Both eight-year-olds and adults showed a P3b to an infrequent target to which a motor response was required. But, surprisingly, only the adults showed a P3a to an infrequent visual stimulus to which no response was required. Instead of a P3a, the children showed a negative waveform—called an Nc—occurring between 250 and 400 msec. This waveform, mediated primarily by low frequencies in the EEG, from 0.1 to 2 Hz, appears to reflect attention to a discrepant event.[48]

The suggestion that the Nc in children reflects a state of enhanced attention to discrepancy is supported by data on ten-year-olds participating in a longitudinal study of temperament. Children vary in their physiological and behavioral responsivity to unfamiliar events. About 20 percent of healthy sixteen-week-old infants—called high reactive—react to unfamiliar sights and sounds by thrashing their arms and legs and crying. This combination of vigorous motor activity and irritability implies a low threshold of response to unfamiliar events, perhaps mediated by the amygdala. About 40 percent of infants show a complementary profile characterized by minimal motor responsivity and no crying; these infants are called low reactive. More children from the high reactive group become shy and timid as toddlers when they encounter unfamiliar people, places, and objects.

When the children in the longitudinal study were ten years old, they were presented with two long series of pictures (169 pictures in each series). In one set, 70 percent of the pictures were of the same fire hydrant but 15 percent were of a flower, and the remaining 15 percent were of discrepant scenes that were ecologically impossible (for example, a man's head on an infant's body or a car in midair). As expected, the pictures of the less frequent flower and the ecologically impossible pictures produced a clear Nc waveform in most children, reflecting a reaction to the discrepant stimuli. However, the children who had been high reactive infants ten years earlier had larger Nc waveforms to both classes of discrepant pictures than those who had been low reactive infants. This intriguing result suggests that the disposition to become cortically responsive (or unresponsive) to discrepant events was preserved over a ten-year interval.

It is not clear why children, but not adults, show a prominent Nc to discrepant pictures to which no cognitive or motor reaction is required. One possibility is that the low-frequency energy mediating the Nc—less than 2 Hz—is suppressed by maturational events that occur at puberty. Another interpretation is that adults, but not preadolescent children, actively relate each discrepant stimulus to other stimuli in the series as part of an attempt to understand the reason for their presentation. Children may be more passive cognitively and treat each picture as an event independent of others in the series.

The hypothesis that preadolescents may fail to relate a discrepant event to prior ones is in accord with the surprising finding that preadolescents are less likely than adults to show an MMN to an infrequent tone if there is an eight-second delay between the last stimulus in a train of identical tones and the discrepant one, but do show an MMN if the delay is only one second. Adolescents and adults, by contrast, show an MMN whether the delay is one or eight seconds.[49]

The sensory buffer for auditory stimuli is estimated to be about three seconds; that is, the brain can hold a stream of auditory events in sensory memory for about three seconds. Thus if adults show an MMN following an eight-second delay between the last train of identical tones and a deviant one, they must be actively relating the discrepant tone to their memory of the train of frequent ones. Children may engage in this activity less regularly.

This hypothesis suggests that the brains of preadolescents are less likely than those of adults to bind present to past when the latter is temporally distant from the former. This possibility has a counterintuitive feeling, for ten-year-olds can hold many events in short-term memory for longer than eight seconds. Why, then, do they not show an MMN to a deviant tone after a delay of eight seconds?

One solution to this paradox is the assumption, noted earlier, that the individual's cognitive biases affect whether the mind/brain automatically relates present to past. The brain organization after puberty guarantees exercise of the cognitive preparation to relate past and present, implying that study of the maturational changes in the brain that occur around puberty will be illuminating. It appears that new fibers from the basolateral nucleus of the rat amygdala begin to grow toward the anterior cingulate at puberty.[50] Should the same anatomical changes occur in human adolescents, this could explain why the binding of present events to past ones is enhanced at puberty.

An Attempt at Synthesis

Ray Johnson has suggested that the N4 and P3 waveforms reflect different processes.[51] There is the possibility, of course, that a more basic state is the foundation of both forms. The P3 and the N4 occur when attention is recruited to an event that is unexpected, not just because it is a discrepant transformation. The first presentation of a word or picture that is not discrepant from the person's stored knowledge often elicits a P3 or an N4. Further, the magnitude of the N4 to words belonging to an infrequent semantic category, or to letters printed in a discrepant size, is larger if the subject is told to attend to the discrepant stimulus.[52] Therefore, it may be that the P3 and N4 are larger to discrepant events because those events recruit more focused attention. This conclusion is in accord with the finding that the magnitude of the N4 to semantically anomalous words decreases in old age.[53]

But it is equally likely that the N4 and the P3a or P3b reflect different psychological processes. The P3b is larger in posterior sites when the subject is instructed to detect a particular infrequent target or has created a category for discrepant events and the discrepancy activates the representation of the new category. This hypothesis would explain why the P3a to novel stimuli decreases over time while the P3b does not. In the latter case the individual has to keep a representation of the target active in posterior association areas. When the target appears, the relevant neurons discharge to produce the P3b waveform.

A P3a is larger in anterior sites when the individual does not expect the discrepant event. When such an event occurs, neurons in medial temporal areas are activated and the resulting dipole creates a larger component in frontal areas. This suggestion implies that even though the P3a and P3b have similar forms, and similar but not identical latencies, the two reflect different psychological processes. Detection of a discrepant event is not equivalent to the recruitment of a reaction to it.[54]

Patients who have a rare and puzzling phenomenon called Capgras syndrome fail to recognize a familiar person and may conclude that the person is an impostor.[55] Perhaps the brain reacts in a special way when we meet a familiar person we do not expect to see, and perhaps that brain event evokes a subtle feeling that we might call "recognition of the familiar." The Capgras patients' failure to generate that brain state may contribute to their odd symptoms.

The total corpus of information on the ERP suggests that the magnitude, latency, and primary scalp site of the largest waveforms occurring after about 100 msec reflect three aspects of schematic and semantic structures: (1) the firmness and coherence of the structure, (2) the degree to which the semantic structure is permeated with schematic representations, and (3) whether the event represents a violation of an expectancy created in the immediate past or a violation of preserved knowledge.

The ERP evidence supports two hypotheses: (1) the brain is exquisitely sensitive to discrepant events that violate a person's expectations, and (2) the contribution of schemata to semantic structures has psychological significance. The unique spectral profile each chemical element produces when heated reveals its structure. The ERP waveforms have the power to reveal varied mental structures. The sight of a picture of a tall boy with a head made of broccoli would elicit a P3a; hearing the sentence "The tall boy had a head of broccoli" would elicit an N4. Because emotional arousal is linked more closely to neural activity in the right hemisphere, activation of schemata increases the probability of an emotional reaction. Photographs and movies evoke intense emotions more readily than words do. When words arouse strong emotions, and they can do so, it is usually because they are penetrated with schemata or are conditioned signals for visceral arousal. I suspect that the preference among academics for arguments composed of abstract language is sustained by an unconscious desire to have the logic of an argument, rather than feelings, determine the validity of propositional claims.

IMPLICATIONS FOR
DEVELOPMENT

Although hominids share many psychological qualities with other primates, evolution awarded our species a number of unique properties. Elaborate semantic networks, a generative syntax, the uncertainty that accompanies detection of inconsistency in those networks, a moral sense, guilt, assignment of self to a web of symbolic categories, and the ability to infer the thoughts and feelings of others are some of the species-specific features that, in combination, distinguish us from all other animals. In this chapter and the next I consider the implications of these talents for three controversial domains of inquiry that engage the arguments presented in Chapters 1–3.

Debates on developmental phenomena are obvious heirs of the prior discussions, especially debates on the nature of the infant mind, the initial establishment of a moral sense, and the process of identification. Our understandings of all three phenomena are informed by evidence about the brain's responses to discrepant experiences.

What Do Infants Understand?

Although infants are biased to attend to events that are discrepant from their schemata, this relation is neither linear nor completely reliable. Failure to recognize these two caveats to what has been a fruitful hypothesis has led to questionable conclusions about the infant's understanding of the world. The bold claims regarding an infant's knowledge of the physical principle of solidity or the concept of number are usually based only on small differences in looking time between two similar events. The problem is that we do not completely understand the meaning of these measurements.

Recruitment of prolonged or differential attention to an unfamiliar, or unexpected, event is not as automatic as the withdrawal of a hand from a hot surface because the infant's brain/mind must first relate the event to an appropriate schematic structure. This process is fragile during the first eight months, and as a result infants do not always devote more attention to a discriminable event that differs from one they have just seen or heard.

A second reason for ambiguity in the meaning of prolonged or differential attention is that the relation between attentiveness and degree of discrepancy between an event and a schema is not linear but curvilinear. Infants will not devote prolonged attention to an unfamiliar event if it has little or no relation to their schemata, or if it shares most of its essential features with a schema. The events that recruit the longest bouts of attention, and the ones that will be remembered for the longest time, are those which share essential features with a schema but do not share less essential ones.

This principle even holds for newborn infants. Newborns were familiarized with the nonsense word "titi" played from one of two speakers placed on either side of the infant's head. As expected, the newborns turned their head to the initial presentations of the word but eventually habituated. They then heard either the same sound or one of four variations created by altering the fundamental frequency of the original sound by 7, 14, 21, or 28 percent. The infants were most likely to orient to the stimulus that altered the fundamental frequency by 14 or 21 percent, and were less likely to orient if the alteration was smaller or larger. That is, the relation between the probability of attending to the new sound and the degree of discrepancy from the original schema was an inverted U function. Similarly, two-to-eight-month-old infants showed their longest looking times and largest heart rate decelerations to an unfamiliar person who shared essential features with their schemata for familiar others—eyes, nose, mouth—but who differed in less essential features, while they showed brief attention and small heart rate decelerations to a geometric arrangement of boxes and bowls with scrambled face-like features taped on the object which did not share essential features with their schemata.[1]

Four-month-olds shown the two faces in Figure 4.1 looked longer at the schematic face with the proper arrangement of facial features

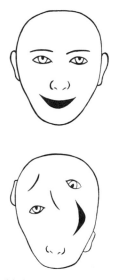

Figure 4.1. Four-month-olds looked longer at the schematic face with the proper arrangement of facial features, but one-year-olds looked longer at the one with reorganized features. Source: J. Kagan, "The determinants of attention in the infant," *American Scientist*, 58 (1970): 300.

than at the one with reorganized features because the former lacked the less essential qualities of the three-dimensional faces the infants had seen in their daily lives, while the rearranged face lacked the essential features of the proper placement of eyes, nose, and mouth. But one-year-olds, whose schemata for human faces have become firmer, paid more attention to the rearranged face because they could relate its features to their schematic knowledge.[2] However, one-year-olds did not devote attention to a mask with no eyes, nose, or mouth because all the essential features of their schema for a face were missing (Figure 4.2).

These findings affirm the principle that duration of attention is an inverted U function of degree of discrepancy from a schema.

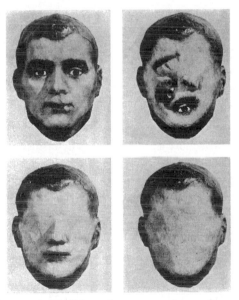

Figure 4.2. One-year-olds did not devote attention to the mask at bottom right, which lacked all the essential features of their schema for a face. Source: J. Kagan, "The determinants of attention in the infant," *American Scientist*, 58 (1970): 303.

Because psychologists can never be certain of the form or firmness of an infant's schema for an event, they cannot always predict which of several alternative events, each of which might appear discrepant to an investigator, will recruit the longest bout of attention. A study of seven-month-olds is illustrative.

The infants saw, simultaneously, two different facial expressions on a screen (for example, a happy face and an angry face) while hearing a voice whose timbre and loudness matched only one of the facial expressions. However, the voice was played five seconds out of synchrony with the mouth movements of the faces. This arrangement meant that the infants were confronted with two different discrepancies: (1) a happy voice asynchronously timed to a happy facial expression and (2) a happy voice paired with an angry facial expression. Although the latter event might seem to some observers to be more discrepant, the infants looked longer at the less serious discrepancy represented by the asynchronous vocal signal.[3] Apparently, the temporal asynchrony between the vocalization and the facial expression transformed the less essential features of the infant's representations while a happy voice coming from an angry face transformed more essential features.

A different procedure also yielded evidence inconsistent with the premise that infants always devote more attention to the less familiar of two discrepant events. A group of six-month-old infants were shown a single toy while hearing a distinct sound coming from one of four locations. On the test trial that followed, two different toys were presented simultaneously: the familiar toy that had just been associated with the sound and a less familiar toy that had been seen earlier in the testing session but had not been associated with any sound. Upon hearing the sound, the infants looked longer at the more familiar toy.[4] Further, seven-month-olds who, at home, heard a twenty-second musical passage once a day for fourteen days were more attentive, during a later test session, to the beginning of the passage than to its middle section because the schema for the latter was less firm than the one for the former.[5] The longest bout of attention was not devoted to the more unfamiliar event.

This principle applies to older children as well as to infants. Young school-age children are much better at recalling pictures or sentences that are moderately discrepant from their knowledge than at recalling familiar or totally novel events. But the discrepant feature has to have some relation to their representation of the events being processed. If it does not, memory is not improved. For example, children did not preferentially remember familiar pictures to which a numeral was attached because the numeral shared no features with the information in the pictures.[6]

It is also important to recognize that duration of orienting to an event is not the only way infants reveal their knowledge. On occasion, a difference in rates of habituation to two events is more sensitive than a difference in total looking time. Further, the magnitude of the discrepancy influences the specific behavior displayed to an unfamiliar event. Infants look longer at a speaker that is playing the babbling sounds of an unfamiliar infant than at a speaker playing their own babbling, but they vocalize more when they hear themselves babble.[7] Both sounds are discrepant, for infants do not usually hear tape recordings of babbling infants. It appears that a long bout of attention reflects a state created by an event that is difficult to assimilate. Vocalization, in contrast, reflects the state created by a discrepant event that is easier to match to a schema and that, as a result, evokes an emotion some might call excitement. If the infant detects a discrepant event but assimilates it easily, attention will be brief but vocalization and perhaps smiling may occur. If the event is difficult to assimilate, attention may be prolonged but there will be no vocalization or smiling. Scientists who only quantify duration of attention will not detect the infant's recognition of the first kind of discrepancy.

On occasion, a fret or a cry, rather than prolonged attention, will occur to a discrepant event. One-year-olds devote more attention to an unfamiliar two-foot-tall robot than to an adult stranger if both are still, but are more likely to cry if the stranger moves toward them than if the robot makes a similar movement. Finally, sometimes infants show equivalent looking times to two events presented simultaneously, but shift their attention back and forth between the two stimuli if one is familiar and the other is not. Infants five, seven, and twelve months old were shown pairs of familiar and unfamiliar pictures simultaneously. Duration of attention to the unfamiliar pictures decreased with age, but the rate of shifting attention back and forth between the familiar and unfamiliar pictures increased with age.[8] Looking, vocalizing, shifting attention, smiling, crying, and operant motor responses contain different information about infants' psychological state and the structure of their schemata. Hence, conclusions about infants' representations should be tempered if the only evidence is that they attended more to one event than another.[9]

DO INFANTS UNDERSTAND PHYSICS?

This caution applies to the claim that infants know that a solid object cannot pass through a solid barrier. The basis for this bold conclusion was a procedure in which four-month-olds first saw a paddle move on a stage in a 180° arc from right to left (see Figure 4.3). The examiner then put a solid block on the stage to signal the infant that the paddle could no longer traverse 180° because the block would obstruct its movement. Some infants then saw the paddle traverse 180° (a physically impossible event), while others saw the paddle move in an arc of 112°, a physically possible event. Because the infants looked longer at the impossible event, the psychologist concluded that they "knew" that the paddle could not pass through the solid block.[10]

But one can argue that the combination of 180° movement with the presence of a block on the stage is optimally discrepant from the familiarization event, while the combination of 112° movement with the block is too discrepant because two features have been

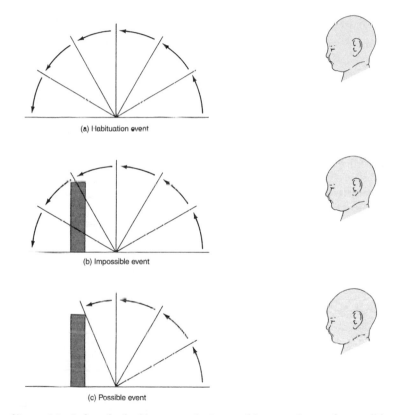

(a) Habituation event

(b) Impossible event

(c) Possible event

Figure 4.3. Infants looked longer at the impossible event than at the possible event.

changed—the amount of movement and the addition of the block. Further, the firmness of an infant's schema for an event always modulates the distribution of attention; if the schema is fragile, generally because of insufficient experience, infants usually attend to an event that is more closely related to their schema rather than to one that is more discrepant. Three-month-olds looked longer at a novel pattern than at a pattern they had studied for three minutes if tested after a one-minute delay, but looked longer at the familiar pattern if they were tested thirty days later. Even one-year-olds will spend more time exploring a set of familiar toys if they have not had sufficient time to create schemata for them, while those allowed more time usually play longer with unfamiliar toys.[11]

Thomas Schilling recognized that four-month-olds might require a great deal of experience to create a firm schema for the complicated sequence of a moving paddle and an obstructing object on a stage.[12] He provided one group of infants with only seven exposures to the paddle moving 180°, but gave another group twelve exposures to the same sequence. He then put the object on the stage and had the paddle move either 180° or 112°. The infants who had only seven exposures, and therefore had a less firmly articulated schema for the 180° movement, looked longer when the paddle moved 180°—the impossible event. However, the infants who had seen the 180° movement twelve times looked longer when the paddle moved 112°—the possible event—because this experience was discrepant from their well-formed schema for the 180° traverse. It is relevant that in the original study the infants who habituated quickly, and therefore had fewer trials, were the ones who looked longer at the impossible event; the infants who had more habituation trials did not do so.

There is another reason to question the claim that four-month-olds "know" that an object cannot pass through a solid barrier. That inference requires the infant to relate what she has just seen to the set of relevant schemata she has previously acquired and to compare the two. The evidence indicates that infants are not capable of this cognitive process until they are at least six to eight months old. That is why most infants show a decrease in duration of attention to a discrepant event—such as a mask with scrambled facial features—from three through seven months, followed by an increase in attentiveness to the same stimulus from seven to twenty-four months. Attention increases after seven months because the infant attempts to relate the discrepant pattern to the acquired schemata for the human face. It is reasonable to suggest that this ability would be necessary for the infant to infer the impossibility of an event. Four-month-olds are not cognitively ready for this inference. It is relevant that five-month-olds, whose attention is recruited by objects in motion, looked longer at 180° rotations than at 112° ones, even when no block was on the stage, because the longer rotation contains more motion.[13]

The potential flaw in the original conclusion becomes obvious if one reflects on the fact that two-year-olds, who have language and better retrieval memory than young infants, are unable to infer the correct location of a ball that has rolled down an incline and struck a tall occluder whose position was visible. The examiner placed the occluder behind one of four doors over a series of trials and asked the child to guess which door should be opened in order to retrieve the ball. Two-year-olds could not solve this problem. That is, they were unable to infer the correct door to open from the location of the visible occluder. If two-year-olds cannot figure out that the ball must be behind the door where the occluder rests, it is unlikely that infants less than a year old know that objects cannot pass through solid barriers.[14]

DO INFANTS INFER WHOLE OBJECTS?

A similar argument applies to the suggestion that four-month-olds watching two visible segments of a rod move together behind a motionless occluder "know" that there is an unbroken rod behind the occluder (see Figure 4.4). The basis for this inference is the finding that, following exposure to this familiarization event, four-month-old infants, but not newborns or two-month-olds, looked longer at two disconnected moving rods than at a complete moving rod.[15] The researchers argued that if the infants knew there was a continuous rod moving behind the occluder, the pair of disconnected rods would be discrepant and attract their attention. A generous meaning of the term "know" in this context is that the infants had created a schema for a connected rod moving behind the stationary occluder.

This restricted meaning of "know" is not synonymous with understanding the occasions when objects that move together do or do not belong to the same object. That knowledge has to be learned over the course of childhood. Five-year-old children know that the

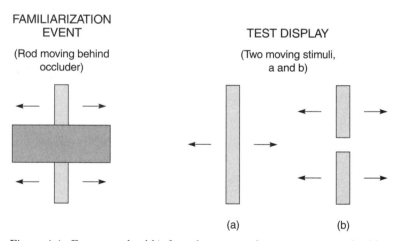

FAMILIARIZATION
EVENT

(Rod moving behind
occluder)

TEST DISPLAY

(Two moving stimuli,
a and b)

(a)   (b)

Figure 4.4. Four-month-old infants, but not newborns or two-month-olds, looked longer at the two disconnected moving rods than at a complete moving rod. Source: P. J. Kellman and E. S. Spelke, "Perception of partially occluded objects in infants," *Cognitive Psychology*, 15 (1983): 483–524.

skis on the top of an automobile racing to the mountains are two discrete objects. By contrast, the Mayan Indians living on Lake Atitlán in northwest Guatemala explain their defeat by the Spaniards in the sixteenth century as a result of a perceptual error. The legend claims that the Mayan warrior fighting a Spanish general mounted on a horse had never seen horses and therefore thought that the horse and Spaniard were one object. Because the Mayan believed he had killed both the animal and the soldier after he had shot an arrow at the horse, he turned away, only to be killed moments later by the Spaniard. A central issue is whether, and at what age, children presented with a display of discrete but connected objects—a toy duck on top of a toy car, for example—know that these are two separate objects.[16] Infants who have seen nipples and nursing bottles lying separately on a table have learned that the two are discrete objects. Infants who have not seen the two separate components will assume they are a unity.

Before we accept the conclusion that the infants created a schema for a complete rod moving behind the stationary occluder, we should consider two other interpretations. I noted that infants presented simultaneously with two different discrepant events often devote more attention to the one that is more difficult to assimilate. Infants can easily differentiate the familiarization event—the moving rod behind the occluder—from both the connected and disconnected rods without the occluder. Both test events are obviously discrepant from the original experience. The longer bout of attention to the disconnected rods implies that this stimulus was more difficult to assimilate. One possible reason is that infants have more often seen connected than disconnected objects (sticks, poles, knives) in their daily lives. Hence the connected rod should be easier to assimilate after the infants were aroused by watching the motion of the rod in the familiarization event, and they should look longer at the disconnected rods.

A second interpretation utilizes the principle of the curvilinear relation between discrepancy and attention. Infants preferentially attend to the overall pattern of a visual event rather than to its subtle features. The familiarization event was a pattern of two moving segments of a rod that appeared to be disconnected because there was a stationary occluder between them. One can argue that a moderately discrepant transformation of this event is one in which the occluder is removed leaving the two disconnected rods. The connected rod shares fewer features with the familiarization event and, therefore, should recruit less attention than the disconnected pair. This interpretation and the one discussed previously do not require the assumption that the infants inferred a continuous rod behind the occluder.

The concept of object unity, like time or space, is not a perceptual schema but a complex symbolic network. It is unlikely that one source of information, in this case a difference in looking time, could supply the needed evidence for this inference. Most psychologists would not rely only on a child's pointing to a picture of a cow when asked "Where is the animal?" to decide whether the child understood the meaning of the word "animal."

Differences in looking time between two events are usually due to the firmness of the infant's schema and/or the amount of symmetry, motion, density, or contour in the events. Hence most current claims as to what infants know will probably be revised when additional evidence is added to the measure of looking time. After a review of the relevant evidence, two scholars agreed that sole reliance on a change in attention to infer an infant's understanding is unwise because "looking times are influenced by many factors . . . [that] preclude clear interpretations of the individual's results."[17]

Perceptual schemata are not to be equated with the semantic knowledge of the older child. The infant's perception of a small ball moving a few inches after being struck by a larger one may not be an early form of the adult's semantic knowledge that a moving object with a large mass causes one with a smaller mass to move. An infant has the former representation but not the latter understanding; a congenitally blind adolescent knows the latter but has no schema for the former.

THE TRANSITION AT EIGHT MONTHS

The meaning of differential looking time is especially ambiguous when infants must relate two or three different events, presented successively over a period of ten to forty seconds, and hold them in working memory. The brain structures and circuits that mediate recognition of an object in a location following a delay—hippocampus, perirhinal cortex, parahippocampal gyrus, entorhinal cortex, and prefrontal cortex—are immature during the first year. Indeed, these structures do not attain maturity in the monkey until late in the first year,[18] which corresponds to the third year in the human child.

The evidence indicates that there is an enhancement in working memory in human infants at eight to nine months because of maturation of brain circuits that involve temporal and frontal lobe structures, especially dorsolateral prefrontal cortex. The new brain organization permits infants to retrieve relevant schemata for objects in locations when there is no incentive in the perceptual field. As a result, infants can now "remember" where an object was hidden seconds earlier and will reach toward its location. The more unfamiliar the object, the more alert the infant and the more likely he will reach to the correct location. The important difference between five-month-olds reaching toward or looking at an unfamiliar object they can see and eight-month-olds reaching to the place where an object was hidden is that the older infants must be able to retrieve a schema for the object's location.

CAN INFANTS ADD?

Because the ability to retrieve the immediate past is fragile during the first eight months, the schemata created to an initial event in a series are apt to fade while succeeding events are processed. As a result, the re-presentation of the first event during later test trials may now be discrepant from the schema for the original event and, therefore, will attract prolonged attention.

This principle can account for the conclusion, which sparked front-page headlines in 1992, that infants are able to add and sub-tract.[19] The infants first saw a single toy on a stage (see Figure 4.5). The examiner then moved a screen to occlude the stage holding the toy, and seconds later the infants saw a human hand place a second toy behind the screen. The screen was then removed and the infants saw either one or two toys. Because most infants looked longer when there was only one toy, the researcher concluded that the infants had "added" their schema for the original toy to their schema for the second toy placed behind the screen and expected to see two toys. Therefore, one toy was a discrepant event and they attended to it.

There is an alternative interpretation of this result. It is likely that the infants' schema for the single toy that was on the stage initially faded during the interval when the examiner lowered the screen, placed the second toy behind the screen, and raised the screen for the test trial. Therefore, the reappearance of the single toy, twenty to thirty seconds later, had become a moderately discrepant event that recruited attention. This interpretation, which requires no assumption about arithmetic ability, is supported by several recent experiments.

Infants saw either a single toy or two toys on a stage, followed by a delay while the examiner occluded the stage. Although no human hand added or subtracted any toy, there was sufficient time for the

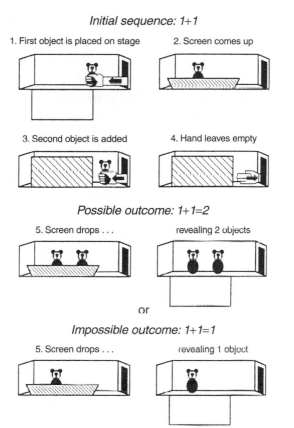

Figure 4.5. Infants looked longer at the impossible outcome; the researcher interpreted this result as evidence that infants could add. Source: K. Wynn, "Addition and subtraction by human infants," *Nature*, 358 (1992): 749–750.

original schema to fade. The infants then saw on a test trial either one or two toys. The infants who had originally seen one toy looked longer when one toy was on the stage, while those who had originally seen two toys were more attentive when two toys were on the stage.[20] This is exactly the pattern that led Karen Wynn in 1992 to infer   infant's ability to add: infants looked longer when the number of toys on the stage was the same number they had seen earlier. But this time no hand had added any toy to the stage. It is relevant that normal adult monkeys tested in the standard delay–nonmatch to sample procedure perform very well if the delay between the initial exposure to the familiarized object and the test trial is about fifteen seconds, but show some impairment if the delay is as long as one minute.[21] The time between the initial familiarization trial and the test trials in the studies of infant addition are much longer than a few seconds. Because the perirhinal cortex and medial temporal structures that mediate recognition memory are immature in infants under one year, it is likely that the schema for the familiarization event fades seriously by the time of the test trials. As a result, the reappearance of the object is discrepant and recruits attention.

Further, when a hand did add a toy to the one already on the stage infants were not particularly attentive when, on the test trial, there was no toy on the stage. If infants could add they should have expected to see two toys and should have been surprised by the empty stage. Infants will attend to an empty stage when they see it just a few seconds after seeing some object on the stage.[22] The total corpus of evidence suggests that infants cannot do arithmetic. The patterns of looking times are more parsimoniously explained as a function of the fading of the original schema and the number of toys on the stage during the test trials.

DO INFANTS HAVE A CONCEPT OF NUMBER?

Other investigators have used a different procedure to argue that the prelinguistic infant's schematic representation of the number of objects in a display shares features with the older child's knowledge of the concept of number. The empirical basis for this claim is that infants who have habituated to one display of dots show increased attention to a display in which the number of dots is changed, say from two to four or from four to two. This argument is not persuasive because an array of four dots is perceptually different from an array of two dots (for example, the density may be greater) and that is a sufficient reason for the increased attention.[23]

It is not obvious that number is a conceptual feature of the infant's schematic representation of a pattern of dots. Scientists assign the property of number to the display, but I am less certain that infants do. Rosa Arriaga varied the shape, color, and location of three different objects over a series of familiarization trials and then showed eight-month-olds a pair of different objects. The infants showed no increase in attention to the change from three to two objects because they had attended to the more salient features of color, shape, and location of the three objects rather than their number.

Some scientists have argued that animals, too, appreciate the number of discrete events that occur over a brief interval, as long as the number is less than four. Rats can be taught, over many, many trials, to make one response when two tones, or two light flashes, occur, but a different response when three tones, or three light flashes, occur. Human infants, too, can distinguish between two- and three-syllable utterances.[24] Monkeys who have seen a human adult place four pieces of apple under one container and three under another usually select the former, but fail to pick the larger number when the comparison involves five versus four pieces of apple. However, these data require only the assumption that animals or infants can discriminate between perceptually different events and can hold those schemata in working memory for a brief period. This evidence does not mean that animals are "counting" or possess a structure that represents a concept of number.

Every philosopher of mathematics regards number as a concept that rests initially on the notions of cardinality and ordinality. A blind person who could not discriminate two from four dots could understand both notions. The Roman symbol for 10 was X; in Greece it was Δ, in Egypt it was ∩, and among the Mayans it was a grotesque face or an equals sign. None of these symbols is perceptually similar to a display of ten objects.

No psychologist would claim that infants who discriminate a cup three-quarters full of liquid from one that is one-quarter full possess the concept of fractions.[25] Infants who show increased attention to a picture of a fly after seeing twenty pictures of different fish do not understand the concepts "vertebrate" and "invertebrate." A male monkey who can discriminate females from males using visual and olfactory cues does not have a concept of gender; a macaque monkey who looks longer at photographs of members of his own species than at those from another species does not have a concept of species.

The capacity to discriminate eight dots from three dots is not a reasonable basis for inferring that infants possess any feature of the semantic concept of number held by school-age children. That is why three-year-olds do not conserve number in a classic conservation procedure and why three-year-olds rarely use counting as a way to compare quantities even when the task focuses on number.[26] But a ten-year-old who wonders about the largest number and knows that the sum of 22 and 23 is 45 does have a number concept. This conceptual network is qualitatively different from the infant's schematic representations of arrays varying in numbers of objects.

Sundials, electric clocks, spring clocks, and atomic clocks all record time, but in different ways. Medieval European villagers without clocks represented time schematically; for example, as "a brief pause," "a long pause," or "the time it takes to travel a league." By contrast, the concepts "month," "year," and "century" are, like the concept "100," semantic structures with minimal schematic contribution.

The brains of many animals are constructed to permit them, with a great deal of training, to create a representation of the number of discrete events (that is, changes in neural activity) over a short interval, as long as that number is small. Although that capacity is a fascinating target of scientific inquiry, it is an insufficient basis for concluding that their brains count the number of events. Otherwise, we should hazard the guess that the brain of a male lobster who has just lost a fight is in a state of defeat. Number is only one of a large number of conceptual attributes that a human agent can apply to an event. It is an inherent property neither of an event nor of a brain.

Frege, too, would not have awarded animals an understanding of number. He argued that number, unlike mass, is a concept and not a property of events. One must specify the particular aspect of an event to which a number applies. Frege used the example of a pile of cards made up of two full decks to ask rhetorically whether there were 104 cards, two decks, or one pile. All three numbers are correct descriptions of the same event.

THE MEANING OF KNOW

Piaget also ascribed conceptual knowledge to infants. He interpreted the infant's reach to the location of a hidden object as signifying that the infant "knew" that objects have a physical permanence and do not disappear without a material intervention. This inference, like the claims that infants know a paddle cannot pass through a solid block and have a concept of number, attributes a profound philosophical idea to an extremely immature human. If eight-month-olds knew that objects had a permanent existence they should not show surprise and laugh during peek-a-boo games when the mother's face reappears from behind her hands; five-year-olds do not laugh. Dogs of some breeds will run hundreds of yards time after time toward a ball thrown by their owner even though they cannot initially see the object they are racing to retrieve. Does the

Labrador "know" that the ball is a physically permanent object that cannot disappear, or is it more accurate to conclude that the animal possesses a schematic representation of the ball and running in the direction in which the ball was thrown is a biologically prepared response in this species. Some breeds, such as Rhodesian ridgebacks, do not retrieve balls thrown by their owners. It is important to distinguish between the persistence of a schema and a belief in the permanence of the object it represents. I have a clearly articulated schema for the muffin I ate with my breakfast coffee but know it exists no more. And I know that the jungles of Borneo exist even though, having never visited them, I have no distinct schemata for their form.

A nine-month-old who has retrieved a hidden object four times from one of two cloths and on the fifth trial watches the object being hidden under the other cloth is likely to reach to the first cloth, even if she can see part of the object in its new place. This behavior, observed most often in nine-month-olds, is called the "A not B error." But this response should not be categorized as an error if the infant had no "desire" for the object and reached toward the first cloth because this habit had been rewarded four times and reaching is a biologically prepared behavior to "being aroused" by the discrepant quality of a hiding game played with a stranger. Seven-month-olds sitting on their mother's lap in a dark room will reach in the direction of a sound even though they cannot see anything and have had no prior experience with the object making the sound.[27] They reach because this action is a biologically prepared response to the sound. The infants may not want the object and may not "know" that they will make contact with it with their hands. It is not obvious therefore that the Labrador racing across the grass "wants" the ball and "knows" it must be lying somewhere in the field.

The problem lies with the meanings of the word "know." Unfortunately, this abstract predicate names very different cognitive states, from simple recognition of a past event through understanding causal sequences, to being able to re-create or to describe the presumed processes mediating these sequences. A two-year-old who, on waking, recognizes that the sun has reappeared does not know why this event is repeated every morning and may not believe that the sun continues to exist during the hours of darkness. The belief that an object has a physical permanence is a semantically rich conviction that develops slowly over the years of childhood. Nine-month-olds do not possess this knowledge, and it is not obvious that a reach toward a hidden toy is an anlage of the adolescent's belief.

In light of the evidence, it is fair to ask why there is enthusiasm among psychologists for awarding infants initial knowledge of some physical principles and the ability to do arithmetic. These claims are reminiscent of an earlier belief in a different form of connectedness between the structures of infancy and those of later childhood. For example, nineteenth-century students of development believed that the grasp reflex of the newborn, which is released by placing an object in the palm, was an early sign of the adult propensity for greed. Sigmund Freud was certain that the frustration of a nursing infant who did not obtain enough milk was preserved and found expression decades later in an adult who was argumentative. Havelock Ellis thought he saw a resemblance between the look of satisfaction on the face of a nursing infant and the faces of lovers lost in the ecstasy of their sexual caresses.[28] These beliefs, like the notion that infants understand the physics of objects, share features with the medieval faith in alchemy.

Several historical facts may help to explain the renascence of the assumption of a continuity between the minds of infants and older children. The preference for attributing the content of children's minds to experience or to inherent human potentialities cycles with changes in political ideology and the branches of scholarship that happen to be in an accelerated stage of discovery. Educated

Europeans at the beginning of the eighteenth century, who wished to be free of the conceptual restraints of the church, Christian philosophy, and the division of a society into those with and without virtue, welcomed Locke's argument that each mind began life unburdened of any perceptual or conceptual biases. However, reflection on human thought revealed the obvious flaws in Locke's assumption, and less than one hundred years later Kant provided the more balanced view that many mental constructions cannot be easily traced to experience. It is not unimportant that the hierarchies in European nation-states were replacing the power of the church when Kant was brooding on the human mind and that the stability of those political structures was aided by loyalty to the rationality in Kant's philosophy.

A century later, mass immigration to America required a return to Locke's premise in order to thwart the politically dangerous view that the brains of the children of the European immigrants were genetically compromised. The behaviorists, first John Watson and a half-century later B. F. Skinner, supplied the rational support for the needed egalitarian philosophy.

History has introduced a trio of new conditions over the last several decades. First, advances in molecular biology and neuroscience provided enough scaffolding for neo-Kantians to suggest that minds are yoked closely to brains. Because the brains of newborns possess structures that mediate many competences, it follows that young minds probably possess some initial cognitive talents. A second significant factor was Noam Chomsky's argument that language was one of these talents. He insisted that children were born with a set of structures that made it easy for them to learn the grammar of their language. It was logical and parsimonious to extend this view and assume that young children possessed many other understandings of the world.

The third historical contribution took the form of an analogy between the behavioral variation noted among related animal species and the human variation in academic achievement, wealth, and social status that, unfortunately, is associated with class and ethnicity in the United States. An increasingly large and affluent middle class, reluctant to permit Congress to vote their hard-earned money for the improvement of the schools and neighborhoods of the poor, preferred the social Darwinist view that all members of a species cannot command equal social potency. (They forgot that, for Darwin, potency meant fecundity, not a college diploma or a family with property.) If the concept of number is an easy discovery for most infants, perhaps eight-year-olds who cannot do arithmetic have a compromised brain.

Thus we have returned to a new version of Kant's philosophy, but for different reasons. The change in the favored explanation of variation in academic achievement and vocational position from differences in education to differences in brain integrity was facilitated by exciting discoveries that made gene and brain circuits more fundamental than the processes that allow experiences to evolve into skills. Scholars felt the importance of their work was enhanced if their ideas and experimental data could be classified as belonging to biology. The idea that physical principles are resting quietly in the brains of eight-month-olds seems to be a biological rather than a psychological fact. I suspect that all of these factors came together to catch some psychologists in a swell of enthusiasm for philosophically deep concepts tucked away in cortical gyri waiting, like beautiful genies, to be released.

Most natural scientists are willing to question appealing ideas when the evidence demands a reappraisal. Physicists gave up their long-standing, aesthetically satisfying assumption that particles had no directional preference when a team of investigators discovered that the electrons emanating from an isotope of cobalt in a magnetic field had a preferred direction. Psychologists are a little more resistant to rejecting pleasing ideas in the face of inconsistent data. The evidence summarized seems sufficiently robust to cast doubt on the belief that infants have some comprehension of the concept of number and the physics of objects. Two distinguished developmental scholars, Marshall Haith and Elizabeth Spelke, acknowledge the controversy surrounding this issue. Spelke points out that an infant's knowledge is domain- and task-specific; that is, a set of structures for one domain is often independent of those for others. She notes, wisely: "There is no consensus among investigators of cognitive development about when knowledge begins . . . how it changes with growth and experience, or what role it plays in the development of thought and action."[29]

Discrepancy and Imitation

The strong tendency of young children to imitate adult behavior is monitored by the uncertainty created by discrepancy. The discrepant quality of the adult's act, as well as uncertainty about the child's ability to perform it, determine the likelihood that the child will imitate a particular adult behavior. Infants, like children, are very selective in the acts they try to copy. Young children are most likely to imitate actions that they are in the process of mastering and therefore are somewhat uncertain about their ability to perform. There is a discrepancy between the schema for the act witnessed and the sensorimotor representation of their ability to display it. One-year-olds will not imitate actions that are beyond their motor talent, like standing on one foot, or acts that are well within their competence, like moving a finger, but will imitate a woman who claps her hands.

Although some psychologists have claimed that one-week-olds can imitate others because they will protrude their tongue at an adult who repeatedly protrudes her tongue at them, it is not obvious that this action should be called imitation. It is more likely that this response is a biologically prepared reaction to a stimulus that moves toward and away from their mouth in a regular rhythm. Young infants also protrude their tongue when a moving pencil is a substitute for the tongue.[30]

Imitation may grow out of a bias, first seen in the last few months of the first year, to follow the direction of gaze of another adult. An infant who sees her mother suddenly look at the ceiling automatically directs her gaze toward the same location. Adult chimpanzees, by contrast, do not usually use the behavior of another animal to guide their own visual exploration and are far less likely to imitate either another animal or a familiar human caretaker.[31] Chimps typically use the behavior of a conspecific to infer what the other may do; children use the actions of others to infer what the other may be thinking.

The emergence of semantic representations during the second year is accompanied by increased generality of the imitative response. Infants twelve and eighteen months old watched an adult perform three discrete acts with a puppet, either in the child's home or in an unfamiliar laboratory. One day later the infants were given either the same or a different puppet in the same or a different location (home or laboratory). The twelve-month-olds were unlikely to imitate the acts they had witnessed a day earlier if the form of the puppet had been altered. The eighteen month-olds imitated the acts, whether the puppet or the setting was new or old.[32] It is likely that the older infants applied a semantic label to the adult behavior and that therefore the shape and color of the puppet and the familiarity of the setting were less important features of their representations.

The Development of Morality

Although children will imitate the behaviors of their parents, including actions regarded as moral, imitation is not the most important foundation of the child's conscience. The more critical basis grows from the representations that belong to the semantic networks defining "good" and "bad." A small proportion of these representations have a link to the emotional reactions called shame, anxiety, and guilt. The combination of semantic and visceral representations that contribute to the meaning of the human moral sense begins its growth in unexpected adult chastisements of children. That is, the initial stage in moral development exploits the alerting power of discrepant experience.

A mother who has just seen her eighteen-month-old spill milk on a table proclaims in a louder voice and with a sterner face than usual, "Don't do that." The unexpected warning is a discrepant event that alerts the child and creates a state of uncertainty. The fact that the child has no control over when the parental criticism will occur adds to its power to alert the child. The child eventually learns that the spilling of food is usually followed by similar chastisements. As a result, he feels uncertain whenever he experiences an intention to violate a family standard and begins to suppress such acts. The child who commits such an act is likely to show signs of sadness, distress, or fear, and may try to make reparations. Most children by the third birthday have created a category of "punishable acts," combining schemata and semantic networks, whose central feature is the potential to create a state of uncertainty regarding the possibility of adults' critical reactions to them or to their behavior. These acts are part of the child's semantic network for "bad."

But children also regard bitter tastes, pain, foul odors, illness, and disfigured objects as bad events. They belong to the same semantic category because they share the feature of being undesirable. It is not yet clear whether these varied experiences share a set of biological features with a single defining referent in brain activity.

In the next phase of morality, which begins its growth by the third birthday, children apply the semantic concepts "good" and "bad" to representations of self. The evaluation of self as good or bad is as central to our species as immobility in rats or the vigilant posture of a subordinate monkey who is approached by an alpha male. The first signs of an awareness of self, present by the end of the second year, include recognizing one's reflection in a mirror, manipulating the behavior of others, and making semantic references to the self in speech.

Young children oscillate their membership in the evaluative categories good and bad depending upon what has happened in the last few hours or days. The experiences of a very small number of children can, over time, slow the oscillation and fix one meaning. Chronic sexual abuse, for example, can persuade a child that she is unredeemably bad. These unfortunate children do not feel much shame, anxiety, and guilt when they violate a community standard, even though they know that the act committed was wrong. A small proportion of these children become unusually aggressive during adolescence.

Mary Bell, an eleven-year-old British girl who murdered two preschool boys, had been sexually abused from an early age by her mother's male clients and also was aware of her father's criminal career.[33] This girl's categorization of herself as a "bad child" made it easier for her to murder without the passion of anger or the desire for material gain. Fortunately, most children are uncertain about their virtue and dread the onset of shame and guilt.

The next stage in the establishment of morality occurs around five to six years of age, when children begin to recognize that they could have suppressed a behavior that violated a standard. This recognition is part of a more general capacity to reflect on a past series of actions and to realize that the sequence could have been different. Piaget regarded this ability as part of the concrete operational stage. This talent permits children to realize that they are responsible for an act that caused harm to another. Hence they are vulnerable to a feeling of guilt. This capacity requires the integration of past with present, a talent that emerges in an early form by four years of age.

Three-year-olds saw an adult display three different actions that formed a coherent sequence, one act on each of three days. When tested on the fourth day they did not retrieve the three temporally separated acts and integrate them into a sequence. Four-year-olds did so at once. Children, some three and one-half and some five years old, first watched themselves in a videotape showing an adult hide a puppet in a particular location. When asked later to find the puppet, the younger children did not retrieve the information they had seen in the video; the older children retrieved the relevant schemata, integrated them with the request, and solved the problem. Three-year-olds do not even integrate the information generated by seeing and hearing an examiner clap her hands twice with the experience a few seconds later of seeing a card illustrating two blocks; four-year-olds automatically integrate the two different events.[34]

Another way to describe this new ability is to state that the child now asks "why" a particular event has occurred. The child searches for a causal sequence linking the present to something that happened in the immediate past. Unlike the younger child, the six-year-old does not treat each event as autonomous, without a relation to a prior condition. It is possible that this bias to ask "why" is aided by the awareness that a glass of spilled milk is the result of the child's clumsy movements. As the child comes to appreciate that the consequences of his actions have a prior cause he generalizes to other events and assumes that they too have a cause.

This analysis applies to the conservation of mass. The child first acknowledges that two balls of clay are equal in size, then watches an adult roll one of the balls of clay into a sausage shape, and then is asked, "Which ball has more clay?" The four-year-old treats that question as independent of any past event. The only information available to answer the question is his current perception of the scene. The sausage appears to have more clay, and that perception determines his answer. The seven-year-old treats the sausage and the untransformed ball as part of a sequence that began earlier when the examiner showed him the two similar balls of clay. The child understands the examiner's question to mean, "Given the sequence you have watched, which object has more clay?" He remembers his prior answer of "same" and integrates that information with his knowledge that the sausage could be transformed into a ball again (this is Piaget's concept of reversibility) and replies that both have the same amount. However, the reversibility cannot explain the child's answer. He also must treat the second event as part of a sequence.

A half-dozen years later the cognitive talents Piaget called formal operations create the next phase of morality by rendering adolescents vulnerable to an additional source of guilt when they detect logical inconsistencies in their sets of related beliefs. For example, the recognition of disloyal thoughts about a friend ("I am a good person; I hope my friend fails the examination") can elicit a moment of guilt even if the friend is not hurt by those thoughts. Czeslaw Milosz left the United States to return to Europe because of an uneasiness produced by the temptations of American culture, which, had he yielded to them, would have compromised his deepest moral values.

Because guilt following detection of inconsistency among thoughts or beliefs increases at adolescence, it is not surprising that suicide attempts, rare before age thirteen, are more frequent after that time. The detection of inconsistencies also motivates youth to find coherence in their beliefs; here are six examples:

1a. Boys and girls should be treated equally.

1b. Boys are more often in positions of leadership.

2a. Adults can be trusted.

2b. Adults often lie.

3a. Look out for self first.

3b. Care about others.

4a. Hard work is rewarded with higher status.

4b. Status is empty.

5a. Loyalty to family values is an ethical obligation.

5b. Loyalty to family values limits freedom of choice.

6a. God loves humans.

6b. God is all-powerful.

6c. There is much human misery in the world.

Many adolescents detect the logical inconsistency among the last three statements, for an all-powerful God could prevent human unhappiness. The existence of human misery implies either that God does not love humans, that God is not all-powerful, or that there is no God.

Elias Canetti recalls his sudden insight that an inconsistency between the irrationality of a crowd and the rationality of each individual was an important cause of historical change. He would later explore this idea in his book *Crowds and Power*. The articulation of this idea was aided by the fact that Canetti, only twenty years old, had lived in five European countries, was aware of the horrors of World War I, and witnessed the unraveling of order in Germany following the Armistice.

Adolescents are rendered especially vulnerable to depression by a second feature of formal operational thought: the ability to be convinced that all possible solutions to a problem have been exhausted. An adolescent who does not dare tell her parents she is pregnant, and has no friend or relative to call for help, is susceptible to a feeling of hopelessness and, perhaps, a suicide attempt if she concludes that there is nothing she can do to resolve her situation.

The new cognitive competences also permit a potentially dangerous insight in adolescents living in societies that contain a great deal of ethical diversity, as our own does. Some adolescents in industrialized democracies experience a temporary lightness of being when they realize the relativity of the surface ethics of their society. A small proportion of contemporary youth entertain the possibility that no ethical standard deserves unquestioned loyalty and therefore feel freed from what they had thought to be absolute moral constraints. A subtle worry trails this discovery, for seventeen-year-olds are reluctant to conclude that no moral imperative is absolutely binding. Some young people indulge in a period of wildness to test whether the premise that no act is absolutely wrong can be true. Most discover that there are some sins and settle down.

The fact that young children rely on semantic networks penetrated with schemata to justify ethical behavior, while adolescents rely more on consistency among semantic networks, illuminates one description of moral development. Lawrence Kohlberg posited a sequence of stages in moral development based entirely on children's verbal explanations of why certain acts were wrong.[35] Most five-year-olds explain that the reason one should conform to family and community norms on stealing, lying, and aggression is to avoid punishment, most adolescents reply that this behavior is necessary for a harmonious society. The concept of a harmonious society has a far leaner set of schemata than the concept of parental punishment. When five-year-olds were asked to describe the conditions that would provoke a certain emotion (for example, "sad," "happy," "guilty," "proud," "angry"), they provided correct answers only for emotional terms that are usually accompanied by distinct facial expressions and events linked closely to schemata (such as a smiling face with happiness). By contrast, children older than seven years understood all the emotional terms, including those, like guilt, not associated with a distinct facial expression or specific concrete event,[36] suggesting that these terms activated semantic networks less penetrated with schemata. If five- and fifteen-year-olds use different structures to think about violations of ethical standards, it is misleading to describe the explanations of young children and those of older children as varying in maturity of moral understanding.

One unfortunate consequence of the frequent viewing of violence on television is that the vivid portrayal of violent acts, which most children do not experience in their daily lives, establishes schemata that need not have a strong link either to the semantic structures for good and bad or to associated emotions of disgust or fear. The schemata created while watching one person stab another repeatedly can remain relatively separate from the semantic representations of the ideas of bad, kill, and hurt. Indeed, aggressive behavior in cartoons often has humor as the background emotion. If the schemata for violent acts seen on a screen are not linked to the semantic structures for bad or wrong, they may not provoke feelings of fear, shame, or anxiety. When these children are frustrated, the schemata for the aggressive behaviors witnessed on the screen can be activated without the restraints usually imposed by the semantic representations for moral standards and the accompanying emotions of fear, shame, or anxiety. Under these conditions, the probability that a child will commit an aggressive act is enhanced. Put plainly, children do not always treat aggressive acts on television and in the movies as if they harmed the victim. I once saw a play in which a chorus chanted regularly, "When Cain killed Abel, he did not realize that he was causing the termination of his brother's life."

DISCREPANCY AND IDENTIFICATION

The content of an adolescent's moral standards is influenced by identifications with others. This process has its origins in the young child's tacit recognition that he and his parents belong to a common category. By the third birthday children have created a category that includes self and other family members based on shared schematic and semantic structures. But the child also detects obvious discrepancies between his behavioral and physical features and those of his parents. This recognition recruits the child's attention and promotes a desire to command those characteristics which are attractive. Size, strength, skill, apparent confidence, and control of fear are five discrepant, attractive adult qualities that children would like to have as their own. Because the mind is biased to believe that if two objects share a few obvious features it is likely they share less obvious ones, children assume that they may possess these attractive adult features because they and adults are members of a common category. The concept of essential features is critical to this process.

Children affirm Plato's intuition that each living thing possesses a core set of features that is the basis for its category name. Most children insist that even if a dog lost its legs, tail, fur, and bark what remained would still be a dog. The bias to assume that a name says something important about its referent is one reason parents rarely select androgynous names like Dale, Dana, or Kim for their children. Less than 3 percent of the infants born in Illinois between 1916 and 1989 were given androgynous names, presumably because parents did not want their children to be uncertain about their gender roles.[37]

Children believe, tacitly, that because they are the biological product of their parents they must share essential, but invisible, features with them, as well as less essential features, like same relatives and same residence. These beliefs persuade children that they and their parents belong to a unique category. Belief in this category is stronger if the shared features are discrepant from the child's understanding of what is normative. Hence a less common surname, like McDonaldfield or Bloomenberg, engenders a stronger identification with family than a common name like Smith or Jones. An American child of European pedigree who shares red hair, freckles, and light blue eyes with a parent is more easily persuaded of common membership than one who shares with a parent the dark hair and eyes of most Caucasian Americans. The child's assumption that she shares desirable (or less desirable) traits with an adult, even though there may be no factual basis for that assumption, is also accompanied by a feeling of pride (or shame) following events that occur to a family member. When that happens the child is said to be identified with that person. Identification requires both belief in a common category and the experience of vicarious affect with another. Each phenomenon can occur separately. A child can feel empathic toward a dog being beaten by an owner without identifying with the animal. A child who recognizes that she and her mother share a common category need not experience any vicarious emotion.

Apparently Elias Canetti identified with his beautiful, sophisticated, and fiercely devoted mother—his father died when he was seven years old—for Canetti recalls the shame he felt as an adolescent when his mother, yielding to childish vanity, asked a second-rate artist to paint her portrait: "I was ashamed for her because she wanted to place the fulfillment of that desire in the hands of another person . . . [a person] who had sold himself [and] . . . whom she regarded as an ignoble slave." Sylvia Plath identified with her husband, Ted Hughes, for she noted in her diary in 1958 how proud she was of other poets' praise of his poetic talent.

IDENTIFICATION WITH A GROUP

Adolescents also know that they are members of groups defined by gender, ethnicity, class, religion, nationality, region, or personality. An identification with any one of these categories often follows recognition that the person shares distinctive features with typical members of those groups. Experience is filtered through these identifications, which can last a lifetime if the category is uncommon and is linked to strong emotions. Both features apply to those who belong to minority groups in a society and to those whose parents had some distinctive experience, such as being Holocaust victims or being raped or murdered.

The child feels an emotion resembling pride if she believes the community respects the category with which she is identified. Canetti recalls his pride in being Sephardic because the Jews in this category in Bulgaria, where he was born, were richer and more religious than other Jews. Canetti's father warned him against marrying a woman whose family were German or Ashkenazi Jews. Michael MacDonald, born to a very poor Irish family in South Boston, remembers his pride in being a part of the neighborhood resistance to the judicial decision to bus school children from South Boston to other neighborhoods in the service of racial integration.[38]

However, the child feels shame, anxiety, or occasionally guilt if she thinks the community regards her category as possessing undesirable qualities. A large number of Germans born just before World War II felt a burden of guilt when they learned, after the war, how their parents, relatives, or countrymen had behaved during the dozen years of Nazi power. Many Americans felt a vicarious shame when they learned about the destruction of Vietnamese villages by American troops.

The American-born offspring of Holocaust survivors are more likely than other American Jews of the same age to suffer from depression or some form of anxiety.[39] One way to understand this fact rests on the assumption that because these children identified with their parents they experience, vicariously, the shame, anxiety, or fear they assume their incarcerated parents felt during World War II.

Czeslaw Milosz confessed to feeling shame over his Lithuanian origins: "I must admit that my region did not produce a single figure who swayed the world's destiny or won recognition for an important discovery." Walter Rathenau, a successful industrialist and moderately prominent political figure in Germany between the two world wars, was deeply ambivalent about his Jewish identity. Although he mocked Jewish dialects and customs when talking with others, he was proud of his membership in this social category. Rathenau described the tension that accompanied his recognition that he belonged to two semantically inconsistent categories: German and Jew. "In the youth of every German Jew, there comes a moment which he remembers with pain as long as he lives: when he becomes for the first time fully conscious of the fact that he has entered the world as a second-class citizen, and that no amount of ability or merit can rid him of that status."[40]

Isaiah Berlin left Russia for England when he was twelve years old to attend a private school outside London at which he was the only foreigner and the only Jewish student. His chronic feeling of being an outsider may have influenced the intellectual positions he took in his mature essays on history and ethics, for he usually arrived at conclusions that would have pleased the upper-middle-class British society that first accepted and later honored him.

Academically talented college students brooding about a vocation before 1950 often felt embarrassed if they chose a career in business rather than medicine, law, or science because becoming rich in a commercial mission evoked representations of merchants exploiting shoppers—the owner of a local department store was the prototype. This vocational choice lost most of its ethical taint a half-century later because accumulation of wealth became more dependent on technical skills exploited in impersonal contexts—a Silicon Valley engineer is a prototypic example. Thus the ethical evaluation of money is affected by how it is gained and therefore by the characteristics of those who accumulate it.

Children, like adults, continually compare the semantic representations of their traits, and those of the groups with which they are identified, with the traits of other salient groups. The detection of features of self that deviate from those of others recruits a special emotional state. Later-born children, for example, detect the differences between their attributes and those of their older siblings. The poor and uneducated detect the differences between their profile and that of those who are advantaged. The current undergraduate body at my university is highly tolerant of differences in religion, ethnicity, and sexual orientation, and there is minimal prejudice toward members of any minority group. Nonetheless, a graduating Caucasian woman with excellent grades told me that she always felt a little ashamed of her family because the parents of her friends were college graduates but neither of her parents had attended college. In this new millennium an educated family has replaced Christianity as a mark of virtue in this liberal college community. Although the culture of Houston, Texas, shares more features with the traditions of Mexico and the Southwest than with those of New England, the building that houses the Junior League of Houston is modeled on an elegant Boston mansion.

Citizens of a small or less developed country detect the difference between their nation's power and that of larger countries. Russia's isolation from Western Europe for most of its history created a defensiveness among the gentry and the small proportion of educated citizens who recognized that their schools were inferior, a majority of their citizens were illiterate, and their religion, derived from ancient Byzantium, was more primitive. One consequence was a jealous hostility toward Poles, whose richer intellectual and cultural history implied that Poland was a more civilized society.

Nations, like children in a neighborhood, compare themselves with others on attributes with an evaluative component, and citizens of the less potent state are motivated to alter the discrepancy. The social unrest in many poor countries would be muted if its citizens were unaware of the affluence and power commanded by other nations. Beijing politicians could sleep more peacefully if Chinese youth did not know about the freedom enjoyed by young adults in Europe and North America.

Reflection on differences in competence, wealth, power, and virtue generates a chronic psychological state in those who are identified with the less potent group. The English language has no good name for this emotion, which blends intimidation with envy in some, with shame or anger in others. Adults in Sumatran communities report experiencing an emotion they call *malu* when they are in the presence of someone who is unusually rich, talented, or powerful, or has exceptionally high status.

DIFFERENTIAL STATUS

The state of a subordinate animal may share some features with this human feeling. If the dominant male monkey is removed from a troop, the animal who had been second in the hierarchy usually assumes the alpha position, and his behavior and physiology change. A dramatic example of this dynamic occurs in a species of fish living in coral reefs in the Pacific Ocean. Each male typically dominates a harem of four to six females who form a dominance hierarchy. If the male dies, the alpha female undergoes anatomical and physiological changes that render her a reproductively competent biological male. Even hens are sensitive to the status differential among roosters in a barnyard, for they prefer mating with high-ranking males. If they are coerced by a male of low rank, contractions of their reproductive tract eject his unwanted sperm.[41]

The significance of differential social status in human societies is reflected in the almost linear relation between social class position, defined by a combination of income, education, and vocation, and both health and life span. College graduates in white-collar jobs earning $100,000 a year have more illnesses and die a little younger than adults with professional degrees earning $200,000 a year. Even though those in the former group have enough money and sufficient knowledge to obtain excellent medical care, their morbidity exceeds those who are higher in the social hierarchy. The social class of a child's family is a better predictor of the child's educational and vocational attainment in adulthood than the child's I.Q. at three years of age.[42] The consequences of being born into families of different social and economic classes are analogous to the final fates of motor neurons in the young embryo. Whether a neuron ends up innervating an arm or a leg depends in an important way on its spatial position as the neural tube is formed. The psychological fate of a child is influenced by the roll of the dice that placed that child in a poor family or an affluent one.

Each adult detects the difference in social status between self and other. The further from the top of the hierarchy a person believes his place to be, the more chronic his uncertainty about domination, criticism, and financial security and, apparently, the greater his susceptibility to illness.

Compare residents of Salem, Massachusetts, in 1700 with contemporary adults living in the same region. Each adult between twenty and thirty years old in eighteenth-century Salem compared himself with about 200 others in the third decade of life. Each person in that age group in contemporary Salem, part of the large Boston Metropolitan area, has about 700,000 other adults in the same cohort who are legitimate targets of comparison, making it harder for anyone to conclude that he or she is a member of the alpha group. Further, the media inform all Americans of the distribution of social positions throughout the United States and might persuade the citizens of Salem to compare themselves with every other American in their age cohort. If so, each has over 40 million peers for comparison. Only the most egomaniacal would conclude that they are in the alpha group.

One reason it will always be difficult to predict the development of a symptom or a talent from a child's genetic constitution is that scientists cannot know the child's eventual adult social position and therefore cannot know the level of uncertainty and physiological stress the person will experience. The inability to confidently predict adult traits from knowledge of an infant's genes is analogous to the biologist's inability to predict the kinds of species that might emerge following a mutation in a population because the scientist cannot know the nature of future ecological niches. These challenges to a strong form of determinism troubled Einstein, who did not want to believe God used dice to make decisions about the form of the world.

THE POWER OF GROUP IDENTITY

Psychologists do not understand why humans are prone to exaggerate the differences between members of their family, class, ethnic group, and religious group and those belonging to other families, classes, ethnic groups, and religious groups. Why do humans create and maintain in-groups and out-groups? There is no persuasive explanation of this obstacle to the idealistic hope that one day all humans might regard themselves as members of one category.

One clue to understanding this enigma is the fact that humans find it hard to reject the premise that some behaviors, ethics, moods, and beliefs must be more virtuous than others. We demand that a good/bad evaluation be applied to many human characteristics. The writer Pär Lagerqvist has God reply to a dead soul who asks about his intention in creating humans: "I only intended humans would never be satisfied with nothing." Because children assume that most of their own family's attributes are virtuous, they are tempted to conclude that other families must be less virtuous. When adolescents combine this judgment with the belief that they are psychologically more similar to their family than to anyone else, they are driven to the happy conclusion that they have a right to feel good about themselves, using a logic that argues: if my family is different from your family and my family's attributes are more virtuous than yours, I must be more virtuous than you.

But many children maintain an identification with a social category they regard as less desirable because they assume that names for objects and categories designate stable essences. The child of poor Mexican immigrants is prepared to believe that this semantic category implies possession of a small set of relatively stable characteristics. Elias Canetti never considered the arbitrariness of his ethnic assignment when he first experienced the anti-Semitic taunts of peers in his school in Zurich. Instead, he remembers becoming hypervigilant and, for the first time, doubting himself.

A second reason why children and adolescents maintain an identification with a group that they believe has undesirable traits is that denying the category to which one has been assigned requires violating an ethical standard of honesty as well as the standard of loyalty to one's family, for parents and other relatives are usually members of the same category. Recall the eleven-year-old British girl who murdered two preschool children. If Mary Bell was convinced that she was "bad," her acts of violence represented loyalty to her self-category and, therefore, at least one sign of personal honesty.

Third, knowledge of one's family, gender, ethnic, or class category provides a guide to action in times of uncertainty. Individuals regularly confront situations in which they must choose one action from a set of alternatives: what college to attend, occupation to pursue, friends to favor, skill to perfect, beliefs to espouse. Membership in a social category absorbs some of the doubt because the values that are associated with varied social categories imply preferences for particular occupations, friendships, skills, and beliefs. Most Asian-American graduate students are unlikely to pursue careers in the social sciences; African Americans rarely pursue careers in genetics. Hence an identification with family, class, or ethnic or national group helps to resolve the uncertainty that accompanies freedom of choice. Youth are susceptible to believing the political philosophy of a despot, and both Hitler and Stalin took advantage of that trait.

Finally, the adolescent who is ashamed of her father's alcoholic binges and wishes for more benign conditions may accept the undesirable category as proper because it protects her self against the terrible feeling of disappointment should substantial efforts to better the self fail. Humans are risk-averse and reluctant to persevere in attempts to gain a goal they value but do not expect to attain. One source of America's vitality is the evaluation of wealth, rather than the pedigree, accomplishment, and ethnicity of one's family, as a sign of virtue—for, on a sunny June morning, becoming rich seems a possibility.

The mismatch between a person's constructions and those of his community are also relevant to judgments about creativity and the validity of personality theory, two themes I address in the final chapter.

5

IMPLICATIONS FOR CREATIVITY
AND PERSONALITY

The community's judgment of a product as creative always depends on the relation between the psychological structures of a particular audience and those of the creative agent. The structures inherent in the celebrated work must be optimally discrepant from those of the local mind. A discussion of human personality profits from the analyses in the earlier chapters because the features of the major constructs in contemporary personality theory are abstract semantic networks that are indifferent to the influence of schemata.

Creativity

The judgment that a poem, a novel, or a play is creative is influenced by the degree to which its central ideas transform the less essential, rather than the most essential, features of the mental structures possessed by the community to which it is addressed. T. S. Eliot's *The Waste Land*, written in 1922, provides an example. The poem was acclaimed as creative by younger poets and college students because it conveyed the profound loss of an idealistic optimism held by many Europeans in the years before World War I and the postwar angst generated by economic uncertainty, high unemployment, and the Bolshevik threat. Eliot's lines capture the doubt and impotence of this period.

It is not unimportant that Eliot was temperamentally a melancholic who was deeply pessimistic over the possibility of humans ever knowing what was true. Eliot's biographer Peter Ackroyd described Eliot's mission in writing the poem: "There is no truth to be found, only a number of styles and interpretations—one laid open to others in an endless and apparently meaningless process . . . This was the informing principle of the original version of 'The Waste Land.'"[1]

I suspect that European and American readers would not have found *The Waste Land* as emotionally powerful had it been written twenty years earlier because it would have altered an essential feature of the buoyant mood of the first decade of the twentieth century. The poem is less appealing to readers today because its cynicism, following the loss of faith in any absolute ethical truth, is too familiar. John Donne's poems, written in the opening years of the seventeenth century, were also full of skepticism, but his English readers were not prepared to understand his dysphoric views and his writings were criticized by many, including Dr. Johnson, who called them "full of disgusting hyperboles." Two centuries later, partly owing to Eliot's advocacy, Donne's work enjoyed a renascence.

Frank McCourt's memoir *Angela's Ashes* was popular with American readers because its ideas transformed the less essential features of their understanding of poverty in the United States. The book describes an impoverished Irish family attempting to cope with their distressed state because of a father who is loving to his sons but indifferent to his family's economic welfare. The essential feature of the concept of poverty is lack of money. The less essential features, for many Americans, include public assistance, inadequately socialized children who do poorly in school, and membership in an ethnic minority.

Although poverty is not a discrepant phenomenon in America, the features of the family in *Angela's Ashes* are transformations of the less essential features of this concept for a majority of Americans: namely, families of color living on welfare whose children are aggressive, take drugs, and are failing in school. The family in *Angela's Ashes* is white, does not rely on government support, and the children are not aggressive, do not take drugs, and do not have problems in school. These transformations of the less essential features of the concept of poverty are one important reason why the book attracted so many fans.

Movies based on Jane Austen's novels have become popular over the last half-dozen years for similar reasons. The primary theme in Austen's novels is the relation between single men and women preparing for marriage. The relation between contemporary American men and women readying for marriage has been marked during recent decades by narcissism, directness, lack of civility, disloyalty, and sexual aggressiveness. The psychological relations between the couples in Austen's novels emphasize civility, concern for the other, and lack of sexual aggression. Thus Austen's novels are transformations of the less essential features of male/female relationships and, as a result, arouse and maintain interest.

An appreciation of nineteenth-century European beliefs about murderers helps to explain the celebration of *Crime and Punishment* following its publication in 1866. The consensual understanding was that these violent agents either were insane and therefore biologically tainted, were overcome by strong jealousy or anger, or killed as part of a robbery. And, of course, they were expected to try to avoid punishment. When Raskolnikov, the central figure in *Crime and Punishment*, tells Sonya that his primary motive for murder was to prove that he had the will necessary to kill someone, and when he confesses at the moment he is likely to escape all punishment, he transforms these popular assumptions about two less essential features of those who commit homicide.

Two other historical facts contributed to the celebration of this novel. The nobles, along with a small proportion of better-educated Russians in St. Petersburg and Moscow, Dostoevsky's main readers in the 1860s, were aware of and shamed by Russia's backwardness. Illiteracy was rampant, the recently freed serfs were unsophisticated, alcoholic, and brutish, and the great Russian army had been defeated in the Crimea. A desire to adopt Western views in order to appear more modern led many Russians to reflect on the validity of two Enlightenment notions that were alien to traditional Russian thought.

The first was that rational humans should act out of self-interest—a premise that continues to be the most essential hypothesis in contemporary economic theory. The second idea was that introspective analysis of one's motives and thoughts enhanced personal maturity, a belief Freud would elaborate a century and a half later. Raskolnikov's behavior refuted both maxims, for he confessed his crime when he did not have to and his incessant self-analysis was one reason for his tragedy. Thus Dostoevsky supported his readers' traditional, more essential understanding of human nature by revealing the flaws in Enlightenment philosophy and pleased them by having Raskolnikov turn to God in the final pages of the novel.

Czeslaw Milosz recognized that the celebrity or indifference awarded to a work depended on the relation between the products of the artist and the beliefs of the community. A writer wishing fame, he wrote, "should not run too far ahead; everything ripens slowly; either we keep advancing one step ahead of the reader, or by going two steps further we exceed his reach." Readers will note in Milosz's insight the same curvilinear function that governs an infant's attentiveness. Very familiar or very novel events, whether objects for the infant or ideas for the adult, are less arousing and less likely to recruit attention than partial transformations of an agent's knowledge. This fact is mysterious. Why should the alerting power of physical events and sentences follow the same curvilinear principle?

One possibility is that the central ideas in most creative novels and plays are semantic networks that are penetrated with schemata. Hester Prynne's adultery and Ahab's pursuit of Moby-Dick are rich in schemata. Alternatively, the mind might be biologically prepared to react in similar ways to any experiences that are only partially assimilable. When a plot, poem, sculpture, melody, or painting shares essential features with an agent's mental structures but transforms less essential ones, the resulting cascade of mental processes creates an "aesthetically satisfying" feeling that might be analogous to the feeling behind the smile of a three-month-old infant who has just recognized her father. Each agent's store of representations determines the likelihood that this state will occur; an educated ear is a prerequisite for enjoying Schönberg; an educated eye for appreciating Picasso; an educated philosophy for applauding Beckett.

CREATIVE SCIENTIFIC IDEAS

A novel scientific idea is also more likely to find acceptance if it replaces the less essential features of an existing theory. Freud's writings provide an excellent illustration. Psychoanalytic theory enjoyed a broad-based popularity in the United States from about 1910 to the late 1960s. These ideas felt intuitively correct to large numbers of psychiatrists, psychologists, and educated citizens because they altered the less, rather than the most, essential features of the previous century's views on personality and psychological symptoms.

Humans always have been, and always will be, vulnerable to episodes of fatigue, depression, worry, tension, insomnia, and irritability.

These complaints, separately or in clusters, have strikingly different causes, including disease, strenuous physical work, and uncertainty over money, job security, health, the possible loss of a loved one, rejection by a friend, the inability to obtain a desired goal, or an imminent threat to one's physical welfare. The unpleasant symptoms are universal because humans have the ability to anticipate calamity in the distant future and to wonder what others might be thinking about them. However, when the occurrence of any one of the above states is unexpected, and therefore discrepant, the agent attempts to interpret it. The local culture influences the individual's interpretation. The most popular interpretations derive their appeal, in part, from the major nodes of uncertainty in the larger community.

A theory held by the ancient Greeks is illustrative. The Greeks relied on the sea for both commerce and conquest, and citizens worried about unexpected, destructive storms. The popular explanation of storms was an imbalance in nature's forces. It may not be a coincidence that both Hippocrates and Galen attributed dysphoric moods and symptoms to an imbalance among the four body humors they believed were present in all individuals.

Industrialization during the latter half of the nineteenth century, which eventually brought steam engines and electricity to daily life, transformed the mood of rural America. Young adults were emigrating from villages to cities, where the accelerating pace of life was accompanied by crime, uncertainty about the possibility of financial loss, diminished status, and some guilt over the necessity of being more competitive and less honest than one wished to be.

Equally relevant was the fact that industrialization, which relied on the energy of wood, coal, and kerosene, had made the country conscious of the importance of these sources of energy. And one of the newly discovered laws of thermodynamics stated that all energy was conserved. It may not be surprising, therefore, that a neurologist, Charles Beard, suggested that each person's brain possessed a fixed amount of energy and that symptoms would appear if the person depleted this resource. Beard coined the term "neurasthenia" in 1869 to describe individuals who experienced fatigue, tension, depression, and insomnia because their nervous systems had run out of energy. Lenin received this diagnosis in 1903 when he was suffering from chronic headaches, insomnia, and fatigue, and his physician told him to stop working so hard.

It is relevant that neurology was a new medical specialty whose members charged higher fees than most physicians. As a result, wealthier citizens, especially those who worked with their minds rather than their muscles, were the typical patients visiting this new class of doctor. Beard's diagnosis was flattering, for it implied that patients with these symptoms were of high intelligence, were devoted to serious mental work, and were using their brains too intensely. The diagnosis of insanity was usually given to lower-class patients whose symptoms were marked by criminality, aggression, delusions, alcoholism, hallucinations, mania, or severe depression. These pathologies were regarded as the result of profound constitutional defects rather than excessive mental activity.[2]

Three other features of nineteenth-century American thought must be noted before I can describe Freud's transformations. The first was the premise that early experience could influence later personality and the possibility of neurotic symptoms. The second was the belief that excessive bouts of sexual pleasure were dangerous. Many Americans believed that frequent masturbation could cause insanity or mental retardation and were ready to believe that an obsession with sex could bring on a mental disturbance. But sexual frustration could do so as well, because some sexual pleasure was necessary for health. The ancient view that female hysteria was a consequence of sexual frustration remained popular, and physicians were massaging the genitals of their female patients, using battery-powered vibrators or their fingers, until the women had therapeutic orgasms[3]—a medical intervention that Galen had used seventeen centuries earlier. The third conviction was that physical therapies, such as cold baths, herbs, drugs, and electrical stimulation, were beneficial to patients with psychological problems.

Freud made three changes in the less essential features of these nineteenth-century assumptions. He accepted the notion that each person inherited a fixed amount of energy, but he attributed the depletion of that energy to the repression of libidinal instincts, rather than to excessive thinking. A person who used energy to repress sexual impulses had less available for adaptive work.

Freud also accepted the significance of early childhood, but he made improper parental socialization of the child's libidinal impulses, especially punishment of sexual interest, the cause of symptoms in adulthood. By attributing power to parental socialization of sexuality, Freud shifted the blame from the patient to the parents. This move was as flattering to patients as Beard's explanation that an insomniac was using her mind too much. For example, the popular explanation of hysterical symptoms among married women during the late nineteenth century was that the wife possessed a constitutional flaw that prevented her from obtaining regular sexual satisfaction. Many physicians also suspected that, in some cases, the husband was not sufficiently sensitive to his wife's sexual desires. These interpretations attributed flaws to the wife, the husband, or both partners. Freud removed the stigma from the couple by awarding causal power to unintentional errors of childrearing on the part of the wife's parents. The fact that the psychological products of these errors were invisible was not an obstacle to understanding, for the bacterial hypothesis of Pasteur and Koch argued that invisible forces within the body, originating in the outside world, could cause serious illness. It is easy to detect a metaphorical relation between invisible bacteria in the bloodstream and repressed thoughts hidden in the brain.

Finally, Freud changed the form of therapeutic intervention from somatic to psychological by insisting that the patient had to gain insight into the causes of the repression by telling the therapist his deepest thoughts. This suggestion found a friendly audience among many American physicians who had become convinced that prolonged conversation with patients led to more efficient cures. Freud turned the seed of this belief into a primary form of treatment.

Thus the claims that each mind has a limited amount of energy, that early family experiences influence later personality, that repression of libidinal energy leads to symptoms, and that introspective analysis alleviates pathology were transformations of the less essential features of late nineteenth-century thought.

Historical changes have motivated a return to the eighteenth-century metaphor of the body as a machine composed of material entities that can be repaired. The two most important changes are the dependence on machines among citizens of industrialized nations and dramatic advances in medicine and biology. Important activities stop if a car, a washing machine, a telephone, or a computer fails; we now know that a single change in one base pair of a gene can disturb an important bodily function. Doctors are replacing defective hearts, kidneys, hip joints, and, perhaps, in the future, parts of brains, as genetic engineers work on cures for our most serious illnesses through replacement of bad genes with good ones.

Today many clinicians assume that children diagnosed with attention deficit disorder have an impaired frontal lobe; impulsive violent criminals have a faulty cingulate cortex; and dyslexics have a compromised temporal lobe. These lesions are probably of influence for a small proportion of such patients. Some children with attention deficit disorder may have abnormal dopamine metabolism in the frontal cortex, and some dyslexics may possess compromised temporal functioning. The error, however, is to generalize these truths broadly and to apply the metaphor of faulty parts to all patients. This attitude leads to an almost exclusive concern with biological therapies and an indifference to the patient's history, cultural background, and daily living conditions. A physician who asks a patient complaining of fatigue about her job, diet, and living conditions is likely to arrive at one diagnosis if the person is an unmarried accountant living on a quiet street, but a different one if the patient is divorced, working sixty hours per week at a restaurant, and living with five children in a three-room apartment.

Social phobia is most common among women working in less-skilled vocations who did not study beyond high school. These women are embarrassed by the comparison of their social condition with that of more accomplished women and worry they may not act appropriately in unfamiliar settings. It is not surprising that they would want to avoid these settings.

Violent aggression is, and has always been, more common in males than females. Although it is likely that a small proportion of violent males are born with a compromised brain physiology, the majority of boys who join gangs and bully smaller boys do so for other reasons, such as anger over having failed the culture's requirements for academic success and, therefore, being plagued by doubts over ever attaining a secure vocational future.

Many Americans are troubled by the excessive self-interest, insufficient shame, violence, and lack of traditional civility that characterize our society, but do not know how to repair this state of affairs. Minds do not like to dwell on conditions that appear unalterable; hence it is understandable that many have become receptive to the idea that such problems are caused by faulty brain parts that can be repaired.

RESISTANCE TO CREATIVE THEORETICAL IDEAS

New scientific ideas that change essential, rather than less essential, features of the older explanations are usually resisted and require firmer proof of their validity before they win broad acceptance. Einstein and many colleagues of his age cohort were initially skeptical of quantum mechanics because it replaced the determinism that was an essential feature of nineteenth-century physical theory with probabilistic descriptions.

A majority of American geologists rejected Alfred Wegener's 1912 proposal of continental drift because it violated the essential premise that land masses were fixed. (It is also relevant that most American geologists spent much of their time searching for minerals that industry could exploit and were reluctant to give up this profitable activity to probe the bases for continental drift.)[4] Most biologists ignored Avery's suggestion in 1944 that genes were composed of DNA because they were certain that genes were proteins.

Most American developmental psychologists did not study Piaget's ideas when *The Child's Conception of Physical Causality* was translated into English in 1930 because the concepts of ensemble, operation, assimilation, and accommodation transformed the essential features of behavioristic descriptions of cognitive development. The essential constructs in Piagetian theory were cognitive structures changed by failures of assimilation rather than by receipt of external rewards. Piaget's ideas encountered much more criticism than current connectionist models of perception and memory because the connectionist models relied only on changes in the strengths of associations among symbols—a notion that is over two hundred years old. It was not until the 1960s, after John Flavell explained Piagetian concepts to English-speaking audiences, that those ideas gained some prominence.[5] Piaget's ideas have lost some of their appeal recently because he insisted on the importance of actions in the gradual establishment of knowledge of the world. The new nativists claim that the infant is born with an initial scaffolding for understanding the world and only has to be nudged with a few perceptual experiences.

THE CONCEPT OF REINFORCEMENT

Although the concept of reinforcement does not have the influence it had a century ago, many psychologists continue to believe that this concept can be defined in absolute terms as a particular pattern of brain activation, and resist acknowledging that most reinforcements are discrepant or unexpected events. The traditional functional definition of reinforcement states that any event that increases the probability of display of the response that preceded it is a reward or reinforcement. But most of the time these events are also unexpected changes in an animal's experience.[6] For example, the initial delivery of a food pellet one second after a rat has pressed a lever for the first time is an unexpected event that activates the amygdala and awards perceptual salience to the event, as well as to the response displayed. That is why exposing an animal to a potential conditioned stimulus before presenting any conditioning trials reduces the likelihood that the stimulus will become associated with a reinforcement or with an unconditioned stimulus, a phenomenon called latent inhibition. Even the basic phenomenon of conditioned taste aversion, created by pairing water that has a distinct taste with a subsequent malaise, is less efficacious if the distinct taste is familiar rather than novel.[7]

A monkey who had learned which of two different objects to touch, depending on the nature of a warning stimulus, was suddenly presented with two new objects never seen before. Dopamine-producing neurons became active when the animal received the food reward after touching one of the new objects, but ceased to respond after the animal had learned the correct response to these objects and delivery of food was no longer a surprise. The dopamine cells were responsive only when the reward was unexpected. A similar principle holds for norepinephrine-producing neurons in the locus ceruleus.[8] The pleasure that accompanies a visit to a new place, a new friendship, or an unexpected promotion rests, in part, on a similar mechanism. Few individuals would accept an invitation to learn about the future times and places when every one of their desired goals would be attained because the lack of surprise would drain each wished-for event of most of its joy.

Because rewards are unexpected events during the early phase of learning a new response, the biological phenomena described above aid the learning of new habits by facilitating synaptic transmission among the neuron ensembles involved in the behavior. Valentin Dragoi and J. E. R. Staddon[9] describe this phenomenon by saying that learning is driven by a comparison between expected reinforcement and current events. If the event that follows a response is surprising, the animal is physiologically aroused and the strength of the response increases. The same principle applies to Pavlovian conditioning paradigms. The values of the three critical terms in the frequently cited Rescorla-Wagner equation that presumably explains the change in associative strength of a conditioned stimulus are influenced by the discrepant or unexpected quality of the conditioned and the unconditioned stimuli.

In essence, rewards, as well as punishments, are punctuation marks that interrupt the stream of experience and by activating many brain structures, including the locus ceruleus, ventral tegmentum, hippocampus, and amygdala, facilitate the establishment of associations between features in the environment (for example, the lever the rat pressed), the action that produced the unexpected event, and the appearance of the reward. It is likely that a similar mechanism explains why humans are most likely to remember rare events, whether pleasant or unpleasant, for a long time.[10] Remember Milosz's memory of the unstable chamber pot.

This view of reward has freed the present cohort of psychologists from the shackling premises of behaviorism, traceable to Alexander Bain's writing in the middle of the nineteenth century, that dominated American psychology from the second decade of the twentieth century to the 1970s. These premises were so powerful at midcentury that Daniel Berlyne, wondering why animals are so responsive to change, was unable to reject the behaviorist assumption that the only reason animals act is to maximize pleasure or to minimize pain. Berlyne was forced to argue that animals always seek an optimal level of arousal.[11] Attainment of that state is rewarding. In this view, a puppy's exploration of an unfamiliar room is a habit that is learned because the activity produces an optimal level of arousal. Fortunately, contemporary scientists appreciate that puppies explore unfamiliar crannies because the novelty activates biologically prepared circuits that provoke the activity. The animal has no particular motive and seeks no specific goal. An adult passively viewing a series of ninety pictures of flowers interspersed with ten pictures of animals will display a distinctive EEG waveform to the less frequent pictures of animals. As with the puppy, no motive is operative and no goal is attained.

The current understanding that every species inherits biologically prepared reactions to novel events was not popular in the 1950s, and William Dember played a seminal role in persuading psychologists to acknowledge the power of unfamiliarity.[12] The central, pragmatic assumption in the older theory was that animals always avoided wasted motion and only acted when they were motivated for a goal. Many scientists remain faithful to this Puritan principle, even though they have watched gulls fly aimlessly across the summer sky, puppies frolic in tall grass, and babies babble to a moving red ring. Dember recognized the more correct meaning of these phenomena and performed a classic experiment. A rat was first allowed to explore a T-maze that had one black and one white arm. A few seconds later the rat was placed back into the T-maze, but now both arms were of the same color, either both black or both white. The rat typically entered the arm whose color was different from the one it had entered on the first trial. Despite the clarity of this result, many psychologists resisted the obvious conclusion that novel events influenced behaviors that did not satisfy any biological need. The commitment to a need-based theory of action that demanded a hedonic reward for its acquisition and maintenance was so powerful that talented scientists denied what they saw in the infant nursery and forgot that they chose a seashore holiday the summer after they had vacationed in the mountains.

The neurosciences have reversed the bias of the 1950s, for, in this new century, the psychological representations of particular goal states have become the repressed idea. The enthusiastic commitment to finding the brain bases for psychological processes is buoyed by the hope that a detailed description of the pattern of brain activity that accompanies thought, feeling, or action will provide a sufficient explanation of these phenomena. The description of the agent's symbolic intentions and willed actions will be irrelevant.

It is true that neurons in the motor cortex become active a few milliseconds before an adult is consciously aware of having made a decision to move his finger. But had the person decided not to move his finger for ten minutes no increase in neural activity would have occurred during that period. The motor neurons became active because the person decided to move his finger. The neuronal excitation in the motor cortex did not cause an intention to move. Thus a half-century after Dember reminded psychologists that some actions do not require the presence of a survival-based need or hedonic reward, it is necessary to declare what is obvious: some human actions are motivated by a conception of a desired goal. It is useful to know what the frontal cortex is doing when a person is rehearsing the telephone number of a friend she plans to invite to dinner. But the activity of the frontal neurons is not the cause of the rehearsal, it is a sign that the rehearsal is occurring. There is a daily flight from Boston to Chicago at 9 A.M. because some people in the East wish to travel to the Midwest. The fuel combustion in the engines and the movement of the plane's flaps on takeoff and landing are the material bases, but not the reason, for the morning flight.

Although most scientists are no longer burdened by the necessity of assuming that animals only act when they have a motive, or only learn a new response when a biological need is gratified, some investigators continue to believe that the concepts of reward and punishment are necessary to explain the acquisition of most behaviors. E. T. Rolls defines a reward as any event that an animal will work to attain; a punishment is any event an animal tries to avoid. These definitions are most useful for those events that satisfy an animal's biological state of hunger, thirst, cold, or sexual arousal, and/or produce hedonically pleasant or painful sensory states. But Rolls's definitions work less well for human adults who impose symbolic meanings on most of their actions. One day a person will walk a mile to a bakery to buy a special cake; another day she will refuse to eat cake because of its calories. Many urban residents avoid roads with heavy traffic on weekends, but commute twenty-five miles or more in heavy traffic during the workweek. Some energetic adults will fly a thousand miles to climb a snow-covered mountain in subfreezing temperatures; others will travel as far to watch a sunset over a tropical beach. It is not obvious that refusing cake, climbing Mt. Hood on a bitterly cold day, and watching a blood-red sunset over Virgin Gorda share a common set of either thoughts, feelings, or neural firing patterns with eating when hungry or drinking when thirsty.

A person's subjective judgment of pleasure, therefore, is not to be equated with the particular patterns of brain activity evoked by a sweet taste, a soft touch, a warm bath, or sexual release. The human judgment usually involves a comparison with a representation of either a prior or an ideal state of affairs. I wrote this paragraph a few minutes after returning from a walk along a beach on Vineyard Sound on a July day with a very cool breeze on my left and a very warm sun on my right. My subjective evaluation of this stroll as pleasant required my knowing that the temperature in Boston was 95 degrees and the humidity 75 percent. If the sensory input from the breeze, sea, sun, rotting seaweed, and old bottles washed up on the sand were the only information available I would have no way of deciding whether the walk was pleasurable.

The historical accident that made rats, rather than monkeys, the favored laboratory animal in studies of learning contributed to the notion that satisfaction of hunger, thirst, or sexual arousal and avoidance of pain are the most important rewards mediating the learning of a new action. Although rats will learn to press a bar if delivery of food follows that action, it is more difficult, though possible, to get monkeys to touch a screen in order to receive a piece of tasty food. The monkeys attend to the lights in the room, the noise outside the laboratory, and the scientist's movements because these events are interesting. Monkeys will also learn an avoidance reaction to a toy snake if they see another monkey display fearful behavior to this object. No rat would acquire a freezing reaction to an unfamiliar location simply by observing another rat. If the founders of stimulus-response learning theory, B. F. Skinner, Neal Miller, and Kenneth Spence, had worked with monkeys rather than with rats they might have invented different constructs and the concept of biological reward might have shared explanatory power with unfamiliarity.

SOCIOBIOLOGY

Some of the bold conclusions of sociobiologists and evolutionary psychologists have encountered resistance among some social scientists because these ideas are inconsistent with the two premises of behaviorism that twentieth-century American psychologists stoutly defended: that experience is the primary sculptor of psychological profiles and that the pleasure or relief from pain that follows an action, which is reinforcing, is the main determinant of the habits and knowledge that will be acquired and maintained. One reason for the growing popularity of the new biological notions is that they appear to render natural the unconflicted self-interest that contemporary society appears to condone. Evolutionary psychologists ignore the role of history in shaping this attitude and argue instead that animals who look out for the self's interest first are most likely to survive and produce the most offspring. Hence human selfishness is assumed to be a biological product of our evolution.

Stephen Jay Gould has also argued that historical events that made unconflicted self-interest congruent with what citizens had to do are one reason why acceptance of Darwin's insights had to wait until the end of the nineteenth century. Thomas Malthus could not have had his seminal intuition about populations outstripping food supplies until social conditions made it possible for large numbers of poor adults living in urban areas to survive past puberty, have many children, and threaten the security of the established middle class. I doubt that any scholar could have generated the Malthusian hypothesis during the height of the Minoan civilization. Unconflicted self-interest, as T. H. Huxley noted late in his life, is an ethical canon and not a biological fact.

Historical changes in American and European society help explain the attractiveness of sociobiology. Members of all societies are prone to accept the social categories assigned to them, most often gender, ethnicity, religion, and category of work. There are, however, periods when the power of some of these categories is eroded and the ethical directives linked to them lose some of their moral force. A woman in fifteenth-century Venice could not participate in political activity; a modern Venetian woman is not so constrained.

These social categories began to erode after World War II when geographic mobility increased and men who would have entered the blue-collar jobs of their fathers and grandfathers went to college to become professionals. At the same time the towns and neighborhoods that had been ethnically homogeneous became more diverse. The civil rights movement required a curbing of the importance of family pedigree so that African Americans and Hispanics could have greater vocational opportunities. Many argued that the categories of gender, family pedigree, race, ethnicity, religion, and type of work were arbitrary and placed women and ethnic minorities at a disadvantage in this society.

When these categories lose their ability to enhance the individual and to provide guides to action, the self is released from the ethical obligations attached to a given category. As a result, each person feels free to pursue personal pleasure, higher status, and greater power in accord with the Darwinian imperative. These historical changes are one reason why sociobiology has enjoyed a period of popularity. These ideas would not have been celebrated two hundred years earlier. I suspect that during the next century there will be a renascence of some social categories ethnicity will certainly be one of them—and that college students reading about today's discussion of evolutionary psychology a hundred years from now will smile.

Advocates of the ideas of sociobiology ignore the fact that many early human societies were communitarian. Each person's welfare rested not on his actions but on the integrity and strength of the extended family, clan, or village with which he was identified. Excessive competitiveness and narcissism would have provoked rejection. I suspect that the ancient Chinese, who knew that each species begets its own kind and animals must kill to survive, would have found the arguments of contemporary sociobiology hard to understand.

Observations of chimpanzees in natural settings reveal that our close relative is motivated primarily by desires for food, mating opportunities, a dominant social position, and avoiding attack—events that are represented primarily as schemata. Most humans, excluding those who are chronically hungry or ill, are motivated by desires that are represented mainly by semantic networks. Humans wish to avoid behaving in ways that provoke guilt, shame, or criticism by others while they try to gain qualities that maintain their personal dignity. Chimpanzees become uncertain when they perceive a more dominant animal display a particular vocalization or gesture. Humans become uncertain when they imagine that a friend might be thinking they are dishonest, disloyal, deviant, or dumb.

More important, it is very difficult for humans to confine their judgment of an event to the context of their current perception, uninfluenced by any reference to the source of the event. The human mind insists on asking: Where did this event originate? I recently viewed a gallery of Ansel Adams's photographs of the American West and realized I was not having as powerful an aesthetic experience as I would have had if the scenes Adams photographed had been painted—for with paintings I would have felt awe at the artist's talent. I was admiring nature in Adams's photographs of the Snake River; I admired Monet when I saw his painting of the Seine at dawn. The human mind automatically activates notions of cause and intent. Both humans and animals implicitly ask of each event "What is it?" "Where is it?" and "How dangerous is it?" Humans add "Why is it?" and each person's answer participates in that person's psychological reaction to the experience.

Even though uniquenesses are common in the animal kingdom, many sociobiologists are unwilling to acknowledge the possibility that *Homo sapiens* possesses distinctive properties. The social insects are unique among invertebrates; the platypus is unique among vertebrates; the bonobo chimpanzee is unique among apes. The human abilities to infer and occasionally brood about the thoughts and emotions of others, and especially to evaluate those thoughts, render us unique among primates.

The seminal principle in evolutionary theory is that stronger, healthier, more competent individuals acquire more territory, greater access to food, and more frequent mating opportunities and, therefore, have greater reproductive fitness, even though the reproductive fitness of males in some bird species is far less heritable than anatomical traits, like beak size, that are not closely related to reproductive fitness.[13] However, the more important point is that human societies create councils of elders, legislatures, judges, and courts that interfere with this evolutionary principle by protecting the weaker and less competent from exploitation by the stronger and more competent. Many citizens in egalitarian societies, like our own, insist that all lives are equally valuable, although this ethical position appears, on the surface, to be inconsistent with evolutionary principles.

The premise of connectivity, which sustains the explanation of the infant nativists, is present in the arguments of the sociobiologists. In this case, the seamless connectedness assumes basic similarities among rats, monkeys, and humans and is indifferent to the unique properties of our species. This assumption has one obvious pragmatic advantage: it rationalizes research on animal models for human emotions, cognitive capacities, and psychopathologies.

Although some human properties are obviously derivative of those seen in animals, not all are continuous with earlier forms. A more critical posture toward such broad generalizations from animals to humans will aid theory.

The mind always has a choice between generality and specificity when classifying an event. Theorists who use evolutionary theory to illuminate human traits emphasize qualities shared with animals, including common brain structures and the capacities for aggression, fear, and competitiveness; theorists who rely on developmental principles emphasize traits that are unique to humans. For example, evolutionary psychologists explain a stepfather's abuse of a child by pointing out that the father is genetically unrelated to the child. Most developmental psychologists explain the same phenomenon by emphasizing qualities unique to humans, such as amount of education, vocation, and the presence of a mental illness, in order to differentiate the very small number of abusive stepfathers from the majority of loving ones.

The Bolshevik revolution left homeless large numbers of Russian children. When the nation was experiencing great privation during the famine of 1922–1923, scholars wrote that social conditions had created the animal-like properties of these children, who originally had been no different from others. A decade later, when life became gentler, new experts announced that these homeless, asocial children were genetically tainted and biologically different from the majority.[14]

A description of *Homo sapiens* that emphasized features shared with primates would refer to anatomy, physiology, and sensory motor systems. A description that emphasized uniquely human traits, more popular in the eighteenth and nineteenth centuries, would refer to the ability to infer the thoughts of others, generative language, morality, logic, and, perhaps, episodic memory. Humans are described correctly by both lists, but the two have different connotations.

The completion of the human genome project guarantees that genes will become reliable additions to descriptions of human traits. The preference for emphasizing qualities humans share with animals, compared with those restricted to our species, has cycled over time. Prior to Darwin, the latter preference was ascendant. After Darwin, and especially following the discovery of the DNA molecule fifty years ago, the former bias became dominant because of the hope that significant biological discoveries, made possible through animal experimentation, would add to our knowledge of the human condition.

Self-Reports and Theories of Personality

The conceptualization of human personality by American psychologists in the nineteenth century and the first half of the twentieth century rested on a desire for a semantic consistency in which the notion of self was central. There was agreement that the proper referent for personality was the whole person, rather than any single trait, a view in accord with Freudian theory. But historical events eroded this position. Psychologists returning to the university after World War II wished to make their discipline more scientific and insisted that concepts rest on data rather than on a philosophical ideal. In addition, Freudian ideas had become more obviously ragged. As a result, a young cadre of technically trained psychologists exploited the niche that psychoanalysts had occupied and declared that factor analysis of the answers provided by young adults, most often middle-class, white college students filling out questionnaires, would reveal the fundamental dimensions of personality.

It is a truism that the source of empirical evidence contributes to the meaning of every scientific concept. The distinction between schemata and semantic structures has special relevance because, currently, the most popular personality dimensions—called the Big Five—are based entirely on the semantic structures activated when adults answer questionnaires. The Big Five dimensions are neuroticism (calm versus worried), extraversion (socially avoidant versus sociable), openness (conservative versus liberal ideas), agreeable (irritable versus good-natured), and conscientiousness (careless versus reliable). These concepts describe dispositions that are unconstrained by the context in which the trait is displayed, as if conscientious individuals were careful and reliable in all contexts, when, in fact, many behave this way only in very particular settings and with selected others. That is why the stability of the personality traits assessed with questionnaires is modest across the college years: the estimated correlation across forty-five different samples is only 0.51.[15]

In addition, each of the Big Five dimensions has an ethical gloss. Most Americans regard serenity, sociability, agreeableness, conscientiousness, and openness to ideas as good traits that residents of a neighborhood would wish for in someone who moved into the house next door.

More important, different personality types would be inferred if the thousands of people who filled out the questionnaires had been filmed for ten hours a month over a six-month period in different contexts (home, work, on holiday) and those observations factor-analyzed. And a third set of personality types would emerge from a factor-analysis of a half-dozen biological measurements (for example, EEG, event-related potentials, muscle tension, sympathetic reactivity) gathered under varied conditions.

The problem, which I hinted at in Chapter 1, is that questionnaires represent a very particular type of incentive, for they activate particular semantic nodes of a person's network of self-representations. An individual who activated semantic concepts referring to loss of behavioral control as he read "Are you angered easily by minor frustrations?" might answer no, while an individual who activated concepts referring to feelings of tension might answer yes to the same question. Behavioral observations might reveal that the two individuals shared equivalent tendencies to raise their voices and become critical when frustrated by another person

Some adults who report on a questionnaire that they feel depressed are suffering from an infection and the depressed mood is a result of the illness rather than a deep-seated personality trait. Further, self-reports of anxiety or depression usually award the greatest weight to recent experiences, especially intense ones. Hence a normally sanguine person who lost a spouse or failed to achieve a goal during the prior year may report greater sadness than someone who has been chronically depressed over the last ten years.

For these reasons there is usually a poor, or at best modest, relation between individuals' verbal reports of their feelings and physiological measurements believed to be the bases for the feelings. Even patients whose biology prevents them from experiencing any visceral feedback from their body report that unpleasant pictures are more emotionally arousing than neutral ones. A final defect of questionnaires is that the semantic structures available to conscious report reveal only a small part of an individual's self-understanding and fail to reflect tacit properties unavailable to consciousness.

Nonetheless, advocates of the Big Five assume, without detailed argument, that conscious semantic judgments about one's behaviors, beliefs, and moods are the most valid bases for inferring fundamental personality dimensions. This claim is surprising. No biologist would use the reports of informants, even sophisticated ones, to decide on the basic dimensions of human diseases. No economist would rely only on interviews with consumers to discover the fundamental economic concepts. No cognitive psychologist would analyze adults' descriptions of their perceptions, memories, and solutions to problems in order to infer the basic cognitive competences.

Several problems trail the use of verbal self-report as the only basis for inferring personality dimensions. First, each semantic representation of a trait is related to other semantic categories. A woman who affirms on a questionnaire that she "likes meeting new people" is biased to respond affirmatively to all questions semantically related to that statement in order to maintain consistency (for example, she is likely to affirm that she is relaxed with strangers and likes holiday excursions).

Further, terms like "sociable" and "shy" are antonyms; hence the features linked to each word are inversely correlated in the semantic networks of most respondents, even though many adults who like meeting new people take equivalent pleasure from frequent periods of reading or hiking alone. The antonymic relation between "outgoing" and "solitary" biases the individual to minimize the co-occurrence of the two dispositions. This tendency compromises the validity of parental answers to questionnaires designed to evaluate their children's behaviors and moods. Because most parents treat the semantic concepts "happy" and "sad" as antonyms, mothers who say their infants laugh frequently will resist describing them as irritable. But films of infants at home and in the laboratory reveal that there is a large group of infants who both laugh and cry frequently. These semantic constraints are absent when the evidence comes from observations of behavior.

My laboratory has been studying two temperamental groups. About 20 percent of four-month-old infants show a combination of vigorous motor activity and distress when they are presented with unfamiliar visual, auditory, and olfactory stimuli. These infants, called high reactive, are biased by their biology to become shy, fearful, and timid during the toddler years and quiet introverts during late childhood and adolescence. By contrast, about 35–40 percent of four-month-olds show a combination of low motor activity and minimal distress to the same battery of stimuli. These infants, called low reactive, are biased to become sociable, bold toddlers and extraverted adolescents.

The mothers of the ten-year-old children participating in this longitudinal study ranked descriptions of twenty-eight traits from most to least characteristic of their preadolescent child. The temperamental classification of low reactivity made when the child was four months old was a better predictor of the child's behavior at ten years than the mothers' contemporary ratings. Five children classified as high reactive infants at four months were described by their mothers as making friends very easily. However, every one of the five children was fearful in the second year, was shy and subdued in the laboratory at ten years, and showed physiological signs suggesting a low threshold for uncertainty.

The children, who were also interviewed, ranked twenty psychological traits from most to least characteristic of themselves. Most ranked qualities like "happy most of the time," "like to visit new places," "play with many friends," and "like roller coasters" as accurate descriptions of the self, and ranked frequent worry, shyness, and fear as least characteristic. Both those who had been high reactive infants, many of whom had become fearful children, and those who had been low reactive infants and fearless children ranked the twenty traits similarly. However, when we compared the physiological reactions of the small number of high and low reactives who described themselves as shy, only the high reactives showed the biological signs expected for this profile. That is, among the children who described themselves as shy and timid, the physiology expected to accompany shyness occurred primarily among those who had been high reactive infants. These data imply that children who report being shy or fearful can belong to different personality categories.

Third, if a human trait does not have a popular name, and therefore is not part of a semantic network, personality questionnaires do

ı

not include relevant items. Some men are loyal to their wives and affectionate with their children but disloyal and hostile in their relations with colleagues at work. There is no semantic concept that reflects this particular constellation of traits, and, of course, it is missing from all current lists of personality types. Variation in the degree of ambivalence over one's motives and beliefs, concern with peer opinion, a capacity to sustain energy, posture with individuals of higher status, desire for domination of others, ease and intensity of sexual arousal, degree of virtue assigned to self, and the balance between living in the future and living in the present are qualities that influence daily behavior and life choices and therefore point to a potentially fruitful set of personality types. Unfortunately, these traits are not measured easily with questionnaires.

Of equal importance is the fact that individuals vary in their usual patterns of biological activity in brain and body. These states contribute to conscious feeling and chronic moods, but no individual has complete conscious access to them, and therefore individuals cannot be asked about them on a questionnaire. To illustrate, children and adults vary in the level of activity of the noradrenergic brain tracts that influence alertness, arousal, and intensity of certain emotions. Two people could report equivalent irritation over commuting to work in bumper-to-bumper traffic but differ in the degree of noradrenergic activity and in the intensity of irritability in the eyes of a friend. This information lies beyond the reach of any questionnaire. This suggestion is not hypothetical. Chinese-American and Mexican-American adults showed similar physiological reactions to the annoying intrusion of bursts of loud noise, but the former reported feeling less emotion than the latter.[16]

In addition, reports of the frequency and intensity of emotional states, such as anger, anxiety, happiness, and sadness, are influenced by a comparison of present with past moods. However, because the accuracy of retrieval of past feelings is usually poor, the report of contemporary feelings is suspect. A follow-up investigation of sixty-seven adults who had been interviewed as high school students thirty years earlier provides an illustration of the fallibility of adults' recollections of the past. The adults were asked the same questions about their adolescent experiences that they had answered thirty years earlier—questions concerning school, peers, sex, and family relations. Their adult recollections bore little relation to what they had reported when they were teenagers. For example, 82 percent of the adolescents remembered some form of physical punishment from parents, but only 33 percent of the adults remembered having been physically punished. Although only 24 percent of the adolescents said they enjoyed their social relations with peers, over twice as many of the adults recalled deriving a great deal of pleasure from peer relations in adolescence. The lack of fidelity of the adult memories led the investigators to conclude that recollections of past psychological events and emotions were fallible reconstructions.[17]

Informants who fill out questionnaires describing a person they know must compare that individual with others, and that mental set biases the informants. For example, mothers of identical twins describe them as more similar than direct observations reveal. That is why parent and teacher ratings of children are not always valid indexes of the child's actual profile and conclusions based only on this form of evidence are suspect.

An informant's answer to the simple question "Are you happy?" can even be influenced by the content of prior questions. The probability than an adult will say that marital satisfaction is either a major or a minor contribution to life satisfaction, for example, depends on the order in which these two questions are asked. Some judgments about self are constructed on the spot from the thoughts that first pierce consciousness.[18]

On some occasions questionnaire evidence leads to conclusions that violate both biology and common sense. One team of investigators interviewed 794 pairs of adult female twins about their physical health and emotional states. The verbal replies to the questions posed by a stranger revealed the surprising fact that "self-esteem" was as heritable as physical health.[19] However, had the evidence consisted of an actual physical examination with laboratory tests plus direct observations of behavior, I suspect that the results would have been very different.

Another group of scientists asked teachers of young adolescents, some of whom were twins, to fill out a questionnaire called the Child's Behavior Checklist for Teachers. The results implied that identical twins were no more similar in propensity to anxious/depressed moods or delinquent behavior than half-siblings living in stepfamilies. Other scientists administered a twelve-item questionnaire measuring a tendency to worry to more than 45,000 adults living in Australia or the United States. This time identical twins were more similar than siblings, but, surprisingly, the statistical analyses revealed no significant influence of shared family experience on the tendency to worry.[20] The authors concluded that "there is no need to invoke any nongenetic causes of family resemblance" for this complex trait. This claim would probably have to be retracted if the evidence came from behavioral observations and physiology. For all these reasons, conclusions about personality that are based only on questionnaires or interviews have a meaning that is as limited as Ptolemy's conclusions about the cosmos based on the reports of observers staring at the sky without telescopes.

MEANINGS OF PERSONALITY

The essential features of a "personality type" are stable profiles of correlated behaviors, beliefs, and moods that differentiate one group of individuals from others. The ancients took the simplistic, but not wildly incorrect, position that bodily substances, presumably inherited although the notion of genes was two thousand years away, formed a critical foundation of the personality categories that Galen called melancholic, sanguine, choleric, and phlegmatic. Galen acknowledged, however, that the blood, bile, and phlegm that were the material bases for these types were subject to the influence of diet and the vicissitudes of climate.

The core elements of the Galenic view persisted until the end of the nineteenth century when Freud invented new personality terms, like "hysterical" and "obsessive-compulsive," that were thought to be partial products of the person's experiential history rather than of body chemistry. Although most of Freud's theoretical edifice has lost the intuitive feeling of truth that supported it for almost half a century, his bold decision to make childhood history an important component of personality type was correct.

The biological concept of species, which parses individuals into groups with relatively stable profiles, is a useful guide to a more fruitful conception of personality types. Biologists accommodate to three sources of information when they define a species: (1) phylogenetic history, (2) a distinctive set of inherited anatomical and physiological features, and (3) reproductive isolation from related groups, which permits natural selection to augment new inherited features. These three criteria provide an orientation to thinking about personality that acknowledges the contribution of schematic and semantic representations to three bases for personality types: (1) sources of uncertainty, (2) inherited temperamental biases, and (3) social experiences.

Although childhood history has to be a component of adult personality, most psychologists have ignored information about childhood because they cannot be certain about what childhood events are most relevant to adult profiles and because they do not possess sensitive ways to evaluate, in adults, the early experiences they suspect are relevant. Even if the popular claim that an infant's secure emotional bond to the mother influences future traits is valid, there is no procedure that could reveal this childhood state in a twenty-five-year-old adult. Adults have very poor memories of their infant experiences and, therefore, cannot be asked about them. Psychologists do not have procedures analogous to the carbon dating of a piece of bone.

Freud, who recognized the significance of childhood, thought that the targets of libidinal cathexes were the significant historical events. I suspect that stable nodes of uncertainty are more important because human minds dwell on and attempt to mute them. These attempts, whether successful or unsuccessful, are important components of personality traits. Benjamin Franklin, who evidently shared this view, wrote that controlling uneasiness was the quintessential human concern.

The primary sources of uncertainty change their hierarchical position with development. Some sources become less salient, others ascend in importance. During the first two years, when semantic structures are fragile, events that lack the less essential features of schemata are the primary cause of uncertainty. If these discrepant events cannot be assimilated and the uncertainty remains unresolved, distress and/or avoidance follows.

Semantic structures, which incorporate schemata, become dominant by school age, and inconsistency between and among networks becomes a more frequent source of uncertainty. The seven-year-old recognizes that boy and girl, child and adult, love and hate, good and bad, happy and sad are semantic opposites. Each person or event can belong to only one member of those pairs. Seven-year-olds insist, for example, that a person cannot be both sad and happy at the same time. One child told an examiner that one part of his body could be happy and another part sad, but that the two feelings could not exist at once in the same place.[21]

Adults in all cultures experience uncertainty over their acceptability to others in the community, relative competence at locally valued skills, status and wealth, and adherence to community ethical standards. These nodes of uncertainty are as potent now as they were millennia ago. A childhood history marked by poverty, for example, is often associated with a perception of marginality and uncertainty about one's worth. The British literary critic Frank Kermode, who grew up in poverty, admitted to feeling like an outsider: "Looking the part while not being quite equal to it seems to be something I do rather well." Michael MacDonald, who grew up in South Boston, recalled feeling ashamed that his family was on welfare. Many Americans believe that hard work and intelligence are all that are needed to gain the wealth that has come to be considered a primary measure of personal virtue. Hence, as noted earlier, a disadvantaged class position has a greater potential for shame in the United States than in many other countries. Adolescents who identify with their poor families are vulnerable to feelings of shame and doubt if they accept society's view that their parents are lazy or incompetent.

The child's temperamental biases, based on inherited biological processes that create visceral schemata, are analogous to the anatomical and physiological features that define a species. These temperaments include energy level, capacity for sustained attention, and the ease with which anger, sadness, fear, guilt, hope, and joy are provoked. Austrian and German nationals living in England as World War II began were arrested and sent to a camp in northwestern Canada. The diary entries of one young prisoner revealed an uncommon capacity for optimism and an ability to rationalize the harshness of camp life that was probably a gift of his sanguine temperament. The entry for May 11, written one year after his arrival, announced: "Today was a fabulous day. The camp surroundings are now so beautiful that you long to be here." The next day he acknowledged that the camp experience had been beneficial: "I've used my time in this camp very well—I have learned a lot and read a lot in my field. I think that I've developed a wider viewpoint during this year in internment."[22]

Knowing an adult's early temperamental bias and the culture in which he was raised can aid prediction and understanding of his current behavior. For example, a small number of ten-year-old American children who had been low reactive infants and sociable bold toddlers were, surprisingly, shy and quiet in the laboratory, and reported being shy with others. But these timid ten-year-olds did not possess three physiological signs that were characteristic of equally shy ten-year-olds who had been high reactive infants and fearful toddlers. In the laboratory the latter, but not the former, showed right frontal activation in the EEG while sitting quietly, a large evoked potential from the inferior colliculus, and sympathetic lability.[23]

In contrast, a small group of these ten-year-olds who had been high reactive infants and timid two-year-olds were, surprisingly, sociable and relaxed with an examiner, and told an interviewer they were neither anxious nor shy. Nonetheless, these children possessed the three physiological signs that characterized many of the other ten-year-olds who had displayed a high reactive temperament during infancy. Thus knowing the infants' temperament aided understanding of their current behavior and biology. Jung appreciated that the persona displayed to others was not always a sensitive reflection of the private anima. The descriptions of behaviors, moods, and motives that individuals report on questionnaires or in interviews represent a construction of their persona.

The third contribution to personality, analogous to the criterion of reproductive isolation, comes from the contexts of social relationships and experiences—some due to chance—that maintain or change the profile developed during childhood and adolescence. A group of monkeys of a particular species that become geographically separated from their conspecifics, perhaps by an earthquake, will, in fewer than four dozen generations, develop different biological and behavioral traits and may become incapable of breeding with members of the original group. The humans who arrived in Europe about forty thousand years ago developed languages and mores that were very different from those of humans who migrated to Asia. Genetically identical collections of the bacteria *E. coli* that were placed in twelve different flasks and subjected to identical stressors became, over thousands of generations, genetically distinct strains as a result of different mutations that occurred in each flask.[24] Equally unpredictable events can have the same effect on personality.

The local context is important because it permits—or fails to permit—individuals to gain the symbolic goals that their values demand. That is one reason why there is variation among immigrants to a new city in their level of satisfaction with their new home. A recent Vietnamese immigrant to California can find more opportunities to exploit his talents and establish friendships than one who settles in rural Maine. Two-year-olds who are temperamentally uninhibited are at high risk for asocial behavior at age ten if they grow up in poor families with harsh mothers. Children who are very shy in the first five years are at greater risk for adult social anxiety if reared in America, where extreme shyness is regarded as maladaptive, than if raised in many other parts of the world.[25]

Many scientists who made important contributions to physics, mathematics, and biology in the early part of the twentieth century were born in Budapest between 1898 and 1908—Szilard, Gabor, Von Neumann, Wigner, and Teller belong to this category. Von Neumann once noted that this urban setting had a combination of features that rendered it unique on the continent: a large German-speaking Jewish population, a multinational ambiance, strong external pressures to achieve, and an "extreme insecurity in the individuals, and the necessity to produce the unusual or else face extinction."[26] Von Neumann implied that if these scholars had lived in Altoona, Athens, or Alexandria their brilliance might not have been actualized.

A particular score on any one of the current Big Five personality dimensions is heterogeneous with respect to the person's childhood history, temperament, and local context. The large number of individuals who are classified as extraverted, on the basis of their answers to a questionnaire, have different early histories, temperaments, and social relationships. If psychologists possessed information on those factors they would have deeper insight into the varied profiles of these so-called extraverts.

Current psychiatric categories are vulnerable to a similar critique. These categories are usually based on the patients' verbal description of their symptoms. This source of evidence guarantees that the patients will emphasize their feelings of distress because those feelings are phenomenologically salient. By contrast, their beliefs, biology, and daily behaviors are less salient, and their physiological state is not available to consciousness.

Anxiety and depressive disorder are two diagnostic classifications frequently given to adolescents and adults on the basis of verbal descriptions of worry or sadness or both. But the vast majority of these patients have other symptoms, including substance abuse, problems in sustaining attention, unsatisfying social relations, asocial behavior, and low expectations of gaining the goals they desire. These properties are as significant for a correct diagnosis as the person's subjective feeling state. About one-third of adults given the diagnosis of panic disorder differ from the majority of panic patients in that they possess sympathetic lability, sensitivity to separation from friends and relatives, and a continuous need for reassurance.[27] They might belong to a distinct diagnostic group.

Feelings of distress are present in most human diseases, but are usually epiphenomenal, and not directly related to the primary etiological cause of the illness. Headache is one feature of a brain tumor; fatigue is a feature of mononucleosis. But the headache and fatigue are only signs and not the most essential features of the two categories of disease. We can apply this reasoning to psychiatric illness. The central features leading to a diagnosis of depressive disorder are reports of sadness, apathy, sleeplessness, and poor appetite. If these symptoms occurred because the person had failed to meet an important moral standard, the cause of the affective profile is more accurately classified as a guilt reaction. The same symptoms reported by an adolescent pessimistic about his future living in poverty with a criminal parent are better classified as a state of hopelessness. Pessimism about one's future is not to be confused with guilt over failing an ethical standard. A third category of patient might report the same symptoms because of an inherited diathesis involving an imbalance in neurochemistry; this category used to be called endogenous depression. These three patients should be placed in different diagnostic categories, even though their reported symptoms are similar, because the causes of their depressed feelings are different. If clinicians probed their patients' beliefs, moral standards, achievements, and social relations as deeply as they probe their feeling states they would discover the different conditions that can produce depression.

Although future research may refine the three types described above, the main point remains valid: the affect states reported by a patient can have different origins, and a psychiatric classification should be based on the complete profile rather than primarily on verbal reports of feelings. If we relied solely on such reports for diagnosing physical illness, the proper categories would be abdominal pain, headache, chest pain, itching, and fatigue.

A similar argument can be made for anxiety. A feeling of worry can be due to concern with one's physical safety, vulnerability to disease, social rejection, failure to complete an important task, financial loss, or status uncertainty. These are different sources of worry. As in depression, a proportion of individuals inherit a diathesis for worry, and this group should be placed in a separate category. Clinicians and investigators must gather behavioral, cognitive, and physiological information as well as self-reports. The exclusive focus on conscious emotional states is retarding discovery of a more fruitful set of concepts for mental illness.

REQUIREMENTS FOR FUTURE THEORY

Three problems must be solved if we are to invent more valid personality concepts. We must find theoretically fruitful ways to conceptualize and measure the products of childhood histories and temperamental biases and determine the contextual factors—both social and historical—that maintain or alter the profiles acquired during earlier stages of development. Hans Krebs, the biochemist who discovered the citric acid cycle, believed his insight was aided by the fact that he recognized that this chemical reaction took place in the context of a living organism and not in a test tube.

Completion of the genome project will permit future scientists to say something about the genetics of temperamental biases that contribute to personality types. But these discoveries will be delayed if the personality categories remain heterogeneous. It is not possible to discover the genetic contribution to a personality category if it consists of genetically diverse individuals. Had physicians insisted on the unity of a disease category called "stomachaches" they would not have discovered the genetic contribution to bowel cancer. I know of no fruitful construct in evolutionary biology that is defined by one measure and ignores the history, genetics, and local ecology of the species. It is unlikely that a deep understanding of adult personality, child temperament, or psychiatric categories will be attained if psychologists and psychiatrists continue to rely only on evidence supplied by questionnaires and interviews.

Finally, it is reasonable to reject, or at least question, the notion that there is a basic set of personality types present in all cultures through history. No animal species is present in all ecologies, and not all species have persisted over the last hundred million years. Many new forms appeared after the Cambrian explosion, many others vanished, and each ecological area contains a limited number of species. Some personality types, like penguins or dinosaurs, are found only in particular places or during certain historical eras.

It is unlikely that the major personality types in medieval French villages were present in ancient Egypt; some types in modern Sweden would not be found in isolated villages in Borneo. One reason for this claim is that human groups that have been reproductively separated for long periods of time probably possess different temperaments. Asians and Europeans are two such groups, and research suggests temperamental differences between them.

Healthy infants born to Asian parents are less aroused by visual and auditory stimulation than those born to Caucasian parents.[28] Further, five-year-old Chinese children living in Beijing were less accurate than American children of the same age when asked what emotion a protagonist in a story might experience, especially when the appropriate emotions were sadness and fear.[29] Chinese university students asked to recall and date their earliest memory were less likely than Americans to describe an acute emotional experience, and the Chinese dated the age of their first memory to about four years, compared with three and a half years for Americans. Because childhood events accompanied by intense, acute emotions are remembered best, this result may imply a temperamentally based muting in the Asian students of the visceral schemata that are components of emotions. Should this speculation have some validity, psychologists might find less variation in traits related to affective exuberance in Asian than in European populations. As a result, extraversion might be a less differentiating trait among the former group. This speculation finds support in a factor analysis of the ratings of Taiwanese college students, using terms that the Chinese language employs to describe personality, which did not yield an extraversion factor. The analysis revealed that a concern for others (versus a concern for self), competence, degree of self-control, and level of optimism were the major personality factors. These concepts are different from those in the Big Five.[30]

Each society's structure and values also restrict or expand the range of variation in beliefs, behaviors, and moods. Some isolated rural societies—Tibet, for example—limit seriously the opportunity for independent striving for wealth. But residents of Tibet will show more variation in "commitment to Buddhist ideas" than citizens of secular societies like Japan. A shy posture with strangers is most prevalent in urban areas with large numbers of people; it is hard to find many social phobics in small, isolated villages where each person knows everyone else. If there is little variation in a quality, it cannot be a major personality type.

Of course the most prevalent personality types will vary with developmental stage. Two-year-olds do not vary in conscientiousness, religiosity, psychopathy, and a host of other traits that differentiate adults. By contrast, adults do not vary very much in the ease with which they cry to a minor frustration or become fearful in the dark. The error in contemporary writing on personality, which was also present in Freud's essays, is the implicit assumption that there is a set of core types present in all places across time.

Some psychologists might complain that awarding too much power to local cultural conditions ignores the possibility that some social structures and temperaments, present in every society, create a small number of universal personality types. This claim has merit. All cultural settings pose threats of attack, domination, insult, ill-

iences can influence a later vulnerability to anxiety,
bility, openness to ideas, conscientiousness, and intro-
mmitment to a set of universal personality types remains
mise.

SORDERS

f profiles psychiatrists call anxiety disorders provides
y to integrate the two seminal ideas in this book. The
toms of the varied categories of anxiety disorder are
nd reports of fear of particular events or objects, such
cts, heights, or the dark; (2) panic attacks; (3) chronic
ess, physical harm, failure, evaluation, or loss; or
ompulsions, and eating disorders. Because a major-
porarily experience a mild form of one or more of
t least once during a lifetime, the diagnosis of anx-
lied only if the symptoms are chronic and impair
usly.
must be explained. Less than 20 percent of
hibit one or more of the anxiety disorders—
ocial class, and ethnicity—and 10 percent of
rcent of men are given this diagnosis.[33] If the
rder were simply external stressors (for ex-
ronic illness, death of a loved one, or failure
many more adults should be given the diag-
percent of the population experience these
, these events occur as often to men as to
alence of anxiety disorder should not be
e females of many animal species are more
n males, it is reasonable to assume that a
phobias, anorexia, panic, or social anxi-
ical diathesis that renders them vulner-

ness, loss of property, or death of a loved one. Thus every community should contain variation in the ease of becoming uncertain,
tense, or worried over one of these future threats. Further, research
with animals indicates that heritable variation in tendency to avoid
the unfamiliar is present in every mammalian species. Humans in all
cultures have to face unfamiliar people, objects, and situations. It is
reasonable to argue, therefore, that vulnerability to uncertainty and
its complement represent two universal personality types.

However, this argument requires the additional assumption that
the nature and interpretation of the threat have no bearing on the
adult profile. A universalist might claim that it makes no difference
if the threat is physical harm, loss of wealth, low social status, or
death of a loved one, or if the individual is living alone or in an
extended family. But the local ecology always influences the fitness
and survival of a species. A species that moves slowly and has few
defenses against attack is at risk for extinction in an ecology with
many predators, but may reproduce successfully in a niche with few
predators and ample food. Similarly, individuals who are vulnerable
to uncertainty, but live in a society with minimal threat or have a
supportive group, should be less anxious in time of threat. That
consideration should be part of the description of the personality
type. The discoveries that criminality and social phobia are overrep-
resented among adults who grew up in poor, less well educated families and that social phobics living in small towns are more likely to
recover than those living in large cities imply that a personality, or a
diagnostic category, must accommodate to the individual's current
social setting. Sadly, no diagnostic term in contemporary psychiatry
does so.

The frequency of depression among adults in Eastern European
countries increased dramatically after these countries were released
from Soviet domination because the high expectations for improvement in their lives were not realized. This depressed state is not to

be equated with the chronic dysthymic mood of Sylvia Plath. Adolf Hitler's mood changed from extreme self-doubt in the 1920s to one of manic confidence when his speeches to cheering audiences catapulted him to the chancellorship of Germany in 1933. Had Hitler been raised by the same parents and had the same set of early adult failures, but lived in Sweden, I suspect he would have remained a disgruntled, anxious adult and world history would have been different. The combination of sexual permissiveness and hostility to authority, which characterized large numbers of young Americans protesting the Vietnam war and racial intolerance during the 1960s, was absent a hundred years earlier and would have been rare in sixteenth-century French villages.

The suggestion that the social context influences the behaviors that are the essential features of each personality type is supported by observations of animals. Young male elephants occasionally experience surges in testosterone that are accompanied by increased aggressive and sexual behavior. This state, called musth, usually lasts for a few weeks. But musth can continue for four or five months if the group contains no adult males. When older males are introduced into such a population the duration of the younger males' musth episodes is decreased dramatically.[31]

The social rank of the female offspring of a macaque mother is closely related to the mother's rank. However, if by chance the daughter is orphaned and bonds herself with an alpha male her social rank can increase dramatically.[32] A very similar sequence occurs in human societies. Herbert Hoover spent his early childhood in a small Iowa town in the late 1870s. But because both his parents died before he reached adolescence he was sent to live with an uncle in Oregon. One of his high school teachers, who thought Herbert was bright, suggested that he apply to the new university being founded in Stanford, California. At Stanford Herbert estab-

lished a friendship with a faculty mer
mines, and when a British minin
manage a mine in Australia the
Hoover made a fortune in a shor
a need for money, decided to g
orphaned and not allied him
mines, he would not have bee

A rat's behavior followir
amygdala, hypothalamus,
nature of the objects in t
contains small unfamili
an aggressive intruder
if the incentive is a t
shock, the animals w
chemistry mediatir
hypothalamus, an
sive if observed
a cage containi
following pre
infants raise
to become
High reac
demic ac
reactive
gressio
adole

E
rie
fo
s

early
anger,
version,
a shaky p

ANXIETY D

The family
an opportuni
primary symp
(1) avoidance a
as animals, inse
worry over illn
(4) obsessions, c
ity of adults tem
these symptoms a
iety disorder is ap
daily activities seri

Two robust fact
American adults ex
depending on age,
women but only 5 p
causes of anxiety disc
ample, loss of a job, ch
to gain a desired goal),
nosis, for more than 20
stressful events. Furthe
women; hence the prev
greater in women. Becau
avoidant and defensive th
proportion of patients wit
ety possess a special biolog

able to developing these attributes. Being female and possessing a chronic dour mood are powerful predictors of the profile that combines panic attack with depression. Panic disorder patients can have an attack even while sleeping or when told exactly what to expect before they are infused with epinephrine.[34] This fact implies a biological vulnerability to such attacks.

One feature of this biological diathesis involves the person's conscious feeling tone. Sensory information from the body, which originates in circulatory vessels, heart, skin, muscles, and gut, is relayed to the nucleus tractus solitarius in the medulla, where epinephrine and norepinephrine potentiate, but opioid receptors mute, the intensity of these signals, which are then sent to the amygdala and from there to the ventromedial prefrontal cortex. If these signals unexpectedly pierce consciousness, the person is motivated to interpret the sudden change in feeling tone. If the experience is unpleasant in quality, the individual will feel dysphoric. A surge of cortisol can excite the limbic and frontal sites that contribute to the perception of a dysphoric body tone. Individuals who had taken corticosteroids during the month prior to being interviewed were more likely than others to report a stressful event (for example, a frightening experience) because the drug had altered body tone and focused attention on unpleasant events.[35]

A small proportion of individuals—the estimate is ten to twenty percent—are born with a temperament that renders them susceptible to more frequent and/or more intense changes in this "unpleasant" feeling tone. The person's culture and history acting together provide a foundation for the interpretation imposed on these perceptions. The phenomenological quality of body tone in most persons during most days is hedonically neutral. When a change in tone is experienced as pleasant, the person is likely to attribute it to a recent activity, for example, exercising, having a glass of wine or a fine dinner, finishing an assignment, or engaging in sexual activity.

But it is more difficult to assign a cause when the change in tone is experienced as unpleasant.

Two interpretations come easily as individuals try to understand the reason for the unexpected, unpleasant feeling. First, the person may interpret the feeling as anxiety about a possible future threat. Some patients with social phobia attribute their emotion to worry over behaving inappropriately in a social situation. Panic patients often report thoughts of possible physical harm when they experience a sudden increase in anxiety before a panic attack.[36] The frequent association between reports of anxiety and being at high risk for coronary heart disease is due, in part, to the fact that sensory feedback from the compromised cardiovascular system is often interpreted as anxiety.

A second popular interpretation for the change in tone is an ethical lapse. Because a failure to honor one's own standards for proper behavior is often followed by a feeling of shame or guilt, a person experiencing a discrepant onset of dysphoric feeling tone, but not knowing why, is biased to regard it as due to such a failure. Each of us can cite many occasions when our behavior did not meet our standards for civility, honesty, or loyalty. The acceptance of this interpretation will be followed by a surge of guilt or shame. The few individuals who are temperamentally prone to more frequent or intense changes in dysphoric tone will be especially vulnerable to the state Galen and Burton called melancholia.

An eminent British psychologist in his forties who developed a temporary but serious depression combined with intense anxiety ascribed the origin of his illness to intense jealousy and anger upon learning that his wife was having an affair with a man he disliked. The psychologist wrote in a memoir that the willful imposition of rational control over his jealousy and anger was among his highest ethical standards. The feelings of wild jealousy, which he could not control, forced him to acknowledge that he had violated an ethical norm that was part of his definition of self. This moral failure contributed to the dysphoria that required hospitalization.[37] Adults who march to a different set of moral imperatives would not have been as bothered by an equally intense jealousy. A British neuroscientist who suffered a serious depression in his fifties imposed a different interpretation on his body tone. He believed that his depressed feelings intensified when he concluded that the distress of his physical symptoms might never abate.[38]

Americans with obsessive-compulsive disorder often report thinking about committing an aggressive act or being contaminated with dirt. Moral standards calling for restraint on aggression and remaining clean are socialized consistently in Western cultures.[39] Arab patients with obsessive-compulsive disorder who are loyal to the Islamic code think more frequently about committing blasphemy or violating religious imperatives.[40]

A temperamental diathesis that results in more intense or more frequent bouts of dysphoric tone can explain why anxiety disorders are not more prevalent, but not why more women than men develop these symptoms. This fact could be explained if (1) the bodily signal arriving at the medulla was more intense in women than in men; (2) the female medulla either was more active or was less effective in muting the bodily signal; (3) the activation of the amygdala by the medullary information was greater in women than in men and therefore amygdalar projections to the ventromedial prefrontal cortex were stronger in women; or (4) the ventromedial surface of the prefrontal cortex was more responsive in women than in men. Adult women have a larger ventromedial cortex than men.[41] Each of these mechanisms relies on a different neurochemistry. Although I favor the second explanation, any one of the four could explain the sex difference.

Nineteenth-century American and European women felt a moral imperative to be faithful wives and selfless mothers. Many contemporary women, especially those who are well educated, are barraged with three standards that are difficult to meet: be beautiful, be loved, and accomplish something important. It is easy to fail any one of these assignments. Thus when dysphoric bodily information penetrates consciousness demanding an interpretation, a woman may decide, "I'm not pretty enough," "I'm not valued enough," or "I'm not accomplished enough." The development of anxious or depressed symptoms becomes a possibility if this interpretation becomes a mantra.

The importance of the interpretation imposed on feelings illuminates the increased prevalence of middle-aged men and women leaving their spouses in quest of a wholeness they feel their marriage denied them. The unpredictability that maintains emotional vitality penetrates the first four to five decades of life. But after grown children have left the home and daily interactions with a partner have become predictable, a perception of boredom and lost vitality pierces consciousness and pushes for an interpretation. Modern Western premises about the virtue of self-actualization supply that interpretation, and fifty-year-olds wander off to rural cottages, new careers, world travel, or love affairs with the expectation that new settings and relationships will sew the ragged pieces of their torn souls into a seamless, beautiful tapestry.

The right hemisphere plays a more important role than the left in provoking and amplifying the visceral schemata that mediate dysphoric feelings. Temporary suppression of the left hemisphere following an injection of amobarbital in the left carotid artery often produces crying and an increase in heart rate; the same injection into the right carotid artery often produces laughter and a decrease in heart rate.[42] In addition, adults with physical complaints usually show larger increases in cortisol and blood pressure than controls when they view an emotionally aversive film with the right rather than the left hemisphere.[43] Among depressed adults activity in the right amygdala is correlated with the intensity of dysphoric feelings; adults with lesions of the right hemisphere are less able to retrieve emotionally toned memories to particular words than those with a compromised left hemisphere.[44] In light of these findings, it is not surprising that individuals with anxious symptoms are more likely than volunteers to show an asymmetry of frontal lobe activation in the EEG that favors a more active right side.[45]

These findings invite the invention of a name for the chronic dysphoric mood resulting from the interpretations imposed on the unexpected visceral signals that pierce consciousness. Robert Burton called this state melancholia; nineteenth-century physicians called it neurasthenia; contemporary psychiatrists call it comorbid anxiety and depression. Everyone has experienced acute worry because of the possibility of failure, acute sadness over loss of a friend, or acute guilt over insufficient loyalty to a loved one. But these feelings typically vanish with time. Melancholia is longer lasting.

The Bases for Conscience

The habit of attributing unpleasant feeling tone to a moral lapse and experiencing a moment of guilt motivates a final point. The discovery of pharmacological interventions that mute the intensity of fear, anxiety, guilt, and depression in some individuals has been a benevolent gift to those who suffer from these disabling states. Although some commentators have wondered about the social consequences of large numbers of asymptomatic persons taking these drugs, few have questioned the advantages for the smaller group of anguished patients.

It is possible, however, that during the next half-century scientists will discover a drug that eliminates the feeling components of guilt and remorse, while leaving intact the semantic knowledge that certain acts are ethically improper. A person who took such a drug regularly would continue to know that deceiving a friend, lying to a client, or stealing from an employer was morally wrong, but would be protected from the uncomfortable feeling of remorse that normally accompanies violation of a personal moral standard. Anticipation of this feeling restrains asocial behavior; hence it is reasonable to wonder whether our society would be changed in a major way if a majority of citizens were protected from guilt and remorse. If these feelings can be controlled, will people become less kind, civil, honest, and nurturant? This question addresses a long-standing debate on the bases for ethical actions and the criteria individuals apply when they are faced with moral choices.

Most Western philosophers, but especially Kant, made reason the bedrock of conscience. People acted properly, Kant believed, because they knew the behavior was morally right. This argument for reason as the guardian of conscience has merit. All individuals wish to regard the self as virtuous and try to avoid the uncertainty that follows detection of the inconsistency that is created when they behave in ways that are not in accord with their view of the self's desirable attributes. Kant argued that although the moral emotions help to restrain asocial acts they are not necessary for the conduct of a moral life. Dostoevsky was imprisoned for five years in an isolated Siberian outpost with peasant convicts who rejected him because of his middle-class origins and moral premises. Although it would have been expedient for Dostoevsky to adopt, temporarily, the values of his debauched fellow prisoners, he continued to honor the standards he brought to this harsh setting. It would have been equally expedient for Thomas More, who enjoyed power and privilege in 1530, to grant Henry VIII's request to ask the Vatican to annul his marriage so that the king could marry Anne Boleyn. Although More was a practical man he could not violate his moral premises, and he paid for this steadfastness with his life. Kant would have understood the inability of both men to act in ways they believed were immoral.

In contrast, some philosophers, including Peirce and Dewey, have argued that anticipation of feelings of anxiety, shame, and guilt motivates a continued loyalty to one's ethical standards. An individual who was certain he was protected from these uncomfortable emotions might find it easier to ignore the moral imperatives acquired during childhood.

The tension between these two positions is especially clear in modern industrialized societies, where the balance between the feeling of virtue that follows enhancing another and the different pleasure that follows the enhancing of self has shifted toward favoring the latter state. A spouse with young children caught in a marriage that has grown stale must decide whether the ethical demand to maintain family integrity should take precedence over the desire to feel happy, excited, or challenged. A young professional eager for a promotion, higher salary, or a brief moment of fame must decide whether to visit a sick friend or continue working.

The conflict nineteenth-century adults in Western societies experienced over this choice has been replaced by a growing consensus, almost universal among the young, that self's potency and pleasures come first. The awarding of high priority to the varied states of self-enhancement when deciding if one is "happy" has eroded an earlier habit of also relying, occasionally, on the judgment that one is loving, charitable, loyal, honest, or nurturant, and has diluted, but not yet destroyed, the power of Kant's argument.

Although it is not certain that a drug that blocked remorse would eliminate the mutual social obligations that make a society habitable, nonetheless a posture of vigilance is appropriate, for, unlike gorillas, humans can hold representations of envy, anger, and dislike, even toward those they have never met, for a very long time.

Hence the visceral schemata that maintain anticipations of guilt and shame are helpful in restraining rudeness, dishonesty, and aggression. While we wait for the future to resolve this question, it is useful to recognize that a satisfying analysis will require a deep appreciation of the profound differences between visceral schemata for bodily events, on the one hand, and semantic networks for good and bad, on the other.

EPILOGUE

Flannery O'Connor once told a reporter who asked about the frame of mind required for a good novel that it is best if the author does not understand the plot completely so that the writing contributes to a deeper comprehension. I empathized with that insight as I worked on this book. In these chapters I have tried to make two points. First, the work of the mind involves qualitatively different psychological structures that, although emergent from brain activity, cannot be described with biological words.

Several implications follow an acceptance of this premise. The most important is that a sole reliance on the products of semantic networks in studies of humans severely limits the depth of understanding. Students of personality and psychiatric disorders should measure the biological signs of the visceral schemata that add meaning to verbal reports of emotions. Developmental scholars who would like to believe that infants understand simple physical principles should acknowledge the profound differences between perceptual schemata and semantic forms. I have a modest set of semantic structures for the notion of black holes but lack the schemata of the astrophysicist poring over the spectral lines coming from a distant star. The distinction between schemata and semantic networks means that the inferences drawn from animal behavior may not have the same meaning as those inferred from human verbal reports. A rat reluctant to enter an unfamiliar area is not to be equated with a person who reports that she avoids large social gatherings. A hound searching for a duck in a marsh is not to be equated with a person mentally tracing his movements over the past hour in order to find a lost key.

The predicate "know," like a gene with varied functions, does not have a single meaning. Consider the following three statements:

1. One-year-old infants know that six dots are different from two dots.
2. Ten-year-olds know that twenty-five is larger than twenty-four.
3. College students know that the square root of −1 is an imaginary number.

Most of my generation, trained in the 1950s, knew that an aloof mother could create an autistic child because they were told this was so and they had never seen such a child. All of their knowledge came from texts and lectures. The public is vulnerable to many false beliefs when all of their information is semantic in form.

The significance of unfamiliarity is my second point. It is difficult to discipline the mind to resist the addiction of attributing causal power to the perceived features of an event—difficult to appreciate that, much of the time, events that either transform a schema or are inconsistent with a semantic network have the greater potential to arouse. This means that predicting an agent's response to an event often requires knowledge of the person's history.

An individual's history is as significant for that person's thoughts and feelings as the evolutionary history of a species is for its form and physiology. A mutation in a base pair that is part of the genetic configuration for body form will have different consequences in flies, mice, and humans. Analogously, the psychological state created by an earthquake or a torrent of praise will depend on each person's past. The challenge for modern neuroscientists is to devise machines and analytic programs that might detect the psychological products of a person's earlier encounters. I am not certain that this achievement is possible. And if it is not, prediction will always be imperfect. Although most of us live in the moment about to be born, Kierkegaard appreciated that a life can only be understood backward.

NOTES

1. Discrepancy and Schemata

1. E. T. Rolls, *The Brain and Emotion* (New York: Oxford University Press, 1999). A. Schutzwohl, "Surprise and schema strength," *Journal of Experimental Psychology: Learning Memory and Cognition*, 24 (1998): 1187–99. C. Milosz, *Native Realm* (Berkeley: University of California Press, 1968).

2. E. Canetti, *The Memoirs of Elias Canetti* (New York: Farrar Straus and Giroux, 1999), 484.

3. D. Rinberg and H. Davidowitz, "Do cockroaches know about fluid dynamics?" *Nature*, 405 (2000): 756. C. H. Rankin, "Context conditioning in habituation in the nematode *Caenorhabiditis elegans*," *Behavioral Neuroscience*, 114 (2000): 496–505. A. Kandiel, S. Chen, and D. E. Hillman, "c-fos gene expression parallels auditory adaptation in the adult rat," *Brain Research*, 839 (1999): 292–297. K. D. Broad, M. L. Mimmack, and K. M. Kendrick, "Is right hemisphere specialization for face discrimination specific to humans?" *European Journal of Neuroscience*, 12 (2000): 731–741.

4. Z. Merali, J. McIntosh, P. Kent, D. Michaud, and H. Anisman, "Aversive and appetitive events evoke the release of corticotropin-releasing hormone and Bombesin-like peptides at the central nucleus of the amygdala," *Journal of Neuroscience*, 18 (1998): 4758–66.

5. R. Eliott and R. J. Dolan, "Neural response during memory judgments for subliminally presented stimuli," *Journal of Neuroscience*, 18 (1998): 4697–4704. I. Fried, K. A. MacDonald, and C. L. Wilson, "Single neuron

activity in human hippocampus and amygdala during recognition of faces and objects," *Neuron*, 18 (1997): 753–765. R. T. Knight and T. Nakada, "Cortico-limbic circuits and novelty," *Reviews in the Neurosciences*, 9 (1998): 57–70. A. Martin, "Automatic activation of the medial temporal lobe during encoding," *Hippocampus*, 9 (1999): 62–70. W. Schultz and A. Dickinson, "Neuronal coding of prediction errors," in W. M. Cowan, E. M. Shooter, C. F. Stevens, and R. F. Thompson, eds., *Annual Review of Neuroscience*, vol. 23 (Palo Alto: Annual Reviews, 2000), 473–500. F. A. Wilson and E. T. Rolls, "The effects of stimulus novelty and familiarity on neuronal activity in the amygdala of monkeys performing recognition memory tasks," *Experimental Brain Research*, 93 (1993): 367–382. K. A. Kiehl, K. R. Laurens, T. L. Duty, D. B. Forester, and P. F. Liddle, "Neural sources involved in auditory target detection and novelty processing," *Psychophysiology*, 38 (2001): 133–142.

6. R. T. Knight, "Contribution of human hippocampal lesion to novelty detection," *Nature*, 383 (1996): 256–259. C. Rossi-Arnaud and M. Ammassari-Teule, "Modifications of open field and novelty behaviors by hippocampal and amygdaloid lesions in two inbred strains of mice," *Behavioral Processes*, 27 (1992): 155–164. S. Dubois, B. Rossion, C. Schlitz, J. M. Bodart, C. Michel, R. Bruyer, and M. Crommelinck, "Effect of familiarity on the processing of human faces," *NeuroImage*, 9 (1999): 278–289.

7. P. J. Whalen, "Fear, vigilance, and ambiguity," *Current Directions in Psychological Science*, 6 (1998): 177–188. P. J. Whalen, S. L. Rauch, N. L. Etcoff, S. C. McInerney, M. B. Lee, and M. A. Jenike, "Masked presentation of emotional facial expressions modulate amygdala activity without explicit knowledge," *Journal of Neuroscience*, 18 (1999): 411–418. C. A. Nelson and K. G. Dolgin, in "The generalized discrimination of facial expressions by seven-month-old infants," *Child Development*, 56 (1985): 58–61, reported that seven-month-olds devote more attention to a photo of a fearful face than to one of a happy expression, probably because the former is less familiar.

8. H. C. Breiter, N. L. Etcoff, P. J. Whalen, W. A. Kennedy, S. L. Rauch, R. L. Buckner, M. M. Strauss, S. E. Hyman, and B. R. Rosen, "Response and habituation of the human amygdala during visual processing and facial expression," *Neuron*, 17 (1996): 875–887. C. Buchel, J. Morris, R. J. Dolan, and K. J. Friston, "Brain systems mediating aversive conditioning," *Neuron*, 20 (1998): 947–957. J. S. Morris, A. Ohman, and R. J. Dolan,

"Conscious and unconscious emotional learning in the human amygdala," *Nature* 393 (1998): 467–470. Davis and Whalen write that ambiguous events activate the amygdala and its projections to create a vigilant state: M. Davis and P. J. Whalen, "The amygdala," *Molecular Psychiatry*, 6 (2001): 13–34.

9. S. Paradiso, D. L. Johnson, N. C. Andreasen, D. S. O'Leary, G. L. Watkins, L. L. Boles, and R. D. Hichura, "Cerebral blood flow changes associated with attribution of emotional valence to pleasant, unpleasant, and neutral visual stimuli in a PET study of normal subjects," *American Journal of Psychiatry*, 156 (1999): 1618–29. However, others have reported that pleasant and unpleasant visual stimuli produced equivalent PET activity in the amygdala and greater than the activity to neutral stimuli: S. B. Hamann, T. D. Ely, S. T. Grafton, and C. D. Kirts, "Amygdala activity related to enhanced memory for pleasant and aversive stimuli," *Nature Neuroscience*, 2 (1999): 289–293. Among adult men exposed to neutral or unpleasant pictures on different occasions the superior recall of the latter was correlated with greater PET activity in the right amygdala. Among women the difference in recall was correlated with greater activity in the left amygdala. L. Cahill, R. J. Harer, N. S. White, J. Fallon, L. Kilpatrick, C. Lawrence, S. C. Potkin, and N. J. Alkire, "Sex-related differences in amygdalar activity during emotionally influenced memory storage," *Neurobiology of Learning and Memory*, 75 (2001): 1–9.

10. T. Canli, Z. Zhao, J. E. Desmond, E. Kang, J. Gross, and J. D. E. Gabrieli, "An fMRI study of personality influences on brain reactivity to emotional stimuli," *Behavioral Neuroscience*, 115 (2001): 33–42.

11. H. Fischer, J. L. R. Andersson, T. Furmack, and M. Fredrickson, "Fear-conditioning and brain activity," *Behavioral Neuroscience*, 114 (2000): 671–680. N. Ramnani, I. Toni, O. Josephs, J. Ashburner, and R. E. Passingham, "Learning- and expectation-related changes in the human brain during motor learning," *Journal of Neurophysiology*, 84 (2000): 3026–35. S. F. Taylor, I. Liberzon, and R. A. Koeppe, "The effect of graded aversive stimuli on limbic and visual activation," *Neuropsychologia*, 39 (2000): 1415–25. Adults who listened to content-free vocalizations designed to reflect sadness, happiness, fear, or a neutral feeling only reported a feeling of surprise to the fearful vocalizations: J. S. Morris, S. K. Scott, and R. J. Dolan, "Saying it with feeling," *Neuropsychologia*, 37 (1999): 1155–60. The administration of a beta-blocker while adults saw slides accompanied by a

narrative with an emotionally rousing section in the middle inhibited amygdalar activity and, as a result, impaired memory for the emotional part of the narrative. The presumed interpretation is that the drug reduced amygdalar activity to the unexpected emotional sentences and therefore the meaning was less salient and was remembered less well. J. L. McGaugh, L. Cahill, and B. Roozendaal, "Involvement of the amygdala in memory storage," *Proceedings of the National Academy of Sciences, USA*, 93 (1996): 13508–514.

12. O. V. Lipp, D. A. T. Siddle, and P. J. Dall, "The effects of change in lead-stimulus modality on the modulation of acoustic blink startle," *Psychophysiology*, 37 (2000): 715–723.

13. V. Ingalls, "Startle and habituation responses of blue jays (Cyanocitta cristata) in a laboratory simulation of anti-predator defenses of catacola moths (lepidoptera noctuide)," *Behavior*, 126 (1993): 77–96. J. D. Vochtello, P. J. Timmermans, J. A. Duijghuisen, and J. M. Vossen, "Responses to novelty in phobic and nonphobic cynomologous monkeys," *Behavioral Research and Therapy*, 29 (1991): 521–538. B. Heinrich, "Neophilia and exploration in juvenile common ravens: Corvus corax," *Animal Behavior*, 50 (1995): 695–704. G. Fontani, F. Farabollini, and G. Carli, "Hippocampal electrical activity and behavior in the presence of novel environmental stimuli in rabbits," *Behavioral Brain Research*, 13 (1984): 231–240.

14. E. D. Kemble, C. M. Garber, and C. Gordon, "Effects of novel odors on intermale attack behavior in mice," *Aggressive Behavior*, 21 (1995): 293–299. D. S. Tuber, M. B. Hennessy, S. Sanders, and J. A. Miller, "Behavioral and glucocorticoid responses of adult domestic dogs (Canis familiaris) to companionship and social separation," *Journal of Comparative Psychology*, 110 (1996): 103–108. S. M. McDonnell, R. M. Kenney, P. E. Meckley, and M. C. Garcia, "Novel event suppression of stallion sexual behavior and the effects of diazepam," *Physiology and Behavior*, 37 (1986): 503–505. L. C. Miller, K. A. Bard, C. J. Juno, and R. D. Nadler, "Behavioral responsiveness of young chimpanzees (Pan troglodytes) to a novel event," *Folia Primatologica*, 47 (1986): 128–142. F. C. Graves and M. B. Hennessy, "Comparison of the effects of the mother and an unfamiliar adult female on cortisol and behavioral responses of pre- and post-weaning guinea pigs," *Developmental Psychobiology*, 36 (2000): 91–100.

15. T. E. Robinson, K. E. Browman, H. S. Crombag, and A. Badiani, "Modulation of the induction of expression of psychostimulant sensitiza-

tion by the circumstances surrounding drug administration," *Neuroscience and Biobehavioral Reviews*, 22 (1998): 347–354. M. Montag-Sallaz, H. Welzl, D. Kuhl, D. Montag, and M. Schachner, "Novelty-induced increased expression of immediate early genes c-fos and arg 3 in the mouse brain," *Journal of Neurobiology*, 38 (1999): 234–246. M. Papa, M. P. Pellicano, A. Cerbone, and C. Lamberti-D'Mello, "Immediate early genes and brain DNA remodeling in the Naples high- and low-excitability rat lines following exposure to a spatial novelty," *Brain Research Bulletin*, 37 (1995): 111–118. A. Badiani, M. M. Oates, H. E. W. Day, S. J. Watson, H. Akil, and T. E. Robinson, "Amphetamine-induced behavior, dopamine release, and c-fos, mRNA expression," *Journal of Neuroscience*, 18 (1998): 10579–593. L. E. Kalynchuk, J. P. J. Pinel, and T. Treit, "Characterization of the defensive nature of kindling induced emotionality," *Behavioral Neuroscience*, 113 (1999): 766–775.

16. J. E. Kerr, S. G. Beck, and R. J. Handa, "Androgens selectively modulate c-fos messenger RNA induction in the rat hippocampus following novelty," *Neuroscience*, 74 (1996): 759–766.

17. A. S. Clarke, W. Mason, and G. P. Moberg, "Differential behavioral and adrenocortical response to stress among three macaque species," *American Journal of Primatology*, 14 (1988): 37–52. G. M. Harrington, "Strain differences in neophobia in the rat," *Bulletin of the Psychonomic Society*, 14 (1979): 424–426. J. H. Van Abeelen and C. M. van den Heuvel, "Behavioral responses to novelty in two inbred mouse strains after intrahippocampal naloxone and morphine," *Behavioral Brain Research*, 5 (1982): 199–207.

18. K. M. Rose, M. Wodzicka-Tomaszewska, and R. B. Cumming, "Agnostic behavior, response to a novel object, and some aspects of maintenance behavior in feral-strain and domestic chickens," *Applied Animal Behavior Science*, 13 (1985): 283–294.

19. S. L. Watson and J. P. Ward, "Temperament and problem solving in the small eared Bushbaby (Otolemur garnettin)," *Journal of Comparative Psychology*, 110 (1996): 377–385. J. Kagan, *Galen's Prophecy* (New York: Basic Books, 1994).

20. M. B. Hennessy, S. P. Mendoza, W. A. Mason, and G. P. Moberg, "Endocrine sensitivity to novelty in squirrel monkeys and titi monkeys," *Physiology and Behavior*, 57 (1995): 331–338.

21. R. P. Ebstein, J. Levine, V. Geller, J. Auerbach, I. Gritsenko, and R. H. Bekmaker, "Dopamine D4 receptor and serotonin transporter

220

number in the detection of neonatal temperament," *Molecular Psychiatry*, 3 (1998): 238–246. E. P. Noble, T. Z. Ozkaragoz, T. L. Ritchie, X. Zhang, T. R. Beilin, and R. S. Sparks, "D2 and D4 dopamine receptor polymorphisms and personality," *American Journal of Medical Genetics*, 81 (1998): 259–267; L. N. Trut, "Early canid domestication," *American Scientist*, 87 (1999): 160–169.

22. M. S. Hooks, G. H. Jones, A. D. Smith, D. B. Neil, and J. B. Justice, "Response to novelty predicts the locomotor and nucleus accumbens dopamine response to cocaine," *Synapse*, 9 (1991): 121–128. P. J. Pierre and P. Vezina, "Predisposition to self administer amphetamine," *Psychopharmacology*, 129 (1997): 277–284.

23. B. C. Jones, X. Hou, and M. N. Cook, "The effect of exposure to novelty on brain monoamines in C57BL/6 and DBA/2 mice," *Physiology and Behavior*, 59 (1996): 361–367.

24. F. H. Allport, *Theories of Perception and the Concept of Structure* (New York: Wiley, 1955), 622. Esther Thelen suggests that all psychological events are processes and there are no structures: E. Thelen, "Motor Development," *American Psychologist*, 50 (1995): 79–95.

25. J. Hochberg, "Gestalt theory and its legacy," in J. Hochberg, ed., *Perception and Cognition at Century's End* (New York: Academic Press, 1998), 253–306.

26. R. P. Hasegawa, A. M. Blitz, N. L. Geller, and M. E. Goldberg, "Neurons in monkey prefrontal cortex that track past or predict future performance," *Science*, 290 (2000): 1786–89. Even the receptive fields of neurons in V1 to a particular visual stimulus can vary depending on the individual's state of vigilance. Thus every neuronal ensemble has to be viewed as a dynamic pattern sensitive to past events and the state of the whole brain: F. Worgotter and W. T. Eysel, "Context, state, and the receptive fields of striatal cortex cells," *Trends in Neuroscience*, 23 (2000): 497–503. M. S. Jog, Y. Kubota, C. I. Connolly, V. Hillegaart, and A. M. Graybiel, "Building neural representations of habits," *Science*, 286 (1999): 1745–49.

27. J. Panksepp, *Affective Neuroscience* (New York: Oxford, 1998). J. Panksepp and M. Y. V. Bekkedal, "The affective cerebral consequence of music," *International Journal of Arts Medicine*, 5 (1997): 18–27.

28. E. A. Kravitz, "Serotonin and aggression," *Journal of Comparative Physiology, A: Sensory, Neural, and Behavioral Physiology*, 186 (2000): 221–238.

29. M. Basoglu, S. Mineka, M. Paker, T. Aker, M. Livanov, and S. Gok, "Psychological preparedness for trauma as a protective factor in survivors of torture," *Psychological Medicine*, 27 (1997): 1421–37. Some argue that a reduction of all psychological events to biology is not possible: G. A. Miller and J. Keller, "Psychology and neuroscience: making peace," *Current Directions in Psychological Science*, 9 (2000): 212–215.

30. E. J. Gibson, *Principles of Perceptual Learning and Development* (New York: Appleton/Century/Crofts, 1969). J. M. Mandler, "Representations," in *Handbook of Child Psychology*, 5th ed., vol. 2, ed. D. Kuhn and R. S. Siegler (New York: Wiley, 1998), 255–308. A. Paivio, *Mental Representations* (New York: Oxford, 1986). M. D. Vernon, *A Further Study of Perception* (Cambridge: Cambridge University Press, 1954).

31. S. M. Kosslyn, *Image and Brain* (Cambridge, Mass.: MIT Press, 1994). S. B. Hamann and L. R. Squire, "Intact perceptual meaning in the absence of conscious memory," *Behavioral Neuroscience*, 111 (1997): 850–854.

32. J. W. Schooler, S. M. Fiore, and M. A. Brandimonte, "At a loss from words," in D. L. Medin, ed., *The Psychology of Learning and Motivation*, vol. 37 (New York: Academic Press, 1997), 291–340.

33. J. Kagan, R. E. Klein, M. M. Haith, and F. J. Morrison, "Memory and meaning in two cultures," *Child Development*, 44 (1973): 221–223.

34. V. E. Stone, S. Baron-Cohen, and R. T. Knight, "Frontal lobe contributions to theory of mind," *Journal of Cognitive Neuroscience*, 10 (1998): 640–656.

35. B. J. Hock and M. P. Bunsey, "Differential effects of dorsal and ventral hippocampal lesions," *Journal of Neuroscience*, 18 (1998): 7025–32. A. Damasio, *The Feeling of What Happens* (New York: Harcourt, 1999).

36. H. Helson, *Adaptational-level Theory* (New York: Harper and Row, 1964).

37. G. L. Wenk, "The nucleus basalis magnocellularis cholinergic system," *Neurobiology of Learning and Memory*, 67 (1997): 85–95.

38. D. C. Rubin, E. Groth, and D. J. Goldsmith, "Olfactory cuing of autobiographical memory," *American Journal of Psychology*, 97 (1984): 493–507.

39. J. Piaget, *The Origins of Intelligence in Children* (New York: International Universities Press, 1952). B. Shapiro, J. Fagen, J. Prigot, M. Carroll, and J. Shalan, "Infants' emotional and regulatory behaviors in response to

violations of expectancies," *Infant Behavior and Development*, 21 (1998): 299–313.

40. R. K. Clifton, P. Rochat, R. Y. Litovsky, and E. E. Perris, "Object representation guides infants' reaching in the dark," *Journal of Experimental Psychology: Human Perception and Performance*, 17 (1991): 323–329. R. K. Clifton, E. E. Perris, and D. D. McCall, "Does reaching in the dark for unseen objects reflect representation in infants?" *Infant Behavior and Development*, 22 (2000): 297–302. Five-month-olds are able to adjust their reach to a moving object even when they cannot see their hands: D. J. Rubin, N. E. Berthier, and R. K. Clifton, "Infants' predicted reaching for moving objects in the dark," *Developmental Psychology*, 32 (1996): 524–535.

41. A. Berthoz, *The Brain's Sense of Movement*, trans. G. Weiss (Cambridge, Mass.: Harvard University Press, 2000).

42. W. F. Asaad, G. Rainer, and E. K. Miller, "Task-specific neural activity in the primate prefrontal cortex," *Journal of Neurophysiology*, 84 (2000): 451–459.

43. M. S. A. Graziano, D. F. Cooke, and C. S. R. Taylor, "Coding the location of the arm by sight," *Science*, 290 (2000): 1782–86. M. A. Goodale and A. Haffenden, "Frames of reference for perception and action in the human visual system," *Neuroscience and Biobehavioral Reviews*, 22 (1998): 161–172.

44. B. A. Morrongiello, K. D. Fenwick, and G. Chance, "Cross-modal learning in newborn infants," *Infant Behavior and Development*, 21 (1998): 543–554. M. Dondi, F. Simion, and G. Caltran, "Can newborns discriminate between their own cry and the cry of another newborn infant?" *Developmental Psychology*, 35 (1999): 418–426. G. B. Martin and R. D. Clark, "Distress crying in neonates," *Developmental Psychology*, 18 (1982): 3–9. J. W. Makin and R. H. Porter, "Attractiveness of lactating females' breast odors to neonates," *Child Development*, 60 (1989): 803–810.

45. K. Wiener and J. Kagan, "Infants' reaction to changes in orientation of figure and frame," *Perception*, 5 (1976): 25–28. S. E. Antell, A. J. Caron, and R. S. Myers, "Perception of relational invariants by newborns," *Developmental Psychology*, 21 (1985): 942–948.

46. A. Slater, C. van den Schulenburg, E. Brown, M. Badenoch, G. Butterworth, S. Parsons, and C. Samuels, "Newborn infants prefer attractive faces," *Infant Behavior and Development*, 21 (1998): 345–354. M. H. Bornstein and S. J. Krinsky, "Perception of symmetry in infancy," *Journal of*

Experimental Child Psychology, 39 (1985): 1–19. M. H. Johnson and J. Morton, *Biology and Cognitive Development* (Oxford: Blackwell, 1991).

47. T. Wilcox, "Object individuation," *Cognition*, 72 (1999): 125–166.

48. A. L. Woodward, "Infants selectively encode the goal object of an actor's reach," *Cognition*, 69 (1998): 1–34.

49. M. L. Courage and M. L. Howe, "The ebb and flow of infant attentional preferences," *Journal of Experimental Child Psychology*, 70 (1998): 26–53. The context in which an infant learns to make a motor response to a stimulus affects the probability of later display of that response: D. Borovsky and C. Rovee-Collier, "Contextual constraints on memory retrieval at six months," *Child Development*, 61 (1990): 1569–83.

50. C. Travis, *Unshadowed Thought* (Cambridge, Mass.: Harvard University Press, 2000), 252.

51. R. B. Ivry and L. C. Robertson, *The Two Sides of Perception* (Cambridge, Mass.: MIT Press, 1998).

52. G. R. Fink, J. C. Marshall, P. W. Halligan, and R. T. Dolan, "Hemispheric asymmetries in global-local processing are modulated by perceptual salience," *Neuropsychologia*, 37 (1999): 37–40.

53. A. J. Doupe and P. K. Kuhl, "Birdsong and human speech," *Annual Review of Neuroscience*, 22 (1999): 567–631.

54. A. J. Rubenstein, I. Kalakanis, and J. H. Langlois, "Infant preferences for attractive faces," *Developmental Psychology*, 35 (1999): 848–855.

55. G. F. Marcus, S. Vijayan, S. Rao, L. Bandi, and P. M. Vishton, "Rule learning by seven month old infants," *Science*, 283 (1999): 77–80.

56. S. Trehub, "Human processing predispositions and musical universals," in N. C. Wallin, B. Merker, and S. Brown, eds., *The Origins of Music* (Cambridge, Mass.: MIT Press, 2000), 427–448.

57. M. Rivera-Gaxiola, G. Csibra, M. H. Johnson, and A. Karmiloff-Smith, "Electrophysiological correlates of cross-linguistic speech perception in native English speakers," *Behavioural Brain Research*, 111 (2000): 13–23. T. Ruusuvirta, T. Korhonen, M. Penttonen, J. Arikoski, and K. Kivirikko, "Hippocampal event-related potentials to pitch deviances in an auditory oddball situation in the cat," *International Journal of Psychophysiology*, 20 (1995): 33–39.

58. M. E. Droller, "The modality of music and its effects on children's perceptions" (honors thesis, Harvard University, 2000).

59. M. T. Wallace and B. E. Stein, "Onset of cross-modal synthesis in the superior colliculus is gated by the development of cortical influence," *Journal of Neurophysiology*, 83 (2000): 3578–82. S. A. Rose, A. W. Gottfried, and W. H. Bridger, "Cross-modal transfer in six-month-old infants," *Developmental Psychology*, 17 (1981): 661–669.

60. D. Maurer, C. L. Stager, and C. J. Mondloch, "Cross-modal transfer of shape is difficult to demonstrate in one month olds," *Child Development*, 70 (1999): 1047–57.

61. L. B. Smith, "Perceptual structure and developmental process," in G. R. Lockhead and J. R. Pomerantz, eds., *The Perception of Structure* (Washington: American Psychological Association, 1991), 297–316.

62. R. L. Goldstone and L. W. Barsalou, "Reuniting perception and conception," *Cognition*, 65 (1998): 231–262. F. C. Keil, *Concepts, Kinds and Cognitive Development* (Cambridge, Mass.: MIT Press, 1989). E. E. Smith, A. L. Patalano, and J. Jonides, "Alternative strategies of categorization," in S. A. Sloman and L. J. Rips, eds., *Similarity and Symbols in Human Thinking* (Cambridge, Mass.: MIT Press, 1998), 81–110. P. Gardenfors, *Conceptual Spaces* (Cambridge, Mass.: MIT Press, 2000).

63. S. Watanabe, R. Kakigi, S. Koyama, and E. Kirino, "Human face perception traced by magneto and electroencephalography," *Cognitive Brain Research*, 8 (1999): 125–142.

64. A. Puce, T. Allison, and G. McCarthy, "Electrophysiological studies of human face perception, III: Effects of top down processing on face-specific potentials," *Cerebral Cortex*, 9 (1999): 445–458.

65. J. Kagan, "Attention and psychological change in the young child," *Science*, 170 (1970): 826–832.

66. J. S. De Loache and L. M. Smith, "Early symbolic representation," in I. E. Sigel, ed., *Development of Mental Representation* (Mahwah, N.J.: Erlbaum, 1999), 61–86.

67. Kagan, *Galen's Prophecy*.

68. L. Daston and K. Park, *Wonders and the Order of Nature* (New York: Zone Books, 1998). The pig had a special symbolic meaning among medieval Europeans and still does among some contemporary Jews. It has been suggested that because the pig combines a cloven hoof with an absence of rumination of food it is a discrepant form and therefore a cause for uncertainty: C. Vassas-Fabre, *The Singular Beast* (New York: Columbia University Press, 1997).

69. D. D. Hoffman and M. Singh, "Salience of visual parts," *Cognition*, 63 (1997): 29–78. D. L. Medin and J. D. Coley, "Concepts and categorization," in Hochberg, ed., *Perception and Cognition at Century's End*, 403–439.

70. D. Bickerton, *Language and Human Behavior* (Seattle: University of Washington Press, 1995).

71. J. D. Ryan, R. R. Althoff, S. Whitlow, and N. J. Cohen, "Amnesia is a deficit in relational memory," *Psychological Science*, 6 (2000): 454–461.

72. D. Magnusson, "Individual development," in P. Moen, G. H. Elder, and K. Luscher, eds., *Examining Lives in Context* (Washington: American Psychological Association, 1995), 19–60. D. Magnusson, "The individual as the organizing principle in psychological inquiry," in L. R. Bergman, R. B. Cairns, L. G. Nilsson, and L. Nystedt, eds., *Developmental Science and the Holistic Approach* (Mahwah, N.J.: Erlbaum, 2000), 33–47.

73. J. Searle, "Consciousness," in Cowan, Shooter, Stevens, and Thompson, eds., *Annual Review of Neuroscience*, vol. 23, 557–578.

74. J. Kagan, *Three Seductive Ideas* (Cambridge, Mass.: Harvard University Press, 1998).

75. P. Shah and A. Miyake, "The separability of working memory resources for spatial thinking and language processing," *Journal of Experimental Psychology: General*, 125 (1996): 4–27.

2. Inconsistency and Semantic Networks

1. F. Ramus, M. D. Hauser, C. Miller, D. Morris, and J. Mehler, "Language discrimination by human newborns and by cotton top tamarin monkeys," *Science*, 288 (2000): 349–351; J. R. Saffran, R. N. Aslin, and E. L. Newport, "Statistical learning by eight-month-old infants," *Science*, 274 (1996): 1926–28.

2. A. E. Hillis and A. Caramazza, "Category specific naming and comprehension impairment," *Brain*, 114 (1991): 2081–94.

3. G. A. Miller, "Practical and lexical knowledge," in E. Rosch and B. B. Lloyd, eds., *Cognition and Categorization* (Hillsdale, N.J.: Erlbaum, 1978), 305–329.

4. B. L. Whorf, *Language, Thought, and Reality* (Cambridge, Mass.: MIT Press, 1956). R. A. Shweder, *A Polytheistic Conception of the Sciences and the Virtue of Deep Variety in Unity of Knowledge* (New York: New York Academy of Sciences, 2001).

226

5. M. Boucart and G. W. Humphreys, "Integration of physical and semantic information in object processing," *Perception*, 26 (1997): 1197–1209.

6. J. F. Werker, L. B. Cohen, V. L. Lloyd, M. Casasola, and C. L. Stager, "Acquisition of word-object associations by 14-month-old infants," *Developmental Psychology*, 34 (1998): 1289–1309.

7. M. Casasola and L. B. Cohen, "Infants' association of linguistic labels with causal actions," *Developmental Psychology*, 36 (2000): 155–168.

8. C. Dalaghan, "Child meets word," *Journal of Speech and Hearing Disorders*, 28 (1985): 449–454. N. Akhtar, M. Carpenter, and M. Tomasello, "The role of novelty in early word learning," *Child Development*, 67 (1996): 635–645. G. J. Hollich, K. Hirsh-Pasek, and R. M. Golinkoff, "Breaking the language barrier," *Monograph of the Society for Research in Child Development*, 65 (2000): v–135.

9. D. A. Baldwin, E. M. Markman, B. Bill, R. N. Desjardins, J. M. Irwin, and G. Tidball, "Infants' reliance on a social criterion for establishing word-object relations," *Child Development*, 67 (1996): 3135–53.

10. M. Tomasello, *The Cultural Origins of Human Cognition* (Cambridge, Mass.: Harvard University Press, 1999).

11. J. C. Goodman, L. McDonough, and N. B. Brown, "The role of semantic context and memory in the acquisition of novel nouns," *Child Development*, 69 (1998): 1330–44. If two-year-olds hear an unfamiliar word applied to an object they know, they assume it is the proper name of the object. But if the same word is applied to an object they do not know, they assume the word names the category of the object. D. G. Hall, "Acquiring proper nouns for familiar and unfamiliar animate objects," *Child Development*, 62 (1991): 1142–54.

12. D. H. Rakison and G. E. Butterworth, "Infants' use of object parts in early categorization," *Developmental Psychology*, 34 (1998): 49–62. S. A. Graham, L. P. Williams, and J. Huber, "Preschoolers' and adults' reliance on object shape and object function for lexical extension," *Journal of Experimental Child Psychology*, 74 (1999): 128–151.

13. S. Chu and J. S. Downes, "Long live Proust," *Cognition*, 25 (2000): B41–B50.

14. Paivio also argues for this distinction. However, he suggests that the two systems are independent while I favor interdependence. Case and Okamoto, in contrast, emphasize the semantic structure as the main con-

struct in conceptual structures and define it as a network of semantic nodes and their relation to a domain of knowledge. Goldstone and Barsalou award priority to schemata, which they call perceptual symbols. Ganis, Kutas, and Sereno argue for multiple semantic networks that vary in their receptivity to being activated by events or words. Baddeley and Andrade also award autonomous status to schemata and semantic structures in short-term memory, calling the former a visuospatial sketch pad and the latter a phonological loop. A. D. Baddeley and J. Andrade, "Working memory and the vividness of imagery," *Journal of Experimental Psychology: General*, 129 (2000): 126–145. R. Case and Y. Okamoto, "The role of central conceptual structures in the development of children's thought," *Monographs of the Society of Research in Child Development*, 61 (1–2, Serial #246) (1996): 1–295. G. Ganis, M. Kutas, and M. I. Sereno, "The search for common sense," *Journal of Cognitive Neuroscience*, 8 (1996): 89–106. A. Paivio, *Mental Representations* (New York: Oxford, 1986). R. L. Goldstone and L. W. Barsalou, "Revisiting perception and conception," *Cognition*, 65 (1998): 231–262.

15. J. B. Gleason and R. Ely, "Input and the acquisition of vocabulary," in C. Mendell and A. McCabe, eds., *The Problem of Meaning* (New York: Elsevier, 1997), 221–260. See M. Devitt and K. Sterelny, *Language and Reality*, 2nd ed. (Cambridge, Mass.: MIT Press, 1999).

16. E. K. Warrington and R. A. McCarthy, "Categories of knowledge," *Brain*, 110 (1987): 1273–96; quotation from 1290.

17. C. J. Johnson, A. Paivio, and J. M. Clark, "Cognitive components of picture naming," *Psychological Bulletin*, 120 (1996): 113–139. L. S. Seifert, "Activating representations in permanent memory," *Journal of Experimental Psychology: Learning Memory and Cognition*, 23 (1997): 1106–21.

18. P. Goalkasian, "Picture-word differences in a sentence verification task," *Memory and Cognition*, 24 (1996): 584–594. J. G. Snodgrass and A. Asiaghi, "The pictorial superiority effect in recognition memory," *Bulletin of the Psychonomic Society*, 10 (1977): 1–4.

19. L. E. Crawford, T. Regier, and J. Huttenlocher, "Linguistic and non-linguistic spatial categorization," *Cognition*, 75 (2000): 209–235.

20. M. Beeman and C. Chiarello, eds., *Right Hemisphere Language Comprehension* (Mahwah, N.J.: Erlbaum, 1998). R. B. Ivry and P. C. Lebby, "The neurology of consonant perception," in Beeman and Chiarello, eds., *Right Hemisphere Language Comprehension*, 3–25. G. Deloche, X. Seron, G. Scius,

and J. Segui, "Right hemisphere language processing," *Brain and Language*, 30 (1987): 197–205.

21. A. S. David and J. C. Cutting, "Categorical-semantic and spatial imagery judgments of nonverbal stimuli by the cerebral hemisphere," *Cortex*, 28 (1992): 39–51. E. Duzel, R. Cabeza, T. W. Picton, A. P. Yonelinas, H. Scheich, H. J. Heinze, and E. Tulving, "Task-related and item-related brain processes of memory retrieval," *Proceedings of the National Academy of Sciences*, 96 (1999): 1794–99. J. Metcalfe, M. Funnell, and M. S. Gazzaniga, "Right hemisphere memory superiority," *Psychological Science*, 6 (1995): 157–164. The integrity of the left hemisphere appears to be critical when a person must make a temporal discrimination. For example, individuals with a compromised left hemisphere heard a pair of briefly separated tones as one tone at temporal intervals in which normal subjects continue to hear two distinct sounds. The competence is critical when we process words and continuous speech flow. However, adults with a compromised right hemisphere who have no difficulty solving the above temporal tasks find it hard to make exact frequency matches. For example, the subject first hears a standard tone followed by two tones and has to say which of the two is identical to the first. Individuals who can do this task easily have perfect pitch. J. T. Coull and A. C. Nobre, "Where and when to pay attention," *Journal of Neuroscience*, 18 (1998): 7426–35.

22. A. Martin, C. L. Wiggs, and J. Weisberg, "Modulation of human medial temporal lobe activity by form, meaning, and experience," *Hippocampus*, 7 (1997): 587–593.

23. R. Vandenberghe, C. Price, R. Wise, O. Josephs, and R. S. J. Frackowiak, "Functional anatomy of a common semantic system for words and pictures," *Nature*, 383 (1996): 254–256. M. Koivisto and M. Laine, "Strategies of semantic categorization in the cerebral hemispheres," *Brain and Language*, 66 (1999): 341–357.

24. G. Ben Shakhar and I. Gati, "Common and distinctive features of verbal and pictorial stimuli as determinants of psychophysiological responsivity," *Journal of Experimental Psychology: General*, 116 (1996): 91–105.

25. J. B. Halberstadt, P. M. Niedenthal, and J. Kushner, "Resolution of lexical ambiguity by emotional state," *Psychological Science*, 6 (1995): 278–282.

26. P. M. Niedenthal, J. B. Halberstadt, and A. H. Innes-Ker, "Emotional response categorization," *Psychological Review*, 106 (1999): 337–361.

27. W. K. Estes, *Classification and Cognition* (New York: Oxford University Press, 1994). J. W. King, G. Gavis, and M. Kutas, "Potential asymmetries in language comprehension," in Beeman and Chiarello, eds., *Right Hemisphere Language Comprehension*, 187–213.

28. A. K. Anderson and E. A. Phelps, "Expression without recognition," *Psychological Science*, 11 (2000): 106–111.

29. D. L. Schacter, L. Israel, and C. Racine, "Suppressing false recognition in younger and older adults," *Journal of Memory and Language*, 40 (1999): 1–24.

30. D. W. Bales and M. P. Sera, "Preschoolers' understanding of stable and changeable characteristics," *Cognitive Development*, 10 (1995): 69–107.

31. R. Sera and L. B. Smith, "New evidence on the development of the word big," *Child Development*, 61 (1990): 1034–52.

32. J. G. W. Raaijmakers and R. M. Shiffrin, "Search of associative memory," *Psychological Review*, 88 (1981): 93–134.

33. J. D. Ryan, R. R. Althoff, S. Whitlow, and N. J. Cohen, "Amnesia is a deficit in relational memory," *Psychological Science*, 6 (2000): 454–461.

34. W. Kintsch, *Comprehension* (New York: Cambridge University Press, 1998).

35. E. Ochs and B. Schieffelin, "The impact of language socialization on grammatical development," in P. Fletcher and B. MacWhinney, eds., *The Handbook of Child Language* (Oxford: Blackwell, 1995), 73–94.

36. F. Graf, *Magic in the Ancient World* (Cambridge, Mass.: Harvard University Press, 1997).

37. M. K. Mullen, "Children's classifications of nature and artifact pictures into female and male categories," *Sex Roles*, 23 (1990): 577–587.

38. R. Service, *Lenin* (Cambridge, Mass.: Harvard University Press, 2000), 45.

39. M. Zentner and J. Kagan, "Infants' perception of consonance and dissonance in music," *Infant Behavior and Development*, 21 (1998): 483–492.

40. G. A. Miller and P. Johnson-Laird, *Language and Perception* (Cambridge, Mass.: Harvard University Press, 1976). G. A. Miller and C. Fellbaum, "Semantic networks of English," *Cognition*, 41 (1991): 197–223.

41. E. DeRenzi and F. Lucchelli, "Are semantic systems separately represented in the brain?" *Cortex*, 30 (1994): 3–25.

42. Warrington and McCarthy, "Categories of knowledge."

43. J. Hart and B. Gordon, "Neural subsystems for object knowledge," *Nature*, 359 (1992): 60–64.

44. A. Caramazza and J. R. Shelton, "Domain-specific knowledge systems in the brain," *Journal of Cognitive Neuroscience*, 10 (1998): 1–34. B. C. Rapp and A. Caramazza, "Disorders of lexical processes and the lexicon," in M. S. Gazzaniga, ed., *The Cognitive Neurosciences* (Cambridge, Mass.: MIT Press, 1995), 901–913. D. H. Rakison and D. Poulin-Dubois, "Developmental origin of the animate-inanimate distinction," *Psychological Bulletin*, 1276 (2001): 209–228.

45. B. S. Mak and A. H. Vera, "The role of motion in children's categorization of objects," *Cognition*, 71 (1999): 11–21. M. D. Hauser, "A nonhuman primate's expectations about object motion and destination," *Developmental Science*, 1 (1998): 31–37.

46. W. W. Eaton, K. Neufeld, L. S. Chen, and G. Cai, "A comparison of self report and clinical diagnostic interviews for depression," *Archives of General Psychiatry*, 57 (2000): 217–226.

47. T. H. Huxley, *Life and Letters of Thomas Henry Huxley* (New York: Appleton, 1901).

48. E. A. Antoniadis and R. J. McDonald, "Amygdala, hippocampus, and discriminative conditioning to context," *Behavioural Brain Research*, 108 (2000): 1–9. The error of positing a unitary fear state is seen in a study of rats whose raphe nucleus was lesioned before they experienced a single electric shock in a distinctive compartment. When the animals and controls were placed in the compartment three minutes after the shock, both groups froze to an equal degree. But forty-eight hours later the lesioned animals froze less than the controls, suggesting that if freezing indexes fear we must assume one fear state after three minutes and another fear state after forty-eight hours. E. Melik, E. Babar-Melik, T. Ozqunen, and S. Binokay, "Median raphe nucleus mediates long term but not short term contextual fear conditioning in rats," *Behavioural Brain Research*, 112 (2000): 145–150. Rhesus monkeys with lesions in most of the amygdala showed less freezing to a snake than controls, but the monkeys who had shown freezing to an unfamiliar human intruder prior to surgery continued to freeze to the intruder after lesions of the amygdala. N. H. Kalin, S. E. Shelton, R. J. Davidson, A. E. Kelley, "The primate amygdala mediates acute fear but not the behavioral and physiological components of anxious temperament"

ration, frequency, and intensity changes," *Clinical Neurophysiology*, 999): 1388–93. R. Naatanen, "The perception of speech sounds by man brain as reflected by the mismatch negativity and its magnetic lent (MMNm)," *Psychophysiology*, 38 (2001): 1–21.

R. N. Desjardins, L. J. Trainor, J. Herenous, and C. P. Polak, "Using tch negativity to measure auditory temporal resolution thresholds," *eport*, 10 (1999): 2079–82. W. Ritter, E. Sussman, D. Deacon, an, and H. G. Vaughan, "Two cognitive systems simultaneously r opposite events," *Psychophysiology*, 36 (1999): 835–838.

Rivera-Gaxiola, G. Csibra, M. H. Johnson, and A. Karmiloff- lectrophysiological correlates of cross-linguistic speech perception nglish speakers," *Behavioural Brain Research*, 111 (2000): 13–23.

tienza, J. L. Cantero, and C. M. Gomez, "The mismatch nega- onent reveals the sensory memory during REM sleep in euroscience Letters*, 237 (1997): 21–24. M. Cheour, K. Alho, , K. Reinikainen, K. Saimio, M. Pohjavouri, O. Aaltonen, and "Maintenance of mismatch negativity in infants," *Interna- f Psychophysiology*, 29 (1998): 217–226. T. Ruusuvirta, M. Pent- Korhonen, "Auditory cortical event-related potentials to rats," *Neuroscience Letters*, 248 (1998): 45–48.

, C. Alain, and T. W. Picton, "Effects of visual attentional rocessing," *NeuroReport*, 11 (2000): 875–880. V. Surraka, kaline, J. K. Hietaner, and M. Sams, "Modulation of n processing by emotional, visual stimuli," *Cognitive* 998): 159–167.

W. von Suchodoletz, "Stability of mismatch negativi- ical Neurophysiology*, 111 (2000): 45–52.

Woods, and R. T. Knight, "A distributed cortical net- ory memory in humans," *Brain Research*, 812 (1998):

hin, and D. L. Woods, "Separate memory-related requency and patterns," *Psychophysiology*, 36 (1999): ambertz, "Cerebral specialization for speech and ants," *Journal of Cognitive Neuroscience*, 12 (2000):

Service, S. Kurjenluoma, M. Cheour, and erformance on pseudoword repetition depends

(manuscript). Finally, the central nucleus of the amygdala is necessary for a freezing reaction to a conditioned stimulus but not for an escape reaction; the basal nucleus is necessary for escape but not for freezing. Thus freezing and escape to a signal for shock are mediated by different brain states. P. Amorapanth, J. E. LeDoux, and K. Nader, "Differential lateral amyg- dalar outputs mediate reactions and actions elicited by a fear arousing stim- ulus," *Nature Neuroscience*, 3 (2000): 74–79.

49. G. Oxley and A. S. Fleming, "The effects of medial preoptic area and amygdala lesions on maternal behavior in the juvenile rat," *Developmental Psychobiology*, 37 (2000): 253–265.

50. N. Ramnani, I. Toni, O. Josephs, J. Ashburner, and R. E. Passing- ham, "Learning and expectation related changes in the human brain during motor learning," *Journal of Neurophysiology*, 84 (2000): 3026–35. R. C. Coghill, C. N. Sang, J. M. Maisog, and M. J. Iadrola, "Pain intensity pro- cessing within the human brain," *Journal of Neurophysiology*, 82 (1999): 1934–43. L. Cahill, N. M. Weinberger, B. Roozendaal, and J. L. McGaugh, "Is the amygdala a locus of conditioned fear?" *Neuron*, 23 (1999): 227–228.

51. E. Laan, W. Everaerd, and P. Evers, "Assessment of female sexual arousal," *Psychophysiology*, 32 (1995): 476–485.

52. B. E. Wiltgen, M. J. Sanders, N. S. Behn, and M. S. Fanselow, "Sex differences, context preexposure, and the shock deficit in Pavlovian context conditioning with mice," *Behavioral Neuroscience*, 115 (2000): 26–32.

53. G. Schino, L. Speranza, and A. Troisi, "Early maternal rejection and later social anxiety in juvenile and adult Japanese macaques," *Developmental Psychobiology*, 38 (2001): 186–190.

54. O. V. Lipp, D. A. T. Siddle, and P. J. Dall, "The effects of change in lead stimulus modality on the modulation of acoustic blink startle," *Psy- chophysiology*, 37 (2000): 715–723.

55. R. Brooks, "Negative genetic correlation between male sexual attractiveness and survival," *Nature*, 406 (2000): 67–70. J. Kagan, J. S. Reznick, and J. Gibbons, "Inhibited and uninhibited types of children," *Child Development*, 60 (1989): 838–845.

56. E. Said, *Out of Place* (New York: Knopf, 1999).

57. E. H. Erikson, *Childhood and Society* (New York: Norton, 1950).

58. M. A. Salinger, *Dream Catcher* (New York: Washington Square Press, 2000).

59. L. M. Diamond, "Sexual identity, attractiveness, and behavior among young sexual-minority women over a two-year period," *Developmental Psychology*, 36 (2000): 241–250.

60. A. Ortony, ed., *Metaphor and Thought*, 2nd ed. (Cambridge: Cambridge University Press, 1993).

61. B. Z. Pearson, "The comprehension of metaphor by preschool children," *Journal of Child Language*, 17 (1990): 185–203.

62. D. Anaki, M. Faust, and S. Kravetz, "Cerebral hemisphere asymmetries in processing lexical metaphors," *Neuropsychologia*, 36 (1998): 691–700.

63. N. L. Etcoff, P. Ekman, J. J. Magee, and M. G. Franks, "Lie detection and language comprehension," *Nature*, 405 (2000): 139.

64. See L. Cahill, R. J. Harer, N. S. White, J. Fallon, L. Kilpatrick, C. Lawrence, S. C. Potkin, and N. J. Alkire, "Sex-related differences in amygdalar activity during emotionally influenced memory storage," *Neurobiology of Learning and Memory*, 75 (2001): 1–9.

65. J. Rawls, *A Theory of Justice*, rev. ed. (Cambridge, Mass.: Harvard University Press, 1999), 3.

66. J. Dewey, *Human Nature and Conduct* (New York: Holt, 1922), 14.

67. I. Kant, *Critique of Pure Reason* (London: Macmillan, 1929).

68. S. Parmigiani, P. Polanza, J. Rodgers, and P. F. Ferrari, "Selection, evolution of behavior, and animal models in behavioral neuroscience," *Neuroscience and Biobehavioral Reviews*, 23 (1999): 957–970.

69. N. N. Cook, R. W. Williams, and L. Flaherty, "Anxiety-related behaviors in the elevated zero-maze are affected by genetic factors and retinal degeneration," *Behavioral Neuroscience*, 115 (2001): 468–476.

70. M. de Haan and C. A. Nelson, "Brain activity differentiates face and object processing in six-month-old infants," *Developmental Psychology*, 35 (1999): 1113–21.

3. Event-related Potentials

1. C. A. Nelson and C. S. Monk, "The use of event-related potentials in the study of cognitive development," in C. A. Nelson and M. Luciano, eds., *Handbook of Developmental Cognitive Neuroscience* (Cambridge, Mass.: MIT Press, in press).

2. E. Halgren, P. Baudena, G. Heit, J. M. Clarke, and K. Marinkovic,

"Spatio-temporal stages in face and word processing 88 (1994): 1–5.

3. W. Skrandies, "Evoked potential correlate *Cognitive Brain Research*, 6 (1998): 173–183. Rec the prefrontal cortex in monkeys trained to res the same category as a prior stimulus (the pict cats) revealed increased activity about 130 m target. D. J. Freedman, M. Riesenhuber, T. egorical representation of visual stimuli i *Science*, 291 (2001): 312–316.

4. S. J. Swithenby, A. J. Bailey, S. maki, and C. D. Teschi, "Neural proc *Brain Research*, 118 (1998): 501–510 and E. Degiovanni, "ERP evidence of faces," *Clinical Neurophysiology*, K. Marinkouk, V. Jousmaki, an the human fusiform face area (2000): 69–81; J. W. Tanaka a recognition," *Psychological S*

5. J. B. Debruille, F. G of face recognition," *New*

6. T. Koenig, K. microstates of the br meaning," *Electroenc* 535–546.

7. S. Yamaguc of the "Top-Do *Journal of Neur*

8. K. R. D W. C. West, trophysiolo *tive Neur* L. F. M. logical

9. mon

th equ 10 misma *Neur* N. Co paired f Smith, " in native tivity com humans," R. Ceponien R. Naatanen *tional Journal o* tonen, and T. pitch deviance i 13. L. J. Otte load on auditory M. Tenlauren-E human informati *Brain Research*, 7 (1 14. R. Uwer an ties in children," *Cli* 15. C. Alain, D. L work for auditory-ser 23–37. 16. C. Alain, A. A processing for auditory 737–744. G. Dehaene-I non-speech stimuli in in 449–460. 17. R. Ceponiene, E R. Naatanen, "Children's on auditory trace quality," *Developmental Psychology*, 35 (1999): 709–720. G. Schulte-Korne, W. Deimel, J. Bartling, and H. Remschmidt, "Auditory processing and dyslexia," *NeuroReport*, 9 (1998): 337–340. T. Baldeweg, A. Richardson, S. Watkins, C. Foale, and J. Gruzelier, "Impaired auditory frequency discrimination in dyslexia detected with mismatched evoked potentials," *Annals of Neurology*, 45 (1999): 495–503.

18. G. Fernandez, A. Effern, T. Grunwald, N. Pezer, K. Lehnertz, M. Dumpelmann, D. Van Roost, and C. E. Elger, "Real-time tracking of memory formation in the human rhinal cortex and hippocampus," *Science*, 285 (1999): 1582–85.

19. P. Luu, P. Collins, and D. M. Tucker, "Mood, personality, and self-monitoring," *Journal of Experimental Psychology: General*, 129 (2000): 43–60. D. Deacon, H. S. Hewitt, C. Yang, and N. C. Nagata, "Event-related potential indices of semantic priming using masked and unmasked words," *Brain Research: Cognitive Brain Research*, 9 (2000): 137–146.

20. B. Opitz, A. Mecklinger, A. D. Friederici, and D. Y. von Cramon, "The functional neuroanatomy of novelty processing," *Cerebral Cortex*, 9 (1999): 379–391. C. A. Nelson and S. J. Webb, "A cognitive neuroscience perspective on early memory development," in M. de Haan and M. Johnson, eds., *The Cognitive Neuroscience of Development* (London: Psychology Press, in press).

21. I. Berlad and H. Pratt, "P300 in response to the subjects' own name," *Electroencephalography and Clinical Neurophysiology*, 96 (1995): 472–474. Y. M. Cycowicz and D. Friedman, "A developmental study of the effect of temporal order on the ERPs elicited by novel environmental sounds," *Electroencephalography and Clinical Neurophysiology*, 103 (1997): 304–318. M. P. Viggiano and M. Kutas, "The covert interplay between perception and memory," *Electroencephalography and Clinical Neurophysiology*, 108 (1998): 435–439.

22. M. Eimer, "Event-related brain potentials distinguish processing stages involved in face perception and recognition," *Clinical Neurophysiology*, 111 (2000): 694–705.

23. C. Escera, K. Alho, I. Winkler, and R. Naatanen, "Neural mechanism of involuntary attention to acoustic novelty and change," *Journal of Cognitive Neurosciences*, 10 (1998): 590–604. V. P. Clark, S. Fannon, S. Lai, R. Benson, and L. Bauer, "Responses to rare visual target and distractor stimuli using event-related fMRI," *Journal of Neurophysiology*, 83 (2000): 3133–35.

24. A. Mecklinger and P. Ullsperger, "The P300 to novel and target events," *NeuroReport*, 7 (1995): 241–245. Patients with damage to the dorso-lateral prefrontal cortex spend less time than controls studying discrepant events. K. R. Daffner, M. M. Mesulam, P. J. Holcomb, V. Calvo, D. Acar, A. Chaberie, R. Kikinis, F. A. Jolesz, D. M. Rentz, and L. F. M. Scinto, "Disruption of attention to novel events after frontal lobe injury in humans," *Journal of Neurology, Neurosurgery, and Psychiatry*, 68 (2000): 18–24.

25. M. M. Mesulam, "From sensation to cognition," *Brain*, 121 (1998): 1012–52.

26. A. M. Dale, A. K. Liu, B. R. Fischl, R. L. Buckner, J. W. Belliveau, J. D. Lewine, and E. Halgren, "Dynamic statistical parametric mapping," *Neuron*, 26 (2000): 55–67.

27. R. T. Knight, "Decreased response to novel stimuli after prefrontal lesions in man," *Electroencephalography and Clinical Neurophysiology*, 59 (1984): 9–20.

28. K. J. Meador, D. W. Loring, H. C. Davis, K. D. Sethi, B. R. Patel, R. J. Adams, and E. J. Hammond, "Cholinergic and serotonergic effects on the P3 potential and recent memory," *Journal of Clinical and Experimental Neuropsychology*, 11 (1989): 252–260. C. Grillon and R. Ameli, "P300 assessment of anxiety effects on processing of novel stimuli," *International Journal of Psychophysiology*, 17 (1994): 205–217.

29. K. M. Spencer, J. Dien, and E. Donchin, "A componential analysis of the ERP elicited by novel events using a dense electrode array," *Psychophysiology*, 36 (1999): 409–414.

30. P. J. Deldin, C. C. Duncan, and G. A. Miller, "Season, gender, and P300," *Biological Psychology*, 39 (1994): 15–28.

31. M. Niedeggen, F. Rosler, and K. Jost, "Processing of incongruous mental calculation problems," *Psychophysiology*, 36 (1999): 307–324. J. Grigor, S. Van Tollen, J. Behan, and A. Richardson, "The effect of odor priming on long latency visual evoked potentials of matching and mismatching objects," *Chemical Senses*, 24 (1999): 137–144. B. deGelder, K. B. Bocker, J. Tuomeinen, M. Hensen, and J. Vroomen, "The combined perception of emotion for voice and face," *Neuroscience Letters*, 260 (1999): 133–136.

32. L. Osterhout and J. Nicol, "On the distinctiveness, independence, and time course of the brain responses to syntactic and semantic anomalies," *Language and Cognitive Processes*, 14 (1999): 283–317.

33. M. Kutas and S. Hillyard, "Event-related brain potentials elicited by novel stimuli during sentence processing," *Annals of the New York Academy of Sciences*, 425 (1984): 236–241.

34. W. C. West, "Common versus multiple semantic systems" (doctoral diss., Tufts University, 2000), 109–110.

35. P. J. Holcomb, J. Kounios, J. E. Anderson, and W. C. West, "Dual-coding, context availability and concreteness effects in sentence comprehension," *Journal of Experimental Psychology: Learning Memory and Cognition*, 25 (1999): 721–742.

36. F. Schlaghecken, "On processing beasts and birds," *Brain and Language*, 64 (1998): 53–82.

37. Ibid.

38. R. Johnson, K. Kreiter, B. Russo, and J. Zhu, "A spatio-temporal analysis of recognition related event-related brain potentials," *International Journal of Psychophysiology*, 29 (1998): 83–104.

39. S. J. Cloud, "Auditory-evoked potentials for words with high positive and high negative connotation value," *Dissertation Abstracts*, 58 (9b) (1998): 95006–356.

40. K. D. Federmeier and M. Kutas, "Right words and left words," *Cognitive Brain Research*, 8 (1999): 373–392.

41. T. S. Eliot, *The Waste Land and Other Poems* (New York: Harcourt, Brace, and World, 1934).

42. D. J. Coch, "Brain and behavior in beginning readers" (doctoral diss., Harvard Graduate School of Education, 1999).

43. J. C. Ziegler, A. Benraiss, and M. Besson, "From print to meaning," *Psychophysiology*, 36 (1999): 775–785.

44. H. J. Heinze, T. F. Muente, and M. Kutas, "Context effects in a category verification task as assessed by event-related brain potential (ERP) measures," *Biological Psychology*, 47 (1998): 121–135.

45. L. J. Otten and E. Donchin, "Relationship between P300 amplitude and subsequent recall for distinctive events," *Psychophysiology*, 37 (2000): 644–661.

46. M. de Haan and C. A. Nelson, "Brain activity differentiates face and object processing in six-month-old infants," *Developmental Psychology*, 35 (1999): 1113–21. P. K. Ackles and K. G. Cook, "Stimulus probability and event-related potentials of the brain in six-month-old human infants," *International Journal of Psychophysiology*, 29 (1998): 115–143.

47. T. R. H. Cutmore and T. D. Muckert, "Event-related potentials can reveal differences between two decision-making groups," *Biological Psychology*, 47 (1998): 159–179.

48. R. Karrer and L. A. Monti, "Event-related potentials of 4–7 week old infants in the visual recognition memory task," *Electroencephalography and Clinical Neurophysiology*, 94 (1995): 414–424. K. M. Thomas and C. A. Nelson, "Age-related changes in the electrophysiological response to visual stimulus novelty," *Electroencephalography and Clinical Neurophysiology*, 98 (1996): 294–308. S. J. Johnstone, R. J. Barry, J. W. Anderson, and S. F. Coyle, "Age-related changes in child and adolescent event-related potential component morphology, amplitude and latency to standard and target stimuli in an auditory oddball task," *International Journal of Psychophysiology*, 24 (1996): 233–238.

49. H. Gomes, E. Sussman, W. Ritter, D. Kurtzberg, N. Cowan, and H. G. Vaughan, "Electrophysiological evidence of developmental changes in the duration of auditory-sensory memory," *Developmental Psychology*, 35 (1999): 294–302. J. Winkler, E. Schroger, and N. Cowan, "The role of large scale memory organization in mismatched negativity event related brain potentials," *Journal of Cognitive Neuroscience*, 13 (2001): 59–71.

50. F. Benes, personal communication.

51. R. Johnson, "On the neural generators of the P300 component of the event-related potential," *Psychophysiology*, 30 (1993): 90–97.

52. D. Deacon, F. Breton, W. Ritter, and H. G. Vaughan, "The relationship between N2 and N400," *Psychophysiology*, 28 (1991): 185–200. A. Mecklinger, B. Opitz, and A. D. Friederici, "Semantic aspects of novelty detection in humans," *Neuroscience Letters*, 235 (1997): 65–68.

53. M. Kutas and V. Iragui, "The N400 in a semantic categorization task across six decades," *Electroencephalography and Clinical Neurophysiology*, 108 (1998): 456–471.

54. V. I. Nenov, E. Halgren, M. Mandelkorn, and M. E. Smith, "Human brain metabolic responses to familiarity during lexical decisions," *Human Brain Mapping*, 1 (1994): 249–268.

55. D. Van Lanaker, "Personal relevance and the human right hemisphere," *Brain and Cognition*, 17 (1991): 64–92.

4. Implications for Development

1. M. J. Weiss, P. R. Zelazo, and I. U. Swain, "Newborn response to auditory stimulus discrepancy," *Child Development*, 59 (1988): 530–541. P. Langsdorf, C. E. Izard, M. Rayais, and E. A. Hembree, "Interest expression, visual fixation, and heart rate changes in two- to eight-month-old infants," *Developmental Psychology*, 19 (1983): 375–386.

2. R. B. McCall and J. Kagan, "Attention in the infant," *Child Development*, 38 (1967): 939–952; R. B. McCall and C. B. Kennedy, "Subjective uncertainty variability of experience, and the infant's response to discrepancies," *Child Development*, 51 (1980): 285–287. P. R. Zelazo, J. R. Hopkins, S. W. Jacobson, and J. Kagan, "Psychological reactivity to discrepant events," *Cognition*, 2 (1974): 385–393.

3. N. H. Soken and A. D. Pick, "Infants' perception of dynamic affective expressions," *Child Development*, 70 (1999): 1275–82.

4. K. D. Fenwick and B. A. Morrongiello, "Spatial co-location and infants' learning of auditory-visual associations," *Infant Behavior and Development*, 21 (1998): 745–760.

5. J. R. Saffran, M. M. Loman, and R. R. W. Robertson, "Infant memory for musical experiences," *Cognition*, 77 (2000): 1315–27. Further, five-month-old infants faced one monitor showing a film of an approaching train and another monitor of a retreating train, but heard only one sound—a lawnmower either increasing or decreasing in loudness. The infants looked longer at the physically possible event—the approaching train when the sound was increasing in loudness and the retreating train when the sound was decreasing. J. Pickens, "Perception of auditory-visual distance relations by five-month-old infants," *Developmental Psychology*, 30 (1994): 537–544.

6. M. L. Howe, M. L. Courage, R. Vernescu, and M. Hunt, "Distinctiveness effects in children's long-term retention," *Developmental Psychology*, 36 (2000): 778–792.

7. M. Legerstee, D. Anderson, and A. Schaffer, "Five and eight month old infants recognize their faces and voices as familiar and social stimuli," *Child Development*, 69 (1998): 37–50.

8. L. S. C. Tan and P. Bryant, "The cues that infants use to distinguish discontinuous quantities," *Child Development*, 71 (2000): 1162–78. S. A. Rose, J. F. Feldman, and J. J. Jankowski, "Attention and recognition memory in the first year of life," *Developmental Psychology*, 37 (2001): 135–151.

9. M. M. Haith, "Who put the cog in infant cognition?" *Infant Behavior*

240

and Development, 21 (1998): 167–179. J. Kagan, S. Linn, R. Mount, and J. S. Reznick, "Asymmetry of inference in the dishabituation paradigm," *Canadian Journal of Psychology*, 33 (1979): 288–305. P. J. Shields and C. Rovee-Colier, "Long-term memory for context specific category information at six months," *Child Development*, 63 (1992): 245–259.

10. R. Baillargeon, "How do infants learn about the physical world?" *Current Directions in Psychological Science*, 3 (1994): 133–140. R. Baillargeon, "Object permanence in 3 1/2- and 4 1/2-month-old infants," *Developmental Psychology*, 23 (1987): 655–664.

11. M. L. Courage and M. L. Howe, "The ebb and flow of infant attentional preferences," *Journal of Experimental Child Psychology*, 70 (1998): 26–53. M. A. Hunter, H. S. Ross, and E. W. Ames, "Preferences for familiar or novel toys," *Developmental Psychology*, 18 (1982): 519–529.

12. T. H. Schilling, "Infants' understanding of physical phenomena" (doctoral diss., University of Massachusetts at Amherst, 1997).

13. S. M. Rivera, A. Wakely, and J. Langer, "The drawbridge phenomenon," *Developmental Psychology*, 35 (1999): 427–435.

14. N. E. Berthier, S. De Bois, C. R. Poirier, M. A. Novak, and R. K. Clifton, "Where's the ball?" *Developmental Psychology*, 36 (2000): 394–401. L. M. Oakes and L. B. Cohen, "Infant perception of a causal event," *Cognitive Development*, 5 (1990): 193–207. T. H. Schilling and R. K. Clifton, "Nine month old infants learn about a physical event in a single session," *Cognitive Development*, 13 (1998): 165–184. M. Tomasello and J. Call, *Primate Cognition* (Oxford University Press, 1997). Hood and colleagues found that two-year-olds showed no evidence of understanding solidity in a different context. B. Hood, S. Carey, and S. Prasada, "Predicting the outcomes of physical events," *Child Development*, 71 (2000): 1540–54.

15. P. J. Kellman and E. S. Spelke, "Perception of partially occluded objects in infants," *Cognitive Psychology*, 15 (1983): 483–524. S. P. Johnson, "The development of visual-space perception," in C. Rovee-Collier, L. P. Lipsitt, and H. Hayne, eds., *Progress in Infancy Research*, vol. 1 (Mahwah, N.J.: Erlbaum, 2000), 113–155. A. M. Slater, V. Morison, M. Somers, A. Matlock, E. O. Brown, and D. Taylor, "Newborn and older infants' perception of partly occluded objects," *Infant Behavior and Development*, 13 (1990): 33–49. Casey and Richards also argue for the ambiguity of duration of attention to an event: B. J. Casey and J. E. Richards, "Sustained visual attention in young infants measured with an adaptive version of the visual preference paradigm," *Child Development*, 59 (1988): 1514–71.

16. F. Xu and S. Carey, "Infants' metaphysics," *Cognitive Psychology*, 30 (1996): 111–153. F. Xu and S. Carey, "The emergence of kind concepts," *Cognition*, 70 (2000): 285–301. A. Needham and R. Baillargeon, "Infants' use of featural and experiential information in segregating and individuating objects," *Cognition*, 70 (2000): 255–284.

17. P. J. Kellman and M. E. Arterberry, *The Cradle of Knowledge* (Cambridge, Mass.: MIT Press, 1998), 317.

18. M. L. Alvarado and J. Bachevalier, "Revisiting the maturation of medial temporal lobe memory functions in primates," *Learning and Memory*, 7 (2000): 244–256.

19. K. Wynn, "Addition and subtraction by human infants," *Nature*, 358 (1992): 749–750.

20. K. S. Marks and L. B. Cohen, "Infants' reactions to addition and subtraction events" (presented at the International Conference on Infant Studies, Brighton, England, July 2000). See also M. E. Arterberry, "Perception of object number through an aperture by human infants," *Infant Behavior and Development*, 18 (1995): 359–362, which shows that when the procedure is altered infants younger than one year do not show evidence of the ability to add. L. B. Cohen and K. S. Marks, "How infants process addition and subtraction events" (manuscript, University of Texas, 2000). K. Wynn and W. C. Chiang, "Limits to infants' knowledge of objects," *Psychological Science*, 9 (1998): 448–455. S. A. Rose, J. F. Feldman, and J. J. Jankowski, in "Attention and recognition memory in the first year of life," *Developmental Psychology*, 37 (2001): 135–151, demonstrate the serious compromise in memory in infants under one year.

21. E. A. Buffalo, S. J. Ramus, L. R. Squire, and S. M. Zola, "Perception and recognition memory in monkeys following lesions of area TE and perirhinal cortex," *Learning and Memory*, 7 (2000): 375–382. A. Diamond, S. Zola-Morgan, and L. R. Squire, "Successful performance by monkeys with lesions of the hippocampal formation on AB and object retrieval to tasks that mark developmental changes in human infants," *Behavioral Neuroscience*, 103 (1989): 526–537.

22. Marks and Cohen, "Infants' reactions to addition and subtraction events."

23. Tan and Bryant, "The cues that infants use to distinguish discontinuous quantities."

24. S. Dehaene, *The Number Sense* (New York: Oxford University Press, 1997). M. D. Hauser, S. Carey, and L. B. Hauser, "Spontaneous number

242

representation in semi-free-ranging rhesus monkeys," *Proceedings of the Royal Society: London B*, 267 (2000): 829–833. M. D. Hauser, *Wild Minds* (New York: Holt, 2000). R. Bijeljac-Babic, J. Bertoncini, and J. Mehler, "How do four-month-old infants categorize multisyllable utterances?" *Developmental Psychology*, 29 (1993): 711–721.

25. F. Gao, S. L. Levine, and J. Huttenlocher, "What do infants know about continuous quantity?" *Journal of Experimental Child Psychology*, 77 (2000): 20–29. K. S. Mix, S. L. Levine, and J. Huttenlocher, "Numerical abstraction in infants," *Developmental Psychology*, 33 (1997): 423–428.

26. A. Wakely, S. Rivera, and J. Langer, "Can young infants add and subtract?" *Child Development*, 71 (2000): 1525–34. C. Sophian, "From objects to quantities," *Developmental Psychology*, 36 (2000): 724–730.

27. R. K. Clifton, E. E. Perris, and D. D. McCall, "Does reaching in the dark for unseen objects reflect representation in infants?" *Infant Behavior and Development*, 22 (2000): 297–302.

28. H. Ellis, "The analysis of the sexual impulse," *The Alienist and the Neurologist*, 21 (1900): 247–262.

29. M. M. Haith and J. B. Benson, "Infant cognition," in *Handbook of Child Psychology*, 5th ed., vol. 2, ed. D. P. Kuhn and R. S. Siegler (New York: Wiley, 1998), 199–254; R. S. Bogartz, J. L. Shinskey, and C. J. Speaker, "Interpreting infant looking," *Developmental Psychology*, 33 (1997): 408–422. E. S. Spelke, "Initial knowledge," *Cognition*, 50 (1994): 431–445, quotation 431. E. S. Spelke, "Core knowledge," *American Psychologist*, 55 (2000): 1233–43.

30. A. N. Meltzoff and M. K. Moore, "Imitation of facial and manual gestures by human neonates," *Science*, 198 (1977): 75–78. S. W. Jacobson, "Matching behavior in the young infant," *Child Development*, 50 (1979): 425–430. L. A. Hayes and J. S. Watson, "Neonatal imitation: Fact or artifact," *Developmental Psychology*, 17 (1981): 655–660.

31. M. Tomasello, *The Cultural Origins of Human Cognition* (Cambridge, Mass.: Harvard University Press, 1999).

32. H. Hayne, J. Boniface, and R. Barr, "The development of declarative memory in human infants," *Behavioral Neuroscience*, 114 (2000): 77–83.

33. G. Sereny, *Cries Unheard* (New York: Henry Holt, 1998).

34. E. Loken, "Memory integration in children" (manuscript, 2000). D. J. Povinelli, A. M. Landry, L. A. Theall, B. R. Clark, and C. M. Castille, "Development of young children's understanding of the recent past is

causally bound to the present," *Developmental Psychology*, 35 (1999): 1426–35. K. S. Mix, J. Huttenlocher, and S. C. Levine, "Do preschool children recognize auditory-visual numerical correspondences?" *Child Development*, 67 (1996): 1592–1608.

35. L. Kohlberg, *The Philosophy of Moral Development* (New York: Harper and Row, 1981). Kochanska relies more on children's behaviors than on verbal justifications to infer moral development. G. Kochanska, "Toward a synthesis of parental socialization and child temperament in early development of conscience," *Child Development*, 64 (1993): 325–347.

36. P. L. Harris, *Children and Emotion* (London: Basil Blackwell, 1989).

37. S. Lieberson, S. Dumais, and S. Baumann, "The instability of androgynous names," *American Journal of Sociology*, 105 (2000): 1249–87.

38. M. P. MacDonald, *All Souls* (Boston: Beacon Press, 1999).

39. R. Yehuda, J. Schmeidler, M. Wainberg, K. Binder-Byrnes, and T. Duvdevani, "Vulnerability to post-traumatic stress disorder in adult offspring of Holocaust survivors," *American Journal of Psychiatry*, 155 (1998): 1167–71.

40. C. Milosz, *Native Realm* (Berkeley: University of California Press, 1968). W. Rathenau, *Gesammelte Schriften* (Berlin, 1918), vol. 1, 188–189 (trans. Hartmut Pogge von Strandmann).

41. W. T. Keaton and J. L. Gould, *Biological Science* (New York: Norton, 1993). T. Pizzari and T. R. Birkhead, "Female feral fowl eject sperm of subdominant males," *Nature*, 405 (2000): 787–789.

42. R. B. McCall, "Childhood IQs as predictors of adult educational and occupational status," *Science*, 197 (1977): 482–483. The social class of a child's family is a better predictor of level of cognitive development than whether or not the mother took cocaine during her pregnancy. H. Kilbride, C. Castor, E. Hoffman, and K. L. Foger, "Thirty-six-month outcome of prenatal cocaine exposure for term or near-term infants," *Developmental and Behavioral Pediatrics*, 21 (2000): 19–26.

5. Implications for Creativity and Personality

1. P. Ackroyd, *T. S. Eliot: A Life* (New York: Simon and Schuster, 1984).

2. F. G. Gosling, *Before Freud* (Urbana: University of Illinois Press, 1987).

3. R. P. Maines, *The Technology of Orgasm: "Hysteria," the Vibrator, and Women's Sexual Satisfaction* (Baltimore: Johns Hopkins University Press, 1999).

4. N. Oreskes, *The Rejection of Continental Drift* (New York: Oxford University Press, 1999).

5. J. H. Flavell, *The Developmental Psychology of Jean Piaget* (Princeton: Van Nostrand, 1963).

6. W. Schultz and A. Dickinson, "Neuronal coding of prediction errors," in W. M. Cowan, E. M. Shooter, C. F. Stevens, and R. F. Thompson, eds., *Annual Review of Neuroscience* (Palo Alto: Annual Reviews, vol. 23, 2000), 473–500. E. T. Rolls, *The Brain and Emotion* (New York: Oxford University Press, 1999).

7. M. Gallagher and P. C. Holland, "Understanding the function of the central nucleus," in J. P. Aggleton, ed., *The Amygdala* (New York: Wiley-Liss, 1992), 307–321; D. E. Berman and Y. Duda, "Memory extinction, learning anew, and learning the new," *Science*, 291 (2001): 2417–19.

8. I. Wickelgren, "Getting the brain's attention," *Science*, 278 (1997): 35–37.

9. V. Dragoi and J. E. R. Staddon, "The dynamics of operant conditioning," *Psychological Review*, 106 (1999): 20–61.

10. R. W. Schrauf and D. L. Rubin, "Bilingual autobiographical memory in older adult immigrants," *Journal of Memory and Language*, 39 (1998): 437–457.

11. D. E. Berlyne, *Conflict, Arousal, and Curiosity* (New York: McGraw-Hill, 1960).

12. W. N. Dember, "Response by the rat to environmental change," *Journal of Comparative and Physiological Psychology*, 49 (1956): 93–95.

13. J. Merila and B. C. Sheldon, "Lifetime reproductive success heritability in nature," *American Naturalist*, 155 (2000): 301–310.

14. A. M. Ball, *And Now My Soul Is Hardened* (Berkeley: University of California Press, 1994).

15. R. R. McCrae and P. T. Costa Jr., "Validation of the five factor model of personality across instruments and observers," *Journal of Personality and Social Psychology*, 52 (1987): 81–90. B. W. Roberts and W. F. Del Vecchio, "The rank order consistency of personality traits from childhood to old age," *Psychological Bulletin*, 126 (2000): 3–25. M. M. Weissman, S. Wolk, P. Wickamarathe, R. B. Goldstein, P. Adams, S. Greenwald, M. D. Ryan,

R. E. Dahl, and D. Steinberg, "Children with prepubertal onset of major depressive disorder and anxiety grown up," *Archives of General Psychiatry*, 56 (1999): 794–801. D. J. DeWit, A. Ogburne, D. R. Offord, and K. MacDonald, "Antecedents of the risk of recovery from DSM-III-R social phobia," *Psychological Medicine*, 29 (1999): 569–582.

16. J. Soto, R. Ebling, and R. W. Levenson, "Emotional expression and experience in Chinese Americans and Mexican Americans" (manuscript, 2000).

17. D. Offer, M. Kaiz, K. I. Howard, and E. S. Bennett, "The altering of reported experiences," *Journal of the American Academy of Child and Adolescent Psychiatry*, 39 (2000): 735–742.

18. N. Schwarz, F. Strack, and H. P. Mai, "Assimilation and contrast effects in part-whole question sequences," *Public Opinion Quarterly*, 55 (1991): 3–23. N. Schwarz, "Self-reports," *American Psychologist*, 54 (1999): 93–105.

19. K. S. Kendler, J. M. Myers, and M. C. Neale, "A multi-dimensional twin study of mental health in women," *American Journal of Psychiatry*, 157 (2000): 506–517.

20. H. Towers, E. Spotts, J. M. Neiderhiser, E. M. Hetherington, R. Plomin, and D. Reiss, "Genetic and environmental influences on teacher ratings of the Child's Behavior Checklist," *International Journal of Behavioral Development*, 24 (2000): 373–381. R. I. E. Lake, L. J. Eves, H. M. H. Maes, A. C. Heath, and N. C. Martin, "Further evidence against the environmental transmission of individual differences in neuroticism from a collaborative study of 45,580 twins and relatives on two continents," *Behavior Genetics*, 30 (2000): 223–233; quotation 232.

21. S. K. Donaldson and M. A. Westerman, "Development of children's understanding of ambivalence and causal theories of emotion," *Developmental Psychology*, 22 (1986): 655–662.

22. H. Seidler, *Internment: The Diaries of Harry Seidler*, trans. J. Winternitz (London: Allen and Unwin, 1986).

23. Unpublished data from the author's laboratory.

24. H. C. Plotkin, "Behavior and evolution," in Plotkin, ed., *The Role of Behavioral Evolution* (Cambridge, Mass.: MIT Press, 1988), 1–18. M. Vulic, R. E. Lenski, and M. Radman, "Mutation, recombination, and incipient speciation of bacteria in the laboratory," *Proceedings of the National Academy of Sciences*, 96 (1999): 7348–51.

25. M. Kerr, "Childhood and adolescent shyness in long term perspective," in W. R. Crozier, ed., *Shyness* (London: Routledge, 2000), 64–87.

26. V. Smil, "Genius loci," *Nature*, 409 (2001): 21.

27. G. Perugi, C. Toni, A. Benedetti, B. Simonetti, M. Simoncini, C. Tonti, L. Musetti, and H. S. Akiskal, "Delineating a putative phobic-anxious temperament in 126 panic-agoraphobic patients," *Journal of Affective Disorders*, 47 (1998): 11–23.

28. J. Kagan, D. Arcus, N. Snidman, W. Yu Feng, J. Hendler, and S. Greene, "Reactivity in infants," *Developmental Psychology*, 30 (1994): 342–345.

29. Q. Wang, "Culture, self, and emotion" (doctoral diss., Harvard University, 2000).

30. K. Yang and M. H. Bond, "Exploring implicit personality theories within indigenous or imported constructs," *Journal of Personality and Social Psychology*, 58 (1990): 1087–95.

31. R. Slotow, G. Van Dyk, J. Poule, B. Page, and A. Klocke, "Older bull elephants control young males," *Nature*, 408 (2000): 425–426.

32. N. Itoigawa, "The role of individuals in the history of a free-ranging group of Japanese macaques," *International Journal of Behavioral Development*, 25 (2001): 184–186.

33. D. A. Regier, W. E. Narrow, and B. S. Rae, "The epidemiology of anxiety disorders," *Journal of Psychiatric Research*, 24 (1990): 3–14. M. Tohen, E. Bromet, J. M. Murphy, and M. T. Tsuang, "Psychiatric epidemiology," *Harvard Review of Psychiatry*, 8 (2000): 111–125. D. S. Pine, P. Cohen, D. Gurley, J. Brook, and Y. Ma, "The risk for early adulthood anxiety and depressed disorders in adolescents with anxiety and depressive disorders," *Archives of General Psychiatry*, 55 (1998): 56–64. C. Hayward, J. D. Killen, H. C. Kraemer, and C. B. Taylor, "Predictors of panic attacks in adolescents," *Journal of the American Academy of Child and Adolescent Psychiatry*, 39 (2000): 207–214.

34. D. J. Veltman, G. A. Van Zijderveld, R. Van Dyck, and A. Bakker, "Predictability, controllability, and fear of symptoms of anxiety in epinephrine induced anxiety," *Biological Psychiatry*, 44 (1998): 1017–26.

35. S. B. Patten, "Exogenous corticosteroid exposures are associated with increased recollection of traumatic life events," *Journal of Affective Disorders*, 53 (1999): 123–128.

36. E. Breitholtz, B. Johansson, and L. G. Ost, "Cognitions in general-

247

ized anxiety disorder and panic disorder patients," *Behavior Research and Therapy*, 37 (1999): 533–544.

37. S. Sutherland, *Breakdown* (London: Weidenfeld and Nicolson, 1976).

38. E. G. Gray, "Severe depression," *British Journal of Psychiatry*, 143 (1983): 319–322.

39. C. Sobin, F. Blundel, F. Weiler, C. Gavigan, C. Haiman, and H. Karayiorgou, "Phenotypic characteristics of obsessive-compulsive disorders ascertained in adulthood," *Journal of Psychiatric Research*, 33 (1999): 265–277.

40. E. Tezcan and B. Millet, "Phenomenology of obsessive-compulsive disorder," *Encephale*, 23 (1997): 342–350.

41. J. M. Goldstein, L. J. Seidman, N. J. Horton, N. Makris, D. N. Kennedy, V. S. Caviness, S. V. Faraone, and M. T. Tsuang, "Normal sexual dimorphism of the adult human brain assessed by in vivo magnetic resonance imaging," *Cerebral Cortex*, 11 (2001): 490–497.

42. G. P. Lee, D. W. Loring, K. J. Meador, and B. B. Brooks, "Hemispheric specialization for emotional expression," *Brain and Cognition*, 12 (1990): 267–280. E. Y. Zamrini, K. J. Meador, D. W. Loring, F. T. Nichols, G. P. Lee, R. E. Figueroa, and W. O. Thompson, "Unilateral cerebral inactivation produces differential left/right heart rate responses," *Neurology*, 40 (1990): 1408–11.

43. W. Wittling and E. Schweiger, "Neuroendocrine brain asymmetry and physical complaints," *Neuropsychologia*, 31 (1993): 591–608. W. Wittling, "Psychophysiological correlates of human brain asymmetry," *Neuropsychologia*, 28 (1996): 457–470. W. Wittling and M. Pfluger, "Neuroendocrine hemisphere asymmetries," *Brain and Cognition*, 14 (1990): 243–265.

44. C. R. Cimino, M. Verfaellie, D. Bowers, and K. M. Heilman, "Autobiographical memory," *Brain and Cognition*, 15 (1991): 106–118. H. C. Abercrombie, S. M. Schaefer, C. L. Larson, T. R. Oakes, K. A. Lindgren, J. E. Holden, S. B. Perlman, P. A. Tursk, D. P. Krahn, R. M. Benca, and R. J. Davidson, "Metabolic rate in the right amygdala predicts negative affect in depressed patients," *NeuroReport*, 9 (1998): 3301–07.

45. R. J. Davidson, "Cerebral asymmetry, emotion, and affective style," in R. J. Davidson and K. Hugdahl, eds., *Brain Asymmetry* (Cambridge, Mass.: MIT Press, 1995), 261–388. L. A. Schmidt, "Frontal brain electrical

activity in shyness and sociability," *Psychological Sciences*, 10 (1999): 316–320. W. Wittling, A. Block, E. Schweiger, and S. Genzels, "Hemisphere asymmetry in sympathetic control of the human myocardium," *Brain and Cognition*, 38 (1998): 17–35. W. Wittling, A. Block, S. Genzels, and E. Schweiger, "Hemispheric asymmetry in parasympathetic control of heart," *Neuropsychologia*, 36 (1998): 461–468.

ACKNOWLEDGMENTS

Other scholars have written on these themes, especially Donald Hebb, George Miller, J. McVicker Hunt, William Dember, Alan Paivio, Jean Mandler, Alan Baddeley, Robert McCall, and Philip Zelazo. But this domain is sufficiently complex that each foray exploits a different set of evidence, arranges different arguments, and invents different implications. I hope this text is not redundant with the insights others have achieved.

I thank Joseph Campos, Alfonso Caramazza, Rachel Clifton, Adele Diamond, Tecumseh Fitch, Marc Hauser, Fred Morrison, Charles Nelson, J. S. Reznick, Elizabeth Spelke, and Philip Zelazo for critical comments on part or all of the text, Tracey Shissler, Paula Mabee, and Blair Boudreau for help in preparing the manuscript, and Camille Smith for her wise editing of the text.

The research from my laboratory cited in the text has been supported, in part, by the W. T. Grant Foundation, NIMH, and Foundation Bial. Many ideas were generated by conversations and lectures supported by Mind/Brain/Behavior Initiative at Harvard University.

INDEX